And they crucified him

Alun Ebenezer

EP BOOKS
1st Floor Venture House, 6 Silver Court, Watchmead,
Welwyn Garden City, UK, AL7 1TS

web: http://www.epbooks.org

e-mail: sales@epbooks.org

EP Books are distributed in the USA by:
JPL Distribution
3741 Linden Avenue Southeast
Grand Rapids, MI 49548
E-mail: orders@jplbooks.com
Tel: 877.683.6935

British Library Cataloguing in Publication Data available

ISBN 978–1–78397–183–1

In 23 illuminating chapters, Alun Ebenezer describes, explains and illustrates the momentous events that are the very foundations of the Christian faith. The style is fresh and punchy, the substance challenging and heart-warming. This is a valuable book for serious enquirers, sincere Christians, and sceptical onlookers. It deserves to be read.

Andrew Davies, Itinerant Preacher and Pastor

In this engaging volume, Alun Ebenezer forces us to fix our eyes and hearts on the centre point of human history; the cross and resurrection of the Lord Jesus Christ. It is a dark but ultimately beautiful story that Alun retells with a combination of biblical rigour, heartfelt passion and an engaging turn of phrase. Tightly packed but accessible, this book, like the story it tells, is a challenging and encouraging read.

Reuben Hunter, Pastor Trinity West Church, Shepherd's Bush

This book centres on the very heart of the Christian religion. All the world must get a right understanding of what happened in the last week of the life of the Lord Jesus Christ and especially in his death on the cross. In a wonderfully winsome and lucid way Alun Ebenezer explains these truths to us. Alun is a delightful, approachable, sensitive and discerning man. Reading this book is like having him sit alongside you, and in the most patient and tender of ways explain to you why it was necessary for the Son of God to be put to death on Calvary. A grasp of this is the greatest benefit that anyone can receive in time or eternity.

Geoff Thomas, retired minister of Alfred Place Baptist Church, Aberystwyth

Alun Ebenezer achieves the objective he set out in the preface! This is a profoundly helpful treatment of the pivotal event of human history.

Alistair Begg, Senior Minister, Parkside Church, Cleveland, Ohio

To mam and dad:
thanks for everything

Contents

Foreword

I HAVE KNOWN ALUN EBENEZER FOR OVER 25 YEARS. WE FIRST met on the promenade at the Aberystwyth conference and didn't immediately get on. I was the sophisticated boy from Swansea whilst Alun was this little valley commando with a mop of blonde hair. As the years rolled a strong friendship was forged. Twenty-five years later, we have been best men at one another's wedding, both of us find ourselves in London, we have seen one another through some tough times. Alun is the best friend a man can have—loyal, candid, thoughtful, pride puncturing, generous and witty.

It's a joy to write the foreword to this book not only for my best friend but because I genuinely think this book is worth reading. Alun is a fine preacher and has the ability to make the difficult understandable without over simplification.

There is no greater topic for us to engage with than the person and work of Jesus Christ. Alun here handles these glorious truths with a deft touch and it's book that deserves to be greatly used in our churches.

This little book will help us keep the apostolic priorities of 1 Corinthians 15—For I delivered to you as of first importance what I also received: that Christ died for our sins in accordance with the Scriptures, that he was buried, that he was raised on the third day in accordance with the Scriptures, and that he appeared to Cephas, then to the twelve.

Paul Levy
Minister of the International Presbyterian Church, Ealing

Preface

I AM VERY AWARE THAT THE SUBJECT OF THIS BOOK FOCUSES ON A section of the Bible that is well known to so many. The death and resurrection of the Lord Jesus Christ, and all that led up to and followed it, have been, and continue to be, the subject and theme of so many books. It is well trodden ground. So why another book? Aren't there enough books? Why read this book?

Well, this book tries to do 10 things in an easy to read, contemporary, bound to the scriptures way. It should interest you whether you are a Christian who wants to learn more, somebody who has never considered these things before, or a sceptic. But the book should be especially relevant if you are a sinner in desperate need of forgiveness.

The 10 things the book tries to do are:

- Be Expositional—The book is based on the last chapters in the four Gospels in the New Testament. It sets out to expound these verses and chapters clearly, accurately and faithfully.

- Tackle Difficulties—there are difficulties, or seeming contradictions, in the four Gospel accounts of the death, resurrection and ascension of the Lord Jesus Christ. This book tackles these difficulties, and shows that while there are difficulties there are no contradictions. It seeks to do this in a readable, untechnical way and demonstrates that the Bible is the inerrant and infallible Word of God.

- Be Evangelistic—The book is intended to convince, with the help of the Holy Spirit, those who are not believers to repent of their sin and put their trust in the Saviour that this book is all about.

- Be Theological—The book seeks to explain the theology and doctrines that come out of these momentous hours, days and weeks.

- Be Historical—Show that what is recorded in the Gospels is real history; these events actually happened.

- Be contextual—The book intends to give the background and context to the events that happened during the hours, days and weeks recorded at the end of the four Gospels. It seeks to give a real flavour of what it was like at the time these proceedings took place.

- Be Applicable—The book seeks to apply, in a lively, fresh, illustrative and contemporary way, all the things that took place in the Spring of AD 30 to the readers' life and situation in the 21st century.

- Be Clear—it is written in a way that even if you have no prior Bible knowledge you will be able to understand the events that are described, explained and applied.

- Give Details—The book seeks to bring to life details that can easily get overlooked in such a familiar part of the Bible. There are no four words that carry such significance, meaning and detail than, 'And they crucified him' (Mark 15:24).

- Bring glory to God!

1

Gethsemane

(Matthew 26:36–46; Mark 14:32–42;
Luke 22:39–46; John 18:1)

A Thursday night in the spring of AD 30

THIS BOOK FOCUSES ON SOME HOURS THAT PASSED IN JERUSALEM in the Spring of AD 30: They are recorded at the end of the Four Gospels (Matthew 26:36–28:20; Mark 14:32–16:20; Luke 22:39–24:53; John 18–21).

They begin late on a Thursday night in a Garden called Gethsemane. Jesus, a carpenter-cum itinerant preacher from Nazareth, and his twelve disciples had come to Jerusalem from Galilee the previous Sunday. They had come to celebrate the most important of all Jewish festivals, the Passover. The festival lasted a week with the climax being the Passover meal which earlier that evening these men had eaten in an upstairs room in the Israeli capital.

After supper, they left this upper room, went out of Jerusalem on foot, crossed the Kidron valley, and entered Gethsemane. Twelve disciples had arrived in the upper room with Jesus earlier that evening but only eleven left with him. One of the disciples, Judas Iscariot, had earlier departed and gone into the night.

The question you may be asking straight away is why would you want to read a book that begins in a garden called Gethsemane involving a Galilean peasant? What in the world has this got to do with you? Why should you care about something that happened nearly two thousand years ago in a Middle Eastern country, probably hundreds of miles from where you live?

Three reasons

Because firstly, the man these hours centre on demands your attention. He is the main character in world history. H.G. Wells commented 'I am not a believer but I must confess as a historian that this penniless preacher from Nazareth is the very centre of history'. Napoleon said, 'I know men and I tell you that Jesus Christ was no mere man'. According to the non-Christian Jewish historian Josephus (Maier 1988, p.264–265).

> About this time there lived a wise man called Jesus, and his conduct was good, and was known to be virtuous. Many people among the Jews and the other nations became his disciples. Pilate condemned him to be crucified and to die. But those who had become his disciples did not abandon his discipleship. They reported that he had appeared to them three days after his crucifixion and that he was alive. Accordingly, he was perhaps the Messiah, concerning whom the prophets have reported wonders. And the tribe of the Christians, so named after him, has not disappeared to this day

Secondly, not only is this book about this man, it concentrates on the most important hours in his life. Jesus was thirty-three years old when he died and therefore spent 1,700 weeks on earth. One third of the Gospels are taken up with the last of those weeks—9 out of 28 chapters in Matthew; 6 out of 16 in Mark; 6 out of 24 in

Luke; 9 out of 21 in John. No other biography gives such lopsided attention to the end of the story. But for Jesus, the ending of his life is the story.

Thirdly, not only are these hours the most significant in his life, they are the most significant in your life too. What you do with the events that took place during these hours determines your eternal destiny.

Gethsemane

With the scene set we come to Gethsemane. John says that after Jesus and his disciples finished supper, they left the upper room, went across the Kidron valley and entered Gethsemane (John 18:1).

It was a busy festival time in Jerusalem. The gates of the temple would have been thrown open at midnight and as Jesus passed through the streets and out of the city for the last time people would still be gathered, hustling and bustling as they prepared to go up to the Temple.

Jesus and his disciples would have gone through the eastern gate located north of the temple and descended into a lonely part of the black Kidron valley which was located between Jerusalem's eastern wall and the Mount of Olives. Crossing the brook that would be swelled this time of year with a winter torrent, they would have continued along to the point where the road divides into three, each leading to the Mount of Olives. They would probably have taken a left and not many steps further the men would have turned aside to the right and reached what tradition says is Gethsemane.

It was a garden in the eastern sense. A lovely, quiet retreat that was probably fenced in among a variety of fruit trees and flowering shrubs. The garden would have contained olive trees and perhaps a grove or small house/sleeping quarters of some kind used in the autumn for an olive press.

In all likelihood the grove belonged to one of Christ's followers, possibly the father of Mark, as in the author of the Gospel of Mark. It was also probably the upstairs room in Mark's father's house where they had eaten the Passover meal earlier in the evening.

It is quite likely that Jesus and his disciples had spent Tuesday and Wednesday night in Gethsemane as well. Jewish law required that Jews remain within an extended city limit for Passover. This limit included Gethsemane but excluded Bethany, another place they were known to stay (Matthew 21:17; Mark 11:11; John 12:1).

Gethsemane was probably one of the Lord Jesus Christ's favourite places on earth. It was a quiet place and we know it was Jesus' custom to go there (Luke 22:39). It was a place he often went for meeting, praying, teaching and sleeping. Judas knew the place (John 18:2) and in all likelihood on many occasions been there all night with Christ.

If you are a Christian, there may be a place you think of which brings back really happy memories. Church holidays, camps or conferences; somewhere that reminds you of times when you enjoyed fellowship with other Christians; the singing was glorious, you heard great preaching, met some of your best friends, felt the presence of God. You love going there. It is the happiest place on earth. Well, this was Gethsemane for Jesus and his disciples. But tonight it was all going to change.

1 The humanity of Jesus

In agony
When they came to Gethsemane Jesus left eight of his disciples waiting while he went further into the garden to pray (Matthew 26:36; Mark 14:32). He took Peter, James and John with him. These were the leaders of the group and as his three closest friends (Mark 5:37; 9:2; 13:3) he shares with them how he is feeling.

Jesus was in torment. The words in the Gospel accounts used to describe his feelings are harrowing (Matthew 26:37, 38; Mark 14:33, 34). Jesus actually says he is swallowed up in sorrow, overwhelmed to the point of collapsing and dying (Matthew 26:38). He feels trapped and hemmed in on every side with the horrible feeling of not being able to get out.

His soul is in such agony that he doesn't know what to do with himself. He doesn't know how he is going to get through what he is about to go through. He is agitated. As he prays, he falls on his face (Matthew 26:39). The Son of God literally 'fell on the ground' (Mark 14:35). He is dreading what he is about to face so much that his sweat turns to blood. Luke, who was a doctor, actually notes that they were great drops of blood falling to the ground (Luke 22:44). Apparently, soldiers in the trenches in World War I, being in such stressful conditions, sweat blood. Not only was he sweating and bleeding, the creator of the universe was crying out with strong tears (Hebrews 5:7).

Being in such a distressed state he sees the need to spend time in prayer, pouring his soul out to his Father. He wants to talk to his Father alone but at the same time doesn't want to be left completely alone. And so he asks his three closest friends to remain with him and stay awake and keep watch over him (Matthew 26:38; Mark 14:34). He wants them nearby and withdraws from them about a stone's throw. (Luke 22:40, 41).

This gives us a real glimpse into the humanity of Jesus. Even though he is God, he is as human as we are and just as there are times in our lives when we need people around us, Jesus was exactly the same. This was no superman in Gethsemane but a real man who needed his friends at a time like this.

If there had been CCTV footage of Gethsemane it would have shown a real man going through physical, mental and spiritual torture; not knowing what to do with himself, throwing himself to the ground, sweating, bleeding and crying, needing to be alone in prayer to his Father, but at the same time needing his friends close by.

The shadow falls

So why was Jesus in such agony in Gethsemane? Why was he going through such torture?

The reason is because the hour he dreaded throughout his life had almost arrived. He is about to be crucified and the shadow of the cross falls heavily. We do not know exactly when it first began to fall on Christ but we do know that during the latter part of his three-year public ministry it haunted him. He spoke of this hour emphatically as 'the hour' (Matthew 26:45; Mark 16:35; Luke 22:53; John 7:30; 8:20; 12:23; 13:1; 17:1) and the thought of it was so terrible that at times his soul shrunk from it. He had to rally his courage and pray fervently in order to compose himself to bear it.

Holman Hunt's painting, 'The shadow of Death', depicts the inside of the carpenter's shop in Nazareth. Stripped to the waist, Jesus stands by a wooden trestle on which he has put down his saw. He lifts up his eyes towards heaven, and the look on his face is one of either pain or ecstasy or both. He also stretches, raising both arms over his head. As he does so, the evening sunlight streaming through the open door casts a dark shadow in the form of a cross on the wall behind him, where his tool-rack looks like a horizontal bar on which his hands have been crucified. The tools themselves remind us of the fateful hammer and nails. In the left foreground a woman kneels among the wood chippings, her hands resting on the chest in which the rich gifts of the magi are kept. We cannot see her face because she has averted it. But we know that she is Mary. She looks startled, or so it seems, at her son's cross-like shadow on the wall. Stott (1991, p.17) says, 'Though the idea is historically fictitious, it is also theologically true. From his youth, indeed even from his birth, the cross cast its shadow ahead of him.'

It is important to stress that Jesus isn't in this state because he is simply afraid of pain or dying. It is because on the cross he is about to face the wrath of God. As awful as the physical pain he is about to face will be, he is overwhelmed by the prospect of taking upon himself the guilt of the sins of millions of people and facing the anger of a sin hating God. Crucifixion is without doubt one of the worst forms of punishment ever to have been invented but it is nothing compared to having to endure the wrath of a holy God.

The sinless Son of God is about to take upon himself the sin of the whole world. We know something of being wracked by guilt and shame but for Christ's sensitive soul to face the tidal wave of God's wrath because of our sin is unimaginable. He had always been in contact with sinners and seen the effects of sin on others around him but now he struggles with the prospect of taking all of this guilt upon himself. On the cross the Lord Jesus Christ would be reckoned among the transgressors (Luke 22:37 quoting Isaiah 53). He will be classed as a transgressor. As we shall see in Chapter 9 of this book, he literally was crucified between two criminals. But it means far more than that. On the cross, God will treat His Son as a sinner; the worst sinner that has ever lived.

Just think how guilty your sins make you feel. Think how bad you feel about the things that go through your mind. How ashamed you are of some of the things you have done and how churned up inside you become at the thought of them ever coming to light. Think how repulsed and outraged you feel when you read of the gross sins of others. Jesus Christ who is sinless is about to take on himself the guilt of all these sins. He is to pay the price of millions and millions of sins and therefore he faced the wrath of God as the worst sinner that had ever lived—the worst liar, sexual deviant, gossip, drunkard, thief ever to have lived. No wonder he is in torment!

The shame and suffering he would endure on the cross was becoming more and more real and his Father would begin to withdraw his presence from him. He is beginning to sense total desertion and utter loneliness. Many people have already left him (John 6:66). In the next few hours the disciples were going to forsake him, one was going to deny him and another was going to betray him into the hands of his enemies. But worst of all, on the cross, God was going to forsake him. He would feel total abandonment.

2 The horror of sin

The Lord Jesus' suffering in Gethsemane shows the sinfulness of sin. It does this in three ways.

Exposes sin for what it really is

Firstly, it exposes sin for what it really is. In Gethsemane the Lord Jesus was beginning to fully feel the guilt of sin and face up to the prospect of taking the blame and paying the price for its consequences. Sin is seen for what it really is in Gethsemane.

Sin at first appears to be so attractive. It always promises it will make us feel so good and we just have to have it. This is illustrated for us in the Old Testament in the life of King David. He was at home in his palace when all his men had gone to war (2 Samuel 11). From the roof of his palace he spots a beautiful woman bathing and thinks to himself I have got to have her. Her husband is away at war and they end up having sex. However, she becomes pregnant and now their illicit affair is in danger of becoming found out. To cover up the mess he is in, David arranges for her husband Uriah to come home from battle to spend the night with her to make it look like he is the father. But being a good soldier he won't go to bed with his wife while he is meant to be on duty and so the plan didn't work. Desperate to cover his tracks David then arranges for Uriah to fight on the front line of the battle and Uriah is killed. What started as an afternoon of fun ended up with lies, betrayal and murder. Sin isn't what it appears. It is destructive. It gives momentary pleasure but destroys people's lives.

There are so many examples of the deceitfulness and destructiveness of sin. Pubs and clubs are full of fun and excitement at the start of a Friday and Saturday night but by the end of the night, people have fallen out, had fights, got jealous, ended up doing things that at the time seemed so much pleasure and fun but now have left them feeling guilty and has wrecked their marriages, families and relationships. They wake up in the middle of the night or in the morning feeling empty, hating themselves and those they've committed shameful acts with. People get infatuated with the pleasures of sin but in the end they loathe themselves.

Sin will always leave you wanting more but it can never satisfy. Behind sin is the father of sin, the Devil. According to Lewis, (1992) 'an ever increasing craving for an ever diminishing pleasure is the Devil's formula. To get the man's soul and give him nothing in return—that is what really gladdens the heart of our father (father of lies).'

Orson Wells, in an interview on the Parkinson show in the 1970s said,

> I believe that I have looked back too optimistically on Hollywood ... because I realised how many great people that town has destroyed since its earliest beginnings; how almost everybody of merit was destroyed or diminished ... and I suddenly thought to myself, why do I look so affectionately on that town? It was because it was funny ... and everything that we're nostalgic about ... but really it was a brutal place ... and the story of that town is a dirty one, and its record is bad.

Sin ois powerful. If you don't kill sin, sin will kill you. It destroys people's lives and traps and ensnares you. People think they can control it but the reality is sin takes hold of a person and controls them. A man sits in his room alone with his computer and just thinks he'll click on an image once. Before he knows it he is addicted to pornography. A lady just talks about a person with some friends a couple of times but in no time that woman is a terrible gossip. The first time the alcoholic got drunk he had no plans on becoming addicted.

The puritan William Gurnall said 'Faith looks behind the curtain of sense, and sees sin before it is dressed up for the stage'. Joel Beeke said that 'faith sees the ugliness and hellishness of sin without its camouflage'. In Gethsemane Jesus was experiencing the effects of sin for what it really was. The pain it caused the Lord Jesus in dealing with its consequences on our behalf should make us see it for what it is. It must be horrible.

Maybe sin has really destroyed your life and caused much suffering. Maybe your conscience is troubled and you are constantly wracked with guilt. All of this was about to be laid on Jesus. As he faced this prospect there is no wonder he was in agony.

The justice of God

Not only does Gethsemane show sin for what it really is, secondly it shows the justice of God. God hates sin and Gethsemane demonstrates just how seriously God takes it. He cannot just let it go. Sin has to be punished. His justice demands it.

This means that forgiveness is one of the profoundest problems for God. He doesn't want to send people into everlasting torment but his justice cannot simply allow him to turn a blind eye to our law-breaking and sin.

In Luke 24:25, 26 the Lord Jesus says that because of this 'it was necessary' that he had to go to the cross. Before the cross people's sins had been overlooked. Christ could say to a woman brought to him who had been caught committing adultery, I don't condemn you, go sin no more (John 8:11). He could tell the parable of the Prodigal Son (Luke 15:11–32) to show how God welcomes back the very worst of sinners. How could a holy God allow this? How could all these sins be allowed to accumulate? Because a day had been appointed when these sins would be dealt with (Romans 3:25). For God to be just and fair and still be able to forgive sins, Jesus had to die. In the place of all those who had sinned, and will sin.

The wrath of God

Thirdly, it shows the wrath of God against sin. Hell, at least the shadow of it, began to come to him in Gethsemane. According to Edersheim (2004) 'That night the fierce wind of Hell was allowed to sweep unbroken over the Saviour.' The Lord Jesus says 'this is your (the devil's) hour and the power of darkness'(Luke 22:53).

What Christ was going through at Gethsemane and would face on the cross was the equivalent of that which people would have suffered if no one had died in their place. It is the terror of punishment which will fall upon those who reject the Lord Jesus Christ and decide to go it alone at the judgement (Hebrews 9:27). Hell is the final destination for everyone who refuses to repent of their sin and trust in Christ. This is a frightening prospect. Hell is a place of torment (Luke 16:28; Revelation 14:11) and the worst thing is it is forever (Matthew 18:8; Matthew 25:46; 2 Thessalonians 1:9).

The Lord Jesus talks of facing the wrath of God as 'this cup' (Luke 22:42). The imagery of the cup of the wrath of God is taken from the Old Testament. Psalm 75:8 says, 'For in the hand of the Lord there is a cup with foaming wine, well mixed, and he pours out from it, and all the wicked of the earth shall drain it down to the dregs'. In the Old Testament when an enemy was captured he would be forced to drink a cup full of spiked wine. His head would be tipped back and the drink forced down his neck. He would be made to drink it all, down to the dregs. It would make him vomit and he would fall over, stagger and die a shameful death. Here in Gethsemane, Jesus talks of drinking the cup of God's wrath. He will drink it to the dregs. We shall see in chapter 7 that drinking this cup quite literally made him stagger. The difference is that Jesus drank from this cup willingly.

Revelation 16:17–21 also throws light on 'the cup'. The picture is of the last day when the cup of God's wrath will be poured out fully on unbelievers. Imagine if we all had a cup each and in it was the wrath of God each of us deserved. But Jesus pours the wrath of all those who trust him into his big cup and drinks the lot! Here, he is about to take this cup and drink every last drop of it so that sinners like you and I don't have to.

This is what caused such 'anguish [to] his soul' (Isaiah 53:11).

He was made to feel the guilt which sin carries, and bear the punishment alone which sin deserves.

To drink this cup he would need to throw his whole heart and energy into it. The words in Isaiah 53:11 were written in Hebrew originally and the translation indicates severity of effort, painful exertion, and exhausting work. For Christ to pay the price for our sin, turn away the anger of God and provide forgiveness, required strenuous labour. It was work which involved extremes of pain, both physical and spiritual. The thought of it turned his sweat into great drops of blood falling to the ground and made him cry out to his Father.

In *The Times* (July 29th 2008) there was a report on a 20-year-old British woman, Samantha Orobator held in Phonthong prison in Laos. Inmates described conditions in the prison as squalid. Kay Danes, an Australian who spent ten months at the prison has described the abuse and neglect at the jail. 'I've heard all the prisoners yelling at the top of their lungs, shouting for guards when one of the inmates was dying and nobody comes. Nobody ever comes'. The Bible describes a place far worse than Phonthong prison where the wrath of God is poured out. Right now people are screaming at the top of their lungs but nobody comes. Nobody ever comes!

It was the prospect of this wrath that Jesus faced in Gethsemane.

3 The heart of God

But not only does Gethsemane show the sinfulness of sin, it also shows how much God loves sinners.

To put this into context, we need to keep in mind how much God loved his Son. They had enjoyed each other's company since eternity. There were occasions during Christ's life when the voice of God was heard from Heaven saying, 'You are my beloved Son; with you I am well pleased' (Luke 3:22).

But here in Gethsemane, the Father is seeing his Son in torment and at any point could have said enough is enough, but doesn't. The Lord Jesus says to him, 'All things are possible for you. Remove this cup from me' (Mark 14:36). So why doesn't he? Why doesn't he just stop all the agony? Why doesn't he stop everything so his Son doesn't have to go to the cross?

The reason is that God so loved the world (John 3:16). He loved you so much that he put his Son through this agony. It was all for us. Jesus didn't die to make God love us, Jesus died for us because God loved us. The cross was motivated by God's love. It was while we were yet sinners Christ died for us (Romans 5:8). It was God's pleasure to do this for us. (Galatians 1:4).

Satan will tell you that God is a hard man. Callous in his sovereignty. Nothing could be further from the truth. In Ezekiel he swears by himself on oath that he takes no pleasure in the death of the wicked (Ezekiel 33:11). He says in effect, 'if this isn't true, let me no longer be God. If there was any grain of pleasure in me sending sinners to Hell, let me un-God myself!' He personally, passionately and persistently pleads. In 2 Corinthians 5:20, Paul on behalf of God says 'on bended knees', 'we beg you' be reconciled to God. The creator of the universe stoops down to where you are and pleads with you to turn back to him (Ezekiel 33:11). He welcomes you, whatever you have done, to come to him. Isaiah says that he holds out his arms all the day long (Isaiah 65:2).

A man would have his hair cut in a certain barber's shop in Australia. The man was a Christian but the barber who always cut his hair was very dismissive about the things of God and would make fun of him. One day he went to have his haircut but the barber was not there. He asked the other gentleman cutting his hair where he was and was told that he had finished work because he had found out he had terminal cancer and didn't have much time left. As the man walked out of the shop he saw his old barber sat in his car crying his eyes out. The man went over to him and the old barber said, 'For 40 years I kicked Him in his face but the minute I called to him He came to me'. The God of the Bible is a big hearted, compassionate God who will abundantly pardon (Isaiah 55:7).

In stressing the love of God for sinners and not removing the cup of wrath from his Son, it is also vital that we stress that Christ voluntarily drank it. Even though the thought of it was overwhelming he drank it willingly. The Father sent the Son but the Son wanted to come. There is no discord between the Father and the Son. He wanted to come as much as the Father wanted to send him and the Father wanted to send him as much as the Son wanted to come.

The writer to the Hebrews says that Jesus endured the cross because of the joy that was set before him (Hebrews 12:2). Despite the agony and torment he had to go through, it was worth it. Isaiah says 'Out of the anguish of his soul he shall see and be satisfied' (Isaiah 53:11). It is hard to believe that when I one day meet the Lord Jesus Christ he will look at me, think back to Gethsemane and say of it all, 'it was worth it!'

Several years before his death the Swiss theologian Karl Barth went to the United States for a series of lectures. After a very impressive lecture a student asked 'Dr Barth, what is the greatest thought that has ever passed through your mind?' The ageing professor paused for a long time as he obviously thought about his answer. Then with great simplicity he said, 'Jesus loves me! This I know, For the Bible tells me so.'

The help from Heaven

Some issues to clear up

Mathew and Mark record that Jesus prayed three times. After he finished praying each time he went back to Peter, James and John. He wanted to see if they were watching and praying with him only to find them fast asleep each time. However, Luke only mentions one prayer. There is no inconsistency here; simply that Luke records the essence of Christ's prayer. Furthermore, there are also particular details included by one of the writers that the other two don't mention. None of these details contradict the others' accounts. They just include details that particularly interested them. For example as we have already seen, Luke, as a doctor, points out that the Lord Jesus sweated 'thick drops of blood'. Luke also refers to the angel that came to strengthen him whereas the other two do not include that detail. Mark says that Christ calls out 'Abba Father' and reminds God that all things are possible with him (Mark 14:36). By putting the accounts together it gives us a fuller picture of what happened.

Why he prayed

As Jesus faced the worst moment of his life, in fact the worst moment of anyone's life, he prays. This shouldn't surprise us at all. He was a busy man and because of that he was a man of prayer. Luke 4:31–44 illustrates the busyness and urgency of Jesus' mission (see especially v.43). Because of that he often retired to a lonely place to pray (5:16; 6:12; 9:18, 28; 11:1).

It is clear that Jesus viewed prayer as something refreshing. He had no sins to confess like we do. He didn't see prayer as something to do when you need something but rather saw prayer as a time to spend with his Father. In all that was going on and all that he had to face, he often went to be alone to lay it all out before his Father.

This is how we should look on prayer; as precious times spent with God. Times we can just enjoy being in his company. Asking him to draw near to us, telling him about our day, thinking about how awesome a God he is, telling him about the temptation we are struggling with, asking him to forgive us all our sins. Viewing prayer like this will be so refreshing. It shouldn't be another thing we have to do but rather the highlight of the day. Imagine having the opportunity to spend time alone with the Queen or the President of the USA every day. As a Christian I can spend time alone, as often as I want, with the God of Heaven and earth!

How he prayed

• Reverently
It would seem that as Jesus begun to pray he knelt (Luke 22:41). I don't think that from one verse in the Bible we should make it a requirement that to pray we have to be in the kneeling position. However, it tells us a lot. If the sinless, perfect Son of God knelt to pray, I cannot come into the presence of a Holy God any-old-how. I need to keep before my mind exactly who it is I am coming to. I am a sinner, entering the presence of a Holy God. I must come with reverence and awe.

• Earnestly
Even though he begun kneeling it would seem that as he prays he becomes more and more earnest and desperate and threw himself to the ground (Mark 14:35). He fell face down and prayed (Matthew 26:39). Luke says 'being in agony he prayed all the more earnestly' (Luke 22:44). The Lord Jesus persevered in prayer. He agonised in prayer. We know it was with strong crying and tears (Hebrews 5:7) that he prayed. He went back three times to pray. He would not or could not finish praying until he knew his prayer was answered.

When was the last time you agonised in prayer? We need to keep on at God until we know he has answered us. Our cat Cookie in the morning meows and meows and meows until we feed him. He won't stop meowing until he is fed. It has been known to go on for hours! He won't give in until he has his food. I get out of bed to feed him just to get him to be quiet. The Bible says our attitude should be that we keep asking until it is given to us, keep seeking until we find and keep knocking until the door is opened. The Lord Jesus told parables to illustrate how people should keep on and on until their prayers are heard (Luke 18:1–8; 11:5–13). God's friends search for him. They wait for him to come. He rewards those who diligently seek him (Hebrews 11:6).

• Intimately
He was intimate in his prayer. He was coming to his Father. It is

the only time in the Gospels where he addresses the father with the possessive pronoun, 'my father'. He cries out 'Abba Father' (Mark 14:36). This is as intimate as saying 'Dad'. We shall see in Chapter 18 that by faith Jesus' father is our father and we too can enjoy this intimate relationship.

There is a great picture of President Obama in the Oval office with one of his little daughters hiding behind the desk. To you and me, he is the president of the USA, the most powerful man in the world. To her he is dad. God is the creator of the universe, the Holy one, the judge. But to us who trust in him, he is also 'Abba Father', dad!

What he prayed

He asks 'If it is possible let this cup pass from me' (Matthew 26:39; Luke 22:42). By this cup he refers to this terrible impending experience. As a man, a real man, facing a holy God in the place of guilty sinners, it seems too much to bear. He doesn't know if his strength will be sufficient.

It cannot be underestimated that the Devil and all the forces of Hell were at this point tempting him. We all know temptation and know that it is at its strongest just before we give in. We can only imagine how powerful temptation would become if we did not give into it at all. It is impossible for us to understand the temptation Christ must have faced in Gethsemane. It was Satan's last few throws of the dice. Give in. Throw the towel in. Just go back to Heaven. Why put yourself through the cross?

But he rests in the will of God. He submits himself to that. He knows that the will of God is perfect and resigns himself to it. This is where true happiness is to be found. It will give you courage and make you brave. You can rest in the fact that even in the biggest difficulty it is working for your good (Romans 8:28). Make his will the matter of your prayer.

Is this how you pray? It is right to cast all our care upon Him (1 Peter 5:7) but at the end, once we know he has heard our prayer, we need to accept he knows best and if we don't get what we ask for it is because it is not for our good.

Even more so, it is to say only give me what is in line with your will. Please don't give me the desires of my heart if it is going to be bad for me (Psalm 106:15). This is what I want but you know best God and whatever comes my way, give me the strength I need. To be able to say 'your will be done' we need to know his will through reading the Bible and the help of the Holy Spirit.

When we pray like this, everything changes. We lay the whole situation out before him and tell him everything we have on our hearts and leave it with him. According to Olyott, p.135

> We pray ourselves empty. We go over it and over it again and again until we have nothing else to say. We hold nothing back. With tears we have confessed every sin we know about and all our foolishness. We have told him every mistake, every worry, every fear, every ache and pain, every difficulty we face. We have told him about every one we love, the sin of the world, the state of the churches. We have cast all our care upon him. It is then that he comes to us and speaks peace to our hearts which cannot be explained (Philippians 4:6–7). We feel the Father's embrace and the atmosphere of the Spirit. We find that Christ has never been so precious to us as now.

What happened when he prayed?

His prayer was answered. He still had to face the cross. He was still going to be betrayed into the hands of sinners. It was still going to be Satan's hour. He would still have to take upon himself the sin of all his people. The cup had not been taken away but he had been given strength to drink it. The cross his soul shrunk from facing still had to be faced but God had answered his prayer by giving him the strength to face it. The Lord Jesus came from Gethsemane with serene and resolute confidence. He says to Peter, 'shall I not drink the cup the Father has given me? (John 18:11). His mind was calm.

He had laid out his case before God. He had said that if there was any other way ... but had then trusted himself to the will of God.

Christ knew his prayer had been answered before it had been. There are times when we may know this. John refers to this as the prayer of faith (1 John 5:14–15). If we pray in line with God's will we can be sure of having what we ask for even before it happens. As soon as I finish praying I know my prayer has been answered.

Norman Grubb records (1934, pp. 98–99) that shortly after marrying in China in 1888, missionaries Charles and Priscilla Studd found themselves short of money. They resolved therefore that they would ask the Lord to supply their need and so planned to spend the night in prayer. Within twenty minutes of getting on their knees both of them knew that there was no need to pray any longer. There was such a sense of release and relief in their spirits that they knew God had heard their prayer.

It was almost two weeks before the postman came, but he did not take out of his bag any letter containing money. C.T. Studd therefore turned the postman's bag upside down so sure was he that his prayer had been answered nearly a fortnight earlier. A letter fell to the floor, containing a cheque and an explanation of why it had been sent. The writer had been unable to sleep because of a mysterious constraint on his spirit urging him to send money to the distant missionary couple.

Strength from another world

This anguish left Jesus so weak that an angel appeared to him to strengthen him (Luke 22:43). The baby who sat on Mary's lap, learnt to walk and talk, read and write; the boy who grew up and passed through puberty like all other boys and like every man got thirsty, tired and hungry, is now in total agony and desperately weak.

We can only imagine that at this point in Heaven, angels are looking down on him. These same angels had worshipped him in Heaven, sung for him at his birth (Luke 2:13, 14), strengthened him in the wilderness (Matthew 4:11), watched over his perfect, wonderful life and now crave permission from his Father to go from Heaven to Gethsemane to help him. You can imagine them saying 'oh let some of us or one of us go to his relief'. Instead of being worshipped he was about to be mocked; instead of being adored he was going to be taunted; in place of glory he was going to suffer real humiliation.

And one of those angels came to strengthen him. Maybe he was strengthened by being in pure angelic company. Or maybe he was brought a message from his Father in Heaven telling him to keep going, to think about what was about to be accomplished.

In the same way, in your times of deepest need you may expect the greatest comforts to come to you

A sympathetic High Priest

In the Old Testament the High Priest represented the people before God. But because of what Christ accomplished on the cross there is no need for priests anymore. Jesus Christ is our great High Priest and we can approach God directly through him. In order to represent the people before God, the High Priest needed to fully understand and sympathise with the people. Because Jesus suffered the way he did in Gethsemane he can fully sympathise with every one of us. The Bible calls him a sympathetic High Priest (Hebrews 4:14–16). He could not be sympathetic if he hadn't gone to Heaven via Gethsemane and the cross.

The Bible says that the Lord Jesus learned obedience (Hebrews 5:8). Jesus never did anything wrong. He was perfect so this cannot mean he learned how to be good. It really means he learned what it was like to be human. He learned what it was like to be me and you.

As you read this book the Lord Jesus is in Heaven at God's right hand. When I pray I need him, want him, must have him, as close as possible to God. But at the same time, I need him to remember what it was like to be me. His time on earth, especially in Gethsemane and on the cross, means he does.

I grew up in a place called Ebbw Vale. Our local MP was Michael Foot. He was the leader of the Labour party and would sit across the dispatch box in the House of Commons from the Prime Minister, Mrs Thatcher. He was right at the centre of things. And the great thing was he never forgot what it was like on the back streets of Ebbw Vale and Brynmawr and Tredegar. He was in Westminster where it mattered but had in his mind those south Wales valley towns and villages. Jesus Christ is in Heaven but as I pray to him from my bedroom or work or in Church or wherever, he represents my cause, remembering exactly what it is like to be me. He remembers when he was in Gethsemane and needed strengthening by his father and ministering angels (Luke 22:43). We should therefore go boldly to the throne of God where we will find grace to help in times of need (Hebrews 4:16).

I taught a girl who had one of the worst lives imaginable. Her mum sat in my office and told me in front of her that she didn't really love her. The girl got into all kinds of trouble and would go off at lunchtimes in cars with strangers and have sex; sometimes for money and sometimes not. I remember one day being so annoyed with her and giving her a huge telling off. I was worried for her, frustrated and angry. I can never forget her dissolving into tears and saying, 'Sir, you've got no idea what it's like to be me'. And I didn't. Maybe you are reading this book and you feel no one knows what it is like to be you. And we don't. But the one who once sweat big drops of blood, cried out with loud groans and threw himself to the ground in Gethsemane, does. And this same man in Heaven now sits, ever living to make intercession for all those who trust in him.

In Hebrews 4:15 it says that we do not have one who cannot. It is a double negative. In English two negatives negate each other. Very often when I am questioning boys who are in trouble they immediately say 'I don't know nothing'. They are absolutely right. They don't know nothing, they know something! A double negative cancels the other out. However, in Greek it strengthens it. By using a double negative, the writer to the Hebrews is saying it isn't that the Lord Jesus can sympathise with us, but that it is impossible for him not to.

A preacher once came to preach at the Heath Evangelical Church in Cardiff and gave a very memorable illustration of this. He said that his niece came in from the garden where she had picked flowers for her mother. What the little girl actually had in her hand was a clump of earth with some flowers mixed up with weeds. Her sentiment was lovely in that she wanted to bring something nice for her mother. The preacher said he spent time with the little girl picking out the weeds and getting rid of the earth to make the flowers a presentable posy for her mother. That is a picture of what Jesus Christ does with our prayers. We come to God in prayer, our theology not always correct; stumbling and stammering; repeating ourselves and not really saying what we want to. But in Heaven, there's a man, the God-man Jesus Christ who remembers Gethsemane, intercedes on our behalf and makes our prayers acceptable to God.

Watch and pray

• Unseen enemy

As we have seen, Jesus wanted to spend time alone praying to his Father but also needed his friends close by. So Peter, James and John go further into the garden with him and the Lord Jesus withdraws from them about a stone's throw. Before he does he tells them to 'remain watchful' 'keep on the alert' so you don't enter into temptation (Matthew 26:41). Christ is conscious that tonight the powers of darkness, the devil and all his minions will be active and dangerous. The only way to stand against such a foe is to watch and pray.

What is true of that night is true of every night. The Bible says that the devil roams the earth like a lion seeking whom he may devour. (1 Peter 5:8). It is important to realise that the struggle to live out the Christian life on earth has a deeper background.

If you are a Christian reading this book and someone asked you what is the biggest problem you face as a Christian maybe you would say the attraction of the world; being left out and not being part of the crowd. Perhaps there are particular temptations you face or sins you really struggle with. There could be a particular person that is giving you a hard time because you are a Christian. You may look at the state of the church today and conclude that the biggest problem the church faces is that she seems marginalised in society, misunderstood and mistreated by the world. You may feel your own church's attempts to evangelise and reach people are ineffective. Maybe your church has suffered a split with people leaving to start up their own church or join another.

All of these struggles are all very real and cause great distress. But none of these are yours or the church's biggest problem. The church's biggest problem is that the struggle on earth has a deeper background. Our real, most dangerous enemy is unseen. According to Lloyd-Jones (2002, p.176)

We all know something about persecution. We know what it is to be confronted by people who are unbelievers and anti-Christian, and how difficult they can make life for us at times. Yes, we know all that, but that is not the whole story. We need to be made aware of the fact that these men and women, these individuals, are but instruments of the great powers behind our world. The Bible impresses upon us the truth that it is the devil who is fighting God. So often we fail to remember that and, therefore, become confused and cannot understand things. What you and I see with our physical eyes is simply the visible part of a great spiritual war that is going on in another realm, in which we are being used, as it were, as the instruments.

This is why Jesus says to his disciples to watch and pray. We do not wrestle against flesh and blood, but against the rulers, against the authorities, against the cosmic powers over this present darkness, against the spiritual forces of evil in the heavenly places

(Ephesians 6:12). The only way to triumph is to be alert in prayer and depend on God. None of us in our own strength is a match for the devil.

• Flesh and the spirit

But the disciples couldn't stay awake, not even for a single hour. Sleeping past this hour was natural. It was probably past midnight. Jesus had told them over supper that one of them would betray him into the hands of his enemies, another would deny him. He has told them that he is about to die and that after his death they will suffer persecution. Quite a night! With all that had gone on that night they were no doubt sleeping for sorrow, worn out by grief.

We know from Matthew and Mark that he came to them three times and found them sleeping. Drowsiness got the better of them. Their hearts were not filled with prayer. Mark says the second time Christ comes to them they don't know how to answer him. The Lord Jesus gently rebukes all three of them but particularly Peter because of his earlier boasts (Matthew 26:33, 35). He asks Peter, 'couldn't you stay awake one hour?'

The Lord Jesus says the spirit is willing but the flesh is weak. Flesh does not have to have sinful connotations, hence the NIV goes wrong in Romans 8 by translating it sinful nature. Flesh is simply flesh but in this world it is woven into the falleness of everything. In a Christian it is a dead weight and hence I can only be changed by the life of the Spirit pouring in it. We are body and soul and because we live in a fallen world our body grows tired. In their spirit they want to watch and pray but they give into their flesh.

Finally

One of the most tender and touching pictures in the gospels is the third time the Lord Jesus Christ comes and finds the disciples sleeping. Jesus became flesh. He knows what it was to be tired and weak. This third time the Saviour is now tenderly keeping vigil over them. He wants them to rest as he thinks of all that is ahead of them. His own victory has been won. He has been strengthened through prayer. They'd failed him completely but he will never fail them.

The vigil was short though; there was a brief interval between Matthew 26:45 and Mark 14:41: He had to rouse the three men and tell them to sleep and take their rest later on as his betrayer is coming (Matthew 26:45, 46). Now they need to go to where the other eight were.

2

'On the night when he was betrayed'

Matthew 26:47–56; Mark 14:43–52;
Luke 22:47–53; John 18:2–11

Setting the scene

The time

THE EVENTS OF THIS CHAPTER TOOK PLACE AT NIGHT, A NIGHT that will always be remembered as 'the night when he was betrayed' (1 Corinthians 11:23). The fact it took place at night is emphasised. John says, 'and it was night' (John 13:30). It was the darkest night since the world begun; the darkest moment ever. The Lord Jesus says to the Devil, 'this is your hour' (Luke 22:53).

Jesus had been celebrating the Last Supper with his twelve disciples but Judas had left early and had hurried off to the chief priests (John 13:30). We can imagine that he said to them, 'We need to act tonight'. There was the worry now that Jesus' followers, especially those from Galilee who were in Jerusalem for the Passover, might gather in his defence.

The place

Jesus and his disciples would have left the upper room, crossed the Kidron valley and entered an olive grove called Gethsemane. We saw in the previous chapter this was one of Jesus' favourite places on earth. It was a familiar place, full of happy memories. It was the time of the Passover and there would have been a full moon. In the background would have been the sound of a gentle brook. But it was soon to be filled with the sound of stomping feet and lit up with torches.

The characters

On the one side you had Jesus and his disciples. Jesus had finished praying in agony and then briefly but tenderly watched vigil over Peter, James and John as they slept. He then told them to wake up because the hour had come and he was about to be betrayed into the hands of sinners (Mark 14:41) at which point they joined the other eight disciples.

On the other side was a large crowd, led by Judas Iscariot who, poignantly, is described as 'one of the twelve' (Mark 14:43). Judas standing there with them, once apparently stood with Jesus. As we shall see in this chapter, it goes to show just how close a man can be and still be lost!

The crowd with him was a large mob with swords and clubs, lanterns and torches. The Greek word for crowd in these accounts describe about 300 people. They would have felt the need of lanterns and torches at the prospect of scrambling around a mountainside looking for one man; and the need for clubs and swords just in case it all 'kicked off'.

This crowd included chief priests, the scribes and the elders of the people. These were three distinct groups within the Sanhedrin, the Jewish ruling council.

The chief priests were the religious leaders and also experts in

God's law. They were the priestly aristocracy that largely controlled the Sanhedrin. They hated Jesus because he had a knack of exposing their secret sins. The fact there were chief priests in the garden underlines the seriousness with which they took the arrest.

The elders of the people were the political leaders. They hated Jesus' popularity as he threatened their authority. A few days before, tens of thousands of people had lined the streets shouting 'hosanna' (John 12:12–19).

As well as the Jewish religious and political leaders, the crowd included Roman auxiliary troops who were usually stationed at Caesarea but during the feast days they were garrisoned in the fortress of Antonia to the north west of the temple complex.

This move to Jerusalem not only ensured more efficient policing of the large throngs that swelled the population of Jerusalem during the feasts but guaranteed that any mob violence bred by the crowding and religious fervour would be efficiently crushed. The risk of mob response was doubtless rather high in the case of an arrest of someone with Jesus' popularity. The cohort would have consisted of 600 men but Pilate probably didn't deplete the garrison to that extent.

Also there were officials from the chief priests and Pharisees, no doubt temple police and the primary arresting officers. These temple police had already been affected by Jesus. They had been sent to arrest him before but didn't because, 'no one ever spoke like this man' (John 7:45, 47). Some of them were in all likelihood the same people here.

The servant of the High Priest was there too, a high ranking personal slave of Caiaphas sent along to observe.

It was such a motley crowd to arrest such a gentle man. But there is safety in numbers. As it says in Shakespeare's Hamlet, 'Conscience makes cowards of us all'. The combination of Jewish and Roman authorities in this arrest indicts the whole world. Religion and politics unite to get rid of Christ. According to

Ramachandra (1996), 'Jesus was condemned to death not by the irreligious and the uncivilized but by the highest representatives of Jewish religion and Roman law.'

But there are two others in the garden, unseen.

Satan himself is in Gethsemane. Since the fall of mankind he knows someone is coming (Genesis 3:15). He didn't know who or when and has rushed breathlessly through history trying to destroy and bring down the only one who can save mankind. He tried his hardest at Jesus' birth (Matthew 2:16–18) and in the wilderness (Matthew 4:1–11) and now sees this as his chance to bring the Saviour down. This was Satan's hour (Luke 22:53).

But thankfully, God was also in the garden. God had planned it all! (Acts 2:23–24, 26).

Preliminary comments

Before we look at Judas' betrayal, we need to make four preliminary comments.

1. 'I was there'

Mark 14:51, 53 says, 'A young man followed him with nothing but a linen cloth about his body. And they seized him but he left the linen cloth and ran away naked'. Only Mark records this incident. It is of no interest to the other three Gospel writers. So why does Mark record it? If every word in the Bible is given by inspiration of God (2 Timothy 3:16) why include two verses about a man running away with no clothes on? Because this naked man is probably Mark. These two verses are Mark's signature. He is telling us, 'I was there'.

In all likelihood Judas and the others go to the upper room supposing Jesus was still there having supper with his disciples. The upper room was probably the upstairs room in Mark's mother's house (the same one that is mentioned in Acts 12:12). When the soldiers arrived at the house, Mark roused from his sleep, hastily cast about himself the loose linen garment or wrapper that lay by his bedside and followed (even runs ahead of) the armed band to see what would happen or try to warn Jesus.

When they bound Jesus the disciples all fled but Mark remained as a deeply interested onlooker. He was on the periphery of it all and lingered in the rear and followed as they led away Jesus, never imagining they would attempt to lay hold of him since he had not been with the disciples in the garden. But they do, and so he wriggles out of his garment and runs away naked.

This is important for us because we know that what we are reading is an eye-witness account. These Gospel writers were good historians. They were eye witnesses, or used eye witnesses. John tells us in his account of the betrayal that the servant's name was Malchus (John 18:10). He knows this because he knows the High Priest (John 18:15). This again is the touch of an eye witness. The gospel writers were close to the action.

In my job I sometimes have to sort out fights between pupils. If a fight has occurred at a lunchtime I have to interview pupils to find out what happened. Everyone wants to get out of last lesson to tell me about it! However, most of them have only heard what others have said about what happened and so they are sent back to lessons rather sharpish. But then someone comes to my office and says, 'Sir, I saw everything. I saw the punches flying in; I could hear the hair being torn; I could smell the sweat and see the blood. I saw everything Sir; I couldn't have been closer to the action; I was ringside!' The men who wrote their accounts about Jesus' death and resurrection could not have been closer to the action. They were ringside!

2 Nothing to hide

When the soldiers take hold of him, Jesus said, 'Have you come out as against a robber, with swords and clubs to capture me? Day after day I was with you in the temple teaching, and you did not seize me' (Mark 14:48, 49). Why were they trying to arrest him slyly? John says he couldn't move freely because word was out on the street to hand him over (John 11). But he had taught openly in the

Temple. Why couldn't they take him during the day, in the open? Jesus is saying to them, 'I have got nothing to hide'.

Christianity stands up to scrutiny. It has nothing to hide. People today try to undermine, take some of its teaching out of context, distort it, misrepresent it, but Jesus invites everyone to examine it. All of it. Christianity never seeks to brainwash people. It is not sect-like or Trojan horse-like in any way, shape or form. It is a reasonable faith. If you are reading this book and have heard things, have already made up your mind, got preconceived ideas, then at least examine him again with an open mind.

If Jesus did have any dirt, then surely Judas, who had been with him at close quarters for three years, would have dished it. Judas had heard every sermon he preached, listened to every parable and seen every miracle. Outside the twelve, no one knew Jesus better than Judas. After three years in his presence, if Jesus had any faults or flaws, or wasn't who he claimed to be, Judas would have known. In the end, Judas is plain proof that Jesus was innocent of every charge laid against him and stands up to the most intense examination.

3 It's me you want, let them go

When the soldiers arrest him they try to take hold of his disciples too, but Jesus steps forward and says, if it is me you seek let these go their way (John 18:8).

This shows Jesus' tender care for his disciples. They had already let him down that evening by sleeping when they should have been watching and praying and things were about to go from bad to worse, but he cares deeply for them. In the hour of his greatest disturbance of mind this shows the care he has towards his people.

It also shows great wisdom. They were not ready to suffer. They needed to be alive so that they could be witnesses of all that is about to happen. If they had died with Jesus that night we wouldn't know about it today.

But this incident illustrates a great truth. It foreshadows the ultimate rescue Christ would accomplish in the next few hours for all those who trust him. Through his death on the cross, sinners can go free. One day I will stand before the judgement seat of God. On that day, people I went to school with, worked with, grew up with, went to church with; my own family will all be able to tell stories of how sinful I am, how hypocritical I have been. God's law will condemn me at every point. My conscience will accuse me of things even those closest to me don't know. And the devil will say, 'aha, got you!' But Jesus will step forward and say 'it's me you've come for, let him go'. Because on that cross all my wrong, my filth, my shame were laid on him. And no one who is trusting in him will be lost or put to shame. Jesus can say, 'Of those whom you gave me I have lost none' (John 18:9) and this is symbolised in this arrest.

In school I had a mate called Huw. He was really hard. There was one occasion when another boy wanted to kick my head in. Just as he was about to carry out his attack, Huw stood between us and said 'if you want him you've got to come through me'. (To which I popped my head out from behind Huw and said 'yeah!')

When I stand at the judgement, Jesus will say to all my accusers, if you want him, you will have to come through me.

4 The weapons of our warfare
When this large crowd marched into the garden with their torches, lanterns, clubs and swords, it must have been quite frightening for the disciples. And when they took hold of Jesus to arrest him Peter drew out his sword and cut off the ear of Malchus, servant of the High Priest (John 18:10; Matthew 26:51; Mark 14:47). We know at least one other of the disciples was armed and ready to strike (Luke 22:49).

In coming to Jerusalem for the festival, some Galileans would have provided themselves with short swords which they concealed under their upper garments. But Jesus tells them to put their swords away. He actually says, 'No more of this! Stop it!' (Matthew 26:52) and then heals the ear of Malchus (Luke 22:51).

As well intentioned as Peter no doubt was, this was the height of foolishness. Jesus says if he wanted to he could call on his father who would at once put at his disposal more than twelve legions of angels. But how then would the Scriptures be fulfilled that say it must happen this way (Matthew 26:52–54)?

Twelve legion of angels is a lot of angels. A Roman legion was 12,000 men. By just saying the word, Jesus could call on about 150,000 invisible angels. He doesn't need a fisherman with a terrible aim (I don't think he was aiming for the ear!) to fight for him.

Few things have done more damage to the cause of Christ than misguided attempts to advance the kingdom with the sword. People who have fought in the name of Christ, taken part in holy wars, have done nothing but bring shame and reproach on the gospel. The Lord Jesus condemns those who use carnal weapons in defence of him and his cause

The Church is engaged in a different kind of warfare (Ephesians 6:17). The weapons of our warfare are not swords, guns, armies and bombs but prayer and preaching. But I guess most, if not all of you reading this book, have no intention of taking up arms to fight for Christ. But do you trust completely in the weapons of our warfare—prayer and preaching? Do you look at this trendy, high tech age and think we need to use more sophisticated weapons? We will never be able to compete with the world on their terms. They will always be able to do things bigger and better. A fisherman brandishing a sword whacking off the ear of a lowly servant will never be a match for a 300 strong army with clubs and swords.

In Cardiff in the 1970s, 80s and early 90s in particular, a frail man stood in a pulpit. He preached from a Bible from the 16th Century and sang hymns mainly from the 17th century and hundreds were won for the gospel. His secret was his unflinching faith in preaching and prayer and an absolute dependence on the Holy Spirit.

Don't lose confidence in the weapons the commanding officer has provided!

Judas
God's sovereignty and man's responsibility

God's sovereignty

The events in Gethsemane at first glance would appear to be the worst in the history of redemption. It was the darkest moment ever. Total depravity. The longed for, promised Messiah has been arrested and bound up by a 300 strong mob, betrayed by one of his own and abandoned by the remaining eleven disciples. But look closer and you will see that it was all planned; eternally planned. Matthew 25:56 says all this happened 'that the scriptures must be fulfilled' (Matthew 26:56). Everything that happened from Gethsemane to Calvary is according to God's Word and was marked out hundreds of years before. On the cross, when he cries out, 'I thirst' it was so that the scripture might be fulfilled (John 19:28). When they don't break his legs it is so the scripture might be fulfilled (John 19:36); when they pierce his side and blood and water flow out it is so the scripture might be fulfilled (John 19:37). All planned!

Jesus was surrounded by a crowd with clubs and swords, but he is majestic. The circumstances are humiliating and degrading but he is in control of the whole situation.

Previous attempted arrests had failed because the time wasn't right (John 7:45, 46; John 8:58, 59; John 10:39) but now he takes the initiative. He went to meet his captors knowing full well 'all that was going to happen to him' and asks them, 'Who are you looking for?' (John 18:4).

The crowd had come looking for Jesus of Nazareth (John 18:5). Nazareth was the village of his childhood. They expected to arrest a carpenter-cum itinerant preacher from a notorious dump of a town up north (John 1:46). But in front of them, in full view stood the master of the winds and waves (Matthew 8:27). He answered them by saying 'I am he' (John 18:6) at which point they fell backwards to the ground. In the Old Testament, 'I AM' was how God disclosed himself to Moses (Exodus 3:14). Jesus is saying here 'I AM'; I am God.

There is a great mystery to God's sovereignty and we can never pretend to have worked it all out. We are not to make out that we know everything and have got all our doctrine sown up. When we do this, we trivialise it.

Why did the Lord Jesus stay up all night praying before he chose his twelve disciples and then choose Judas? (Luke 6:12–16). A man of whom he also said it would better for him if he had not been born (Mark 14:21). Why did God choose Israel who would turn against him? We must at these points acknowledge that the secret things belong to God (Deuteronomy 29:29). We mustn't invade his privacy. We will never speculate our way to faith. That which appears contradictory isn't so from Heaven's vantage point. We have secrets from our children for their good. I don't sit down with my son and go through the family finances. There are things his mum and I discuss after he has gone to bed. He doesn't need to know and his little mind wouldn't cope with it. It is infinitely more the case with God. Our minds, even the cleverest, are still tiny compared to the creator of heaven and earth. Just because I don't understand doesn't mean it can't all make perfect sense. I go as far as I can in understanding and knowing the God of the Bible but there comes points where I have to simply trust and acknowledge, 'who has understood the mind of God?' (1 Corinthians 2:16). The unknowability of God expresses his glory.

Man's responsibility

But while the Bible teaches on every page the sovereignty of God, it also teaches man's responsibility. Even though all of this was planned by God, it doesn't excuse Judas. This is impossible to understand but Judas' actions are Judas' actions. He is not a pawn. He is responsible. He hasn't been pre-programmed, but acts against his conscience. God overrules the evil that people do but doesn't make that evil right. Joseph says in Genesis 50:20, 'You meant evil but God meant it for good'.

Some of you reading this book may be guilty of misusing or misunderstanding the sovereignty of God. You play down man's responsibility. Maybe you struggle with the idea that God elects some to be saved and not others (Romans 8:29; Ephesians 1:4–5, 11; Romans 9:6–29; 1 Peter 2:8; Jude 4). You believe that the Lord Jesus died on the cross just for the elect and view the whole thing as already sown-up, pre-programmed and mechanical. You've got every drop of blood that was shed by the Son of God accounted for. You may think it seems so unfair; that some people have no chance. You may even worry that you are not among the elect and think to yourself that he couldn't possibly choose you. It may leave you with the impression that God is a hard, cold, calculating being.

But while the Bible does teach particular redemption it also teaches that whosoever will may come (John 6:37) that whoever calls on the name of the Lord shall be saved (Acts 2:21) that it is his will that none should perish (2 Peter 3:9), that he holds his arms open all the day long (Romans 10:21) and that even though they had stoned the prophets he would have done anything to gather the people of Jerusalem like a hen gathers her chicks but they would not (Matthew 23:37). These truths are equally true. I can't reconcile the two. But as the 19th-century preacher Charles Spurgeon said, there is no need to reconcile friends; and God's sovereignty and man's responsibility are friends. The best of friends.

The Bible teaches that every Christian has been elected before the foundation of the earth. But Jesus also said, whoever comes to me I will never turn away. And that isn't the peg I am hanging my hat on, nor the peg I am hanging my coat on. But the peg I am hanging my eternal soul on!

The worst kind of betrayal

The chief priests, elders of the people and scribes were desperately trying to find a way to get Jesus. They had assembled earlier at the palace of the High Priest, Caiaphas, and plotted to take Jesus by trickery and kill him. They didn't want to do it during the Feast in case of an uproar among the people (Matthew 26:3–5). So they couldn't believe their 'luck' when Judas, one of the twelve, came along with his plan of handing him over at night. This golden opportunity came from the most unexpected quarter. He had probably gone to them the previous day and asked them what they would give him if he delivered them over to him and from that moment had looked for an opportunity to betray him (Matthew 26:14–16).

No one would have imagined it would be one of Jesus' own. If you read the Bible for the first time without knowing anything you would think 'are you kidding me? One of his disciples?'

And to make matters even worse, he doesn't betray Jesus by pointing him out but by kissing him. He says to the crowd the one I kiss is the man, seize him (Matthew 26:48). He then goes on ahead a bit and says, 'greetings Rabbi' (Matthew 26:49) and kisses him. In fact, the word used indicates he kissed him fervently and repeatedly.

It was customary for Jesus' disciples to greet Jesus like this. It was what friends did when they met in an eastern country. This wasn't the kiss a British person would give a fellow Brit when they meet; a peck on the cheek or even the 'air' kiss! This was an uninhibited embrace between two good friends. It shows Jesus was not an austere man and the kiss from Judas expressed love and friendship.

Isn't it the case that the worst and most wicked acts may be done under a show of love for Christ? Hasn't more damage been done to the Lord Jesus and his cause by the so called church? There are so many issues that are hotly debated in the media, by the apparently brightest academics, by talking heads and by politicians—how the world was made, ways of life, leadership in the church, other faiths. So many making real assaults at the living God and ripping the Bible to shreds. But who lets the side down the most? Isn't it the so called church who dumbs down her message, takes the difficult bits out and tells a world that is hurtling full throttle to Hell, 'Peace, peace when there is no peace' (Jeremiah 6:14).

Why do it Judas?

So why did Judas betray him? The most obvious answer is he did it for 30 pieces of silver. We know he loved money, was greedy and a thief. He was the treasurer of the group and helped himself from the money bag (John 12:5, 6). The tipping point probably came for Judas a couple of days before when Mary anointed Jesus' feet with expensive perfume. He couldn't handle it any more. Even though he pretended to be outraged because the money could have been used to help the poor, it was really because he would have loved to have got his hands on the money (John 12:6). It is after this that he goes straight to the priests and says, 'what are you willing to give me and I'll hand him over.'

Judas loved money more than God. What do you love more than God? What are you prepared to hand God over for? What do you want so much that you are prepared to hold on to at the expense of Jesus Christ? Perhaps it is your love of money or drink or sex or whatever. The question is, are you willing to go to Hell for it?

It could also be that Judas became disillusioned. He may have thought that Jesus would overthrow the Romans and bring the Jews back to political power. If that was the case, Judas could get something out of all this. Judas' attitude to Jesus is in stark contrast with the lady who anointed his feet with expensive perfume. Her attitude was what can I give Jesus whereas Judas' was what can I get out of Jesus. He wanted Jesus to do what he wanted him to do. He followed him for all the wrong reasons and when things were turning out in a different way to how Judas imagined he walked out on him. He never loved Jesus.

Maybe that is you as you read this book. You can follow Jesus when it fits in with you or when it seems that it is going to be to your advantage. But what about when suffering comes. When you get left out of things. When you have to deny yourself something. When you're the only young person in your youth group. These are the times that show if you genuinely love him.

The deceitfulness of sin

Judas' betrayal shows the deceitfulness of sin. There are sins we all enjoy and think we will have our fun with them and then when we are done we will give them up and at that point may even turn to Christ. But sin is dangerous and if we play with it, instead of us having sin, sin has us.

Early on the evening of the Last Supper, John says the devil had already put it into the heart of Judas Iscariot to betray him (John 13:2). But by the end of the evening John says 'Satan entered him' (John 13:27). Satan entered him! What a petrifying thought. But however strong the satanic influences it was because there was a time when Judas opened himself to them. Judas opened the door to Satan. It wasn't an unwanted invasion but a welcome invitation.

If we yield to sin, keep giving into it, it will enslave you. It is no longer that you tell lies but you are a liar; you no longer steal, but you are a thief. One click on a pornographic website could lead to addiction. Like an addict you won't think straight and will just do whatever it takes to get your fix of your particular sin. Judas says to the chief priest 'What will you give me for him' (Matthew 26:15). Judas is not setting the price. Thirty pieces of silver wasn't a huge amount of money. It was the price of a slave (Exodus 21). It was probably a third of the price of the perfume Mary had used to anoint his feet (John 12:3). And yet that is what Judas was prepared to get in exchange for Jesus Christ.

That is the same as us. Whatever sin it is in the end it will cheapen you and you will end up selling Jesus Christ for something that is just not worth it. Sin ends up being totally in control. It is the devil's lie, a total illusion that you believe you can stop sinning when you decide. You can't! Repent now before it is too late and you will not want or be able to (Hebrews 12:17; Exodus 10:20). If you don't kill sin, sin will kill you.

Sin also promises so much but always leaves you feeling dirty and guilty. It feels so good at the time but it ruins lives, breaks up families and causes untold pain. The journalist Malcolm Muggeridge once met a woman who, he was told, had slept with the writer H.G. Wells. He asked her how it had happened. She told him that Wells had approached her at a party and said, 'Shall we go upstairs and do something funny?' 'And was it funny?' asked Muggeridge. 'No sir, it was not funny' she replied. 'That evening has caused me more misery than any other evening in my life.'

Even the best things in life will not fulfil you totally. You could gain the whole world only to find out the world is not enough.

Johnny Wilkinson (*The Times*, November 21st 2009) powerfully proves this point when he described what it was like winning the rugby world cup for England. It was the pinnacle of his career and something almost every school boy in the country dreams of. But this is what he said:

> I had already begun to feel the elation slipping away from me during the lap of honour around the field. I couldn't believe that all the effort was losing its worth so soon. This was something I had fantasised about achieving since I was a child. In my head I had reached the peak of the mountain and now all that was left was to slowly descend the other side. I'd just achieved my greatest ambition and it felt a bit empty.

So near and yet so far

This incident also shows that those who pretend to follow Christ are not saved. You can appear to all intents and purposes to be a Christian but actually be eternally lost. You can be so close and yet so far. No one was closer to Jesus than Judas but today no one is further from him.

As they ate the Last Supper in the upper room all thirteen of them would have been gathered around a low meal table, reclining on cushions on the floor. They had just walked to Jerusalem from Bethany and their feet would have been dirty, smelly, tired and no doubt a bit sore. It was a servant's job to wash people's feet and it was the most menial of all their tasks. Just imagine washing off the sweat and grime from people's feet after they'd walked in sandals along those dirty, dusty roads! Anything to do with feet was seen as the lowest of the low. John the Baptist, in trying to emphasise his inferiority to Jesus said that he was not even worthy to carry his sandals (Matthew 3:11).

In the upper room would have stood the pitcher together with the wash basin and the linen cloth but there was no servant in attendance to carry out this task. The disciples had just been arguing about who was the greatest (Luke 22:24) and every one of them would have viewed this job as totally beneath them and all would be hoping someone else would do it. But no one expected what happened next and it left an indelible impression on John's mind. As he writes his Gospel years later he remembers every detail.

The Authorised Version of the Bible says that what happened next took place after supper (John 13:2) but this translation is to be rejected in favour of more accurate translations which say it took place as the meal was being served (New American Standard, English Standard Version, New International Version, Amplified Bible). The Lord Jesus Christ, the eternal Son of God and creator of the universe, put on a slave's apron, poured water into a basin and went around the disciples one by one washing their feet. Even when he got to Judas, the man who in a few hours was going to betray him to his enemies in the cruellest way, he took his dirty feet, washed them and then wiped them with the towel tied around his waist.

It was after this as the supper was in full swing that Jesus became troubled in his spirit and predicted that one of the assembled disciples would betray him (John 13:21). This evoked stunned silence and the disciples looked at one another, uncertain of whom he spoke (John 13:22). No one had a clue who it was.

No one suspected Judas. He was trusted to look after the finances. It would seem he was morally admirable. When Jesus said one of them would betray him, no one suspected him. They didn't all turn around and look at Judas and say, 'I bet it's him.' There is no reference to him being a boaster like Peter. He didn't ask dull questions like some of the others nor did he ask to sit at the right hand, the place of honour in Heaven, like James and John. Tradition says he was the best preacher of the twelve, but we can't be sure of this.

After this bombshell, it was Peter who recovered first and signalled to John to prompt him to ask the question discreetly. John would have been reclining next to Jesus but on his right, therefore his back towards the Master. The easiest way for him to do what Peter had asked him to was to lean back until his head was literally on Jesus' breast (chest). It is clear that Jesus answers the question in quiet tones (John 13:27–30). Jesus says that the one he gives the morsel of bread to after he has dipped it (John 13:26). The dish would have contained a sauce of dried fruit and spices with wine and at Passover Jews would dip bitter herbs into it to remind them of the bitterness of slavery. The host of a feast might well dip into a common bowl and pick out a particularly tasty bit and pass it to a guest as a mark of honour and friendship. This morsel Jesus passes to Judas. He passed it so easily it would suggest Judas was close, probably on his left, the place of honour.

After taking the morsel Judas leaves, with the majority of disciples still none the wiser. They thought Jesus asked Judas to buy whatever was needed for the feast or to give something the poor. But John 13:30 rather chillingly says of Judas, 'He went out and it was night'

Judas was sat right next to Jesus and had his feet washed by him. So close, but so far! The apostle Paul says, 'examine yourself to see if you are in the faith'. You can be in the group, hear a thousand sermons but be eternally lost!

Not too late

The morsel of bread that Jesus passes to Judas is the final act of supreme love by the Lord Jesus towards Judas but instead of breaking his heart it hardens his resolve. Knowing full well what he was about to do, Judas asks, 'Is it I, Rabbi?' (Matthew 26:25).

It is impossible for us to understand how overwhelming this was for the Lord Jesus. He was as much a man as you and I with the same emotions and feelings. One of his closest friends was about to betray him into the hands of his enemies. The original Greek, which was the language the New Testament was first written in, underlines the depth of anguish and hurt Christ felt when he said, 'he has taken cruel advantage of me'; 'he has walked out on me' (John 13:18) and Christ clearly wanted him to get what he is about to do over and done with as quickly as possible when he says in John 13:27 'Do it quickly' (more quickly than you were planning).

Judas' betrayal broke his heart. After he washed the disciples' feet (a symbol of spiritual cleansing) he said you are all clean but not all of you and turned a tearful eye towards Judas (John 13:10).

Some say that warning or admonition to Judas at this stage was impossible. They say that this had all been planned and programmed. But as we have already seen in this chapter, who can know the mind of God (1 Corinthians 2:16)?

After Judas kissed him, Jesus said 'Friend why have you come?' (Matthew 26:50 NKJV). Friend, are you sure. It is not too late. You can still turn back.

And this same kind Saviour says to you, whatever you have

done, and however many times you have done it, friend, it is not too late. Come unto me (Matthew 11:28).

The worst possible end

In Gethsemane as Judas led the procession he was bold. He felt important and part of the crowd. But as the night passes and the dawn breaks Judas is now alone and remorseful. It is a powerful picture of what things are like before and after we sin. As we have seen sin is bewitching and intoxicating but once it is over it leaves you feeling dirty, guilty and scared. Only the naked facts remain. All the glamour has been dispelled; all the reality remains

The bag with the 30 pieces of silver in I imagine now feels like it is weighing so much and Judas just has to get rid of it. He goes back to the place where he could find the chief priests and elders. And without help and hope, totally isolated he goes through the Jerusalem streets.

At this point Jesus has been arrested. He is probably with Herod (as we shall see in Chapter 6) or immediately after it (Matthew 27:3–5). And by now all Jerusalem is talking about it. Judas realises Jesus is condemned. He goes to the chief priests and the elders and says I have sinned and betrayed innocent blood (Matthew 27:3). He rushed towards the sanctuary itself, probably to where priests gathered in the court of Israel, where generally the penitents stood in waiting while at the priests' court the sacrifice was offered for them. He is sorry for the mess he is in but not sorry to Christ. The elders and chief priests have no interest. They say to him, 'what is that to us?' (Matthew 27:4). In effect they say to him that's your problem, you deal with it! He has served his purpose. They are impatient and full of contempt. They've chewed him up and spat him out.

The Jewish leaders can't use the money because they view it as tainted money even though they had created this kind of money. So they bought a field and transformed it into a burial ground for foreigners: People who came to Jerusalem to attend feasts but died there and were unable to be provided with a funeral because they had no relative or friend. But this good deed couldn't cleanse their hearts or hands. It became known as the Field of Blood (Acts 1:19).

Even this was a fulfilment of prophecy. Again, critics of the Bible find it hard to see which prophecy it is referring to. But good students look carefully and find that the prophecy combines Jeremiah 19 and Zechariah 11:13: The fact that Matthew says it was spoken by the prophet Jeremiah (Matthew 27:9) and no mention of Zechariah is because the title Jeremiah, as the major prophet, would be given to the entire book of the prophets and they would not see the need to mention Zechariah as the minor prophet. The main point is that prophecy again is being fulfilled

And so completely alone, without a friend in the world, no help, no escape, no counsel or hope anywhere, Judas throws the coins down so that each resounded as it fell on the marble pavement. Matthew 27:5 says that he then 'went and hanged himself' Matthew 27:5: whereas Acts 1:18 says 'falling headlong he burst open in the middle and all his bowels gushed out'.

Putting the two together, it would appear Judas rushed out of the temple, out of Jerusalem and down into the solitude of the valley of Hinnom. He heads to the Potter's field somewhat to the west above where the Kidron and Hinnom valleys merge and jagged rocks rise perpendicularly. He runs up the steep side of the rocky mountain looking for a tree. He takes off his outer garment and puts it over the tree and ties it around his neck and throws himself off from that jagged rock. The branch snaps and down he comes falling heavily among the jagged rocks beneath and into the sea. His guts spill out and he dies a horrible death. The minute he closes his eyes in death, he opens them in Hell. Forever!

And hours before the Son of God had washed his feet. He had been at all the services. He had heard every parable, seen every miracle and listened to every sermon. He had been at the Last Supper; had sat next to the Lord Jesus. He was the treasurer. But now he is in Hell, and the darkest, deepest part of it!

Sin is the hardest, cruellest, and most deceitful of all masters. What a miserable end a man comes to if he has great privileges and does not use them rightly!

The Puritan John Bunyan, in his famous book *Pilgrims Progress* which he wrote whilst in prison in 1676, describes the glorious scene at the end of the book when Christian enters Heaven. He also describes Ignorance arriving at the gates. Ignorance thought he was a Christian but he wasn't and on arrival at Heaven he gets turned away. His hands and feet are bound and he is thrown out. Bunyan (1997, p.189) comments, 'Then I saw that there was a way to Hell even from the gates of Heaven'.

The same is true of every church and chapel; every Christian camp, conference and youth group. There is a way to Hell from every one of them.

3

At least give him a fair trial

(John 18:12–14, 19–23; Matthew 26:57–68; Mark 14:53–65; Luke 22:54–71)

How the events unfolded

BEFORE THEY WENT UP TO JERUSALEM FOR THE PASSOVER, JESUS Christ told his disciples he would be delivered up and handed over to the chief priests and the scribes and they will condemn him to death and deliver him over to the Gentiles (Mark 10:33). And that is precisely what happened. The events that took place in Gethsemane and the events that are about to take place were planned meticulously by God in eternity past (Ephesians 1:4, 5; 3:8–11).

In the previous chapter we saw how Jesus was betrayed into the hands of his enemies by Judas Iscariot. Now the Son of God, the creator and upholder of Heaven and earth, the holy one, the one at whose command nations rise and fall, the judge of all the earth, the one in whom are hid all the treasures of wisdom and knowledge (Colossians 2:3) is impeached as a villain before the chief priests and elders and scribes. The heads of the Jewish nation combine together to judge and kill their own Messiah. The problem was, the Jews had no power to put Jesus to death. So once they find him guilty according to Jewish law, they hand him over to be sentenced to death by the Roman governor, Pontius Pilate.

The trial took place in three stages on the Thursday night and early hours of Friday morning. After the arrest in Gethsemane, Jesus was initially tied up and taken to the former High Priest, Annas, for questioning. After Annas had questioned him he sent him bound to the High Priest, Caiaphas; and then very early on the Friday morning he appeared before the Jewish council, the Sanhedrin.

While Jesus stood trial before Annas and Caiaphas, Peter was in the courtyard denying that he knew Jesus. We will pick up that part of the story in the next chapter.

Where it all took place

Jesus wasn't taken to the Temple for questioning. This is a virtual certainty with the mention of a girl on duty at the gate (John 18:16) as only men held such assignments in the Temple precincts. It appears that Jesus was taken from Gethsemane to the upper city where stood the palace of Annas. After Annas had informally examined him, Jesus was then taken bound from Annas' palace to Caiaphas'.

The question has been raised how Jesus could be transported from Annas to Caiaphas so easily. But it would seem that Annas and Caiaphas' quarters were in close proximity to one another. It is likely that there was a quadrangle courtyard in the centre of the High Priest's residence. Above the courtyard were apartments (Mark 14:66 says that Peter was below in the courtyard). One wing was occupied by Caiaphas and another by Annas. This would explain how the prisoner was easily sent from the one to the other; it was just across the courtyard.

We know that John followed Jesus into the courtyard of the High Priest (John 18:15). He was able to walk into this courtyard without being questioned and speak to the servant girl attending the gate to get Peter in (John 18:16). This has caused some to wonder how a lowly Galilean fisherman like John would be known by the High Priest in Jerusalem. But it must be borne in mind that John's father was wealthy enough to have hired hands (Mark 1:19–20) and so could very well have had connections to the High Priest; perhaps a relative or two on the inside track in Jerusalem, which means the connection between a Galilean fisherman and the Jerusalem High Priest doesn't seem so far-fetched, especially in a society which did not erect barriers between manual labour and educational or priestly roles.

What is obvious is that John's recollection of that night is one of an eye witness. There are touches which show he was there. He remembers it was a cold night and doesn't just say people warmed themselves by fires but that they were 'charcoal fires' (John 18:18).

Annas

So the detachment of troops and the captain and the officers of the Jews arrested Jesus, tied him up and led him first to Annas who would have dismissed the Roman soldiers as quickly as possible before informally examining Jesus (John 18:12–14; 19–23). This examination possibly took place while some members of the Sanhedrin were being hurriedly assembled and getting themselves together.

Annas had been the High Priest from AD 6 until AD 15 when Valerius Gratus, Pilate's predecessor, deposed him. Even so, Annas continued to hold enormous influence, not only because many Jews resented the deposition and appointment of a High Priest by a foreign power (under Mosaic legislation the appointment of High Priest was for life) but also because no fewer than five of Annas' sons and his son-in-law Caiaphas held the office at one time or another. Annas was viewed as the patriarch of a High Priestly family and regarded as the real High Priest. Whatever Caiaphas said, people would no doubt ask, 'have you cleared it with Annas?'

Annas enjoyed a lot of influence with the Romans. This was largely down to the religious views he professed; to his open partisanship of the foreigner and his enormous wealth. Annas was a Sadducee which was on the liberal side of Judaism as opposed to the strict Pharisees. He was therefore not troubled with any special convictions nor with Jewish fanaticism. As far as the Romans were concerned, he was as Edersheim (2004, p.851) comments, 'a pleasant and useful man who was able to furnish his friends in the Praetorium with large sums of money'.

As a person, he was greedy, serpent-like and vindictive (John 18:13) and he would have hated Jesus. This had a lot to do with the fact that Jesus had on a number of occasions interfered with temple-traffic (John 2:13–22; Mark 11:15–19); something that was so despicable and unpopular with the people. One can only imagine the immense revenues the family of Annas must have derived from the Temple booths. If Jesus' authority had prevailed it would have been fatal to it. In this, and other respects, it is easy to see how antithetic such a Messiah as Jesus must have been to Annas. Jesus on the scene would cost Annas too much, so he had to be got rid of.

Annas' questions centred on Jesus' disciples and his teaching (John 18:19) but Jesus told Annas that he had spoken openly to the world. He says, 'I have always taught in synagogues and in the temple, where all Jews come together. I have said nothing in secret. Why do you ask me? Ask those who have heard me what I said to them; they know what I said' (John 18:21).

As we saw in the last chapter, Jesus has got nothing to hide. Christianity isn't a sect that is surrounded in secrecy and full of things to be ashamed of. The Christian message stands up to intense scrutiny. The church should preach the Bible openly and clearly. Like Paul we should be unashamed of the gospel as it is the power of God for salvation to everyone who believes (Romans 1:16). The gospel is good news which should be proclaimed to all. We shouldn't apologise for its message or try to sanitise parts of it and dumb things down. We have nothing to hide or be embarrassed about. It is a reasonable faith; it makes sense and we should do all that we can to give a reason for the hope that is in us (1 Peter 3:15).

Even so, the way Jesus answered Annas resulted in one of the officers standing up and striking Jesus saying, 'Is that how you answer the high priest?' (John 18:22). We hate the truth when it says what we don't want to hear!

Once Annas realised he was getting nowhere with him he sent him bound to Caiaphas the High Priest (18:24).

Caiaphas

As a man, Caiaphas was rude, sly and hypocritical (John 11:49, 50). He was the High Priest at this time and as far as the Romans were concerned (as they had put him in that position) the one they recognised as the leader of the Jews. In their eyes he was the chairman of the Sanhedrin, the Jewish ruling council.

We know that some of the scribes and the elders who were members of the Sanhedrin were with Caiaphas (Matthew 26:57). However this second stage of the investigation (John 18:24) in all likelihood was still relatively private with some, but not all, of the members of the Sanhedrin present. The formal meeting and action of the Sanhedrin took place at about dawn.

Jesus standing before Caiaphas wasn't so much a trial but a plot. The religious leaders' problem with Jesus had been building up for a while and it is clear they had decided long ago to put him to death. They had no interest in the evidence or conducting a fair trial but just wanted to find something they could take to the Romans to justify the death of Jesus of Nazareth.

There was so much about him they despised. Jesus called the

temple court from where they derived much of their profit a 'den of thieves' and he said that he would break down the temple and in three days would raise it up again (John 2:19). They didn't like the friends he associated with (Matthew 9:11) and he didn't keep the Sabbath according to their traditions (Matthew 12:9–14; Mark 2:22–27; John 5:1–18). Jesus had criticised the Pharisees for exalting their traditions over scripture (Mark 7:9). They thought he posed as a rabbi with no formal training or authorisation (John 7:15). They cared more about the externals of religion and appearing to keep the rules, than loving God. They placed more emphasis on ceremonial cleansing than moral purity (Matthew 15:1–11). They were hypocrites and Jesus exposed their hypocrisy (Matthew 23).

But mainly behind their decision was envy. They hated Jesus' popularity with the people and the authority he had and their envy towards Jesus really exposed their pride. No one is ever envious if they are not first proud of themselves. These men were proud of their nation's long history of a special relationship with God, proud of their own leadership role of this nation, proud of their authority. With Jesus on the scene all of this was threatened. Not realising the profundity of what he was actually saying, Caiaphas had advised the Jews it was expedient for one man to die for the people (John 18:14; Luke 11:49–52). As far as he was concerned, if the status quo was to continue and they were to carry on enjoying life the way it was then Jesus had to go.

Their motives were evil and the actions they took were unlawful and deeply biased (Mark 14:55). They had already decided he was guilty and should die; they just needed to find the evidence.

I wonder if that is true of you in regard to Jesus Christ. You have already made your mind up. You are not a genuine, open minded enquirer. You have got a vested interest in not believing him. You don't want to consider him with an open mind because if it is true then you have got too much to lose. Deep down you know you are a sinner. You know there is a judgement. You know that there is a Heaven and Hell. But all of this means you are answerable and there are things in your life that have to change and you don't want them to. We are fallen human beings, ruled by our dark passions which make us biased against God. We will do anything for all of this not to be true.

Plus, like these men, our biggest problem is pride. No one tells us what to do. We know best. To admit we are wrong and need to change is hard. We like to think of ourselves at our best. But the real you and the real me is what we are like at our worst; when no one is watching; when we can do what we want; when we speak, think and act when we are not trying our hardest or when things are not going our way. That's the real you and me. None of us want to face up to all of this. To accept and admit this and then to bow the knee to another is just too much.

In examining Jesus Christ, the reality is evidence has very little to do with it. It all comes down to a power struggle. You don't want to hand over the reins of your life to Jesus Christ.

Witnesses

There were many illegalities in Christ's trial. These included the arrest and trial by night. The use of a traitor and bribe to identify and secure Jesus' arrest. The absence of any formal charge. The rushed one-day duration of the trial; the fact that the trial, sentence and crucifixion all took place within twenty-four hours. A capital trial had to be in public and held at the Temple not at night. The way the High Priest intervened in the proceedings was not allowed. Neither was the lack of defence for the Lord Jesus and the unjustified verdict. And the fact that they couldn't get two or three witnesses to agree. All of this made the trial illegal.

However, underneath these many illegalities ran a strong undercurrent of adherence to certain points of law. These Jewish leaders, amongst all the wrongfulness, needed to feel they were still doing things by the book.

Most obvious was the calling of witnesses (Mark 14:55, 56).

Jewish law, which they wanted to show some semblance of keeping, prohibited that judges themselves could be witnesses.

So they go out and look for witnesses. But where in Jerusalem in the middle of the night would they find witnesses to Jesus alleged crimes? Especially if it is a certain type of witness you want. Can you imagine if the widow of Nain (Luke 7:11–17) or Legion (Luke 8:28–34) or Jairus (Matthew 9:18–26) would have come forward to testify about Jesus? The answer from the religious leaders would have been, 'Unfortunately, what you are telling us are not the kind of things we're looking for'. They wanted 'false witnesses' (Matthew 26:59).

We don't know how they got their witnesses. Perhaps, as with Judas, they paid them. But in their search that night, many came forward and testified falsely against him (Mark 14:56). The problem was they needed two people to agree on the false testimony they gave.

But at last two false witnesses came forward with a piece of evidence that put the 'trial' on a promising footing. Perhaps the witness had been present when Jesus had first purged the temple (John 2:18, 19) and said 'this fellow said I am able to destroy the temple of God and to build it in three days' (Matthew 26:59–61; Mark 14:58).

The religious leaders, especially one as astute as the High Priest would have known exactly what this saying implied. Jesus was speaking of his body. This is proved by an event after the crucifixion (Matthew 27:63–64). But by distorting what he said they could bring forward a criminal charge which manipulated properly could lead to two charges. It could show Jesus as a dangerous seducer of the people and could lead to a revolt. It showed him to be disloyal to the present order of religion and worship. While the supposed assertion that he would (Mark 14:58) or was able (Matthew 26:61) to build the temple again within three days might be made to imply divine or magical pretensions. It was nothing short of blasphemy.

However, even the testimony of these witnesses did not agree so was overthrown (Mark 14:59). We don't know why but maybe they disagreed on the exact place he said it or other minor variations. But as we all know, it is very hard to agree on a lie.

As you look at this trial, I imagine you are struck with the unfairness and bias of it all. It is clear to see that these men had no interest in properly considering the evidence. But what is more difficult to see is your own bias against Jesus Christ. Who or what do you call on as witnesses against Jesus? As we have already said, we don't want all of this to be true. So we call on witnesses to prove our point of view and confirm our lifestyle.

Maybe you are relying on evolution to come through. If all of this evolved then there is no God and no one to answer to.

Or maybe you are trying to convince yourself that the Bible is not true. You assume it is strewn with errors but can you actually name one?

Or you say that there can't be a God because there is so much suffering. If God is loving and powerful why does he allow so much pain and evil? The fact the world we live in is no longer perfect is down to the fall, not God. The Bible not only gives the only real explanation to the world's problems but also provides the remedy.

When you cross-examine your 'witnesses' they don't add up. Like these men, the top and the bottom of it is that the way you live makes you deeply biased against considering the evidence objectively. Deep down you know there is a God. You know you need a Saviour and that Jesus Christ is the only Saviour but the implications of all of this are massive so you suppress it and tell yourself it is not true and call on the witnesses that support that.

Why not properly call on the Bible as a witness? Look at it carefully and listen objectively to what it has to say? Consider the Lord Jesus Christ. As you read through this book, examine the resurrection and see if it did really take place. Call upon your conscience as a witness. Look at the lives of Christians who say that the Lord Jesus has changed their lives. At least look at all the evidence and not just bring in the witnesses you know will tell you what you want to hear. Give Jesus Christ a fair hearing. Your eternal destiny hangs on it.

Are you the Christ?

At the point when the trial appeared to be going nowhere, the High Priest pulled a bold stroke which revealed the acumen which is undoubtedly why the Romans had made him the chief Jewish ruler.

Caiaphas got up and said in a sarcastic tone, 'I adjure you by the living God, tell us if you are the Christ, the Son of God' (Matthew 26:62, 63), 'the blessed one' (Mark 14:61). He invites Jesus to incriminate himself. This was an illegal move by Caiaphas. The High Priest was forbidden to intervene in a capital trial and was only allowed to cast his vote after the other court members had cast theirs. But needs must. He sprang from his seat to confront, and if possible, browbeat his prisoner, extract from him any reply. He says in effect, 'Let's cut to the chase, are you the Christ?'

Jesus had remained silent up until now but to this he answered, 'You have said so. But I tell you, from now on you will see the Son of Man seated at the right hand of Power and coming on the clouds of heaven' (Matthew 26:64). Luke adds that he said, 'If I tell you, you will not believe' (Luke 22:67).

Throughout the Gospel of Mark, Jesus had been at pains for people not to tell others who he is. He was operating to a set plan and purpose and building up to revealing himself as the Messiah at the right time (Mark 3:12; 8:30). But now the right time had come. Christ as good as says, 'You said it, yes indeed, I'm the Messiah, the Son of God' (Luke 22:70).

At this point the High priest tore his clothes saying, 'He has uttered blasphemy. What further witnesses do we need?' (Matthew 26:65).

But why didn't Caiaphas check out Jesus' claims to be the Messiah? If he had, he would have seen that the one stood before him was the long promised Messiah. According to the scriptures, the Messiah was to have been born in Bethlehem and Jesus was born in Bethlehem (Micah 5:2; Luke 2:1–7). The Messiah was to be born of a virgin (Isaiah 7:14; Matthew 1:24–25; Luke 1:26–30) just as Jesus was. The Messiah was to be born of David's line (2 Samuel 7:12, 16; Isaiah 11:1–2; Matthew 1:1–16; Luke 23–37). The Messiah was to be proceeded by a figure like Elijah (Malachi 3:1; 4:5; Matthew 17:12–13; John 1:19–23). The Messiah was to do many great works and Jesus performed the miracles that were prophesied (Isaiah 61:1–2; Matthew 11:1–6; Luke 4:16–21). The Messiah was to make a public entry into Jerusalem on a donkey (Zechariah 9:9; Matthew 21:1–11; John 12:12–16). The Messiah was to be betrayed by a close friend (Psalm 41:9; Matthew 26:14, 15; 27:3–8). The Messiah was to be despised and rejected by his people and to become familiar with suffering (Isaiah 53:2–3). There are references in the Old Testament to precisely the kind of unique Son of God Jesus claimed to be (Psalm 2:7; Isaiah 9:6). The Old Testament speaks of God becoming flesh (Isaiah 7:14). Many Old Testament passages show that the Lord God appeared among men (Genesis 16:13; 18:13, 17, 26; Exodus 3:1–6; Judges 13; Daniel 3:25).

Jesus is the Messiah. The Son of God. But the High Priest didn't consider for a minute that what Jesus said was true because he didn't want it to be true!

However, Jesus says to Caiaphas, 'you judge me but I will soon judge you'. The Saviour's condition when he said this was such that he could not have looked less like a Messiah. He looked poor, defenceless and in a right mess. He had just been led from the garden of Gethsemane and covered in bloody sweat. In contrast, he was surrounded by those with earthly power, in fine robes and expensive palaces.

Even today it is hard to see that Jesus Christ is the king of kings, the Christ, the Messiah. In 21st century Western society

Jesus is portrayed as anything but the Messiah. But he is and he's coming back! Not to a stable. Not growing up in Nazareth. Not as a Galilean carpenter. Not to be judged but to judge. You will see the Son of Man seated at the right hand of Power and coming on the clouds of Heaven. Can you imagine when Caiaphas and Jesus meet again? Can you imagine when Caiaphas realises that the one he had slapped and spat at and sentenced to death, has risen again and is exalted above every other name?

Like Caiaphas, we will one day stand before Christ. If you don't believe it or can't see it, pray that God would give you the faith to. Jesus said to Caiaphas 'If I tell you, you will not believe, and if I ask you, you will not answer' (Luke 22:67, 68). To fall into the hands of the living God is a fearful thing (Hebrews 10:31). You need to meet him as Saviour before you meet him as judge. Faith is a gift from God (Ephesians 2:8) so ask him to give it to you. And he will (Matthew 7:7).

Sanhedrin

Following Jesus' trial before Annas and then Caiaphas, after daybreak came the formal trial before the Sanhedrin (Matthew 27:1). Caiaphas and some members of the Sanhedrin had got what they thought was enough to go to Pontius Pilate and get the death penalty for Jesus. They just needed the whole Sanhedrin to ratify it (Matthew 27:1). They waited until daybreak to render their official verdict (cf. Matthew 26:66). It is this daytime trial that Luke speaks of (Luke 22:66–71). But all of it happened at speed. Mark says 'as soon as it was morning' (Mark 15:1). These men were in a hurry!

Law and order

The Sanhedrin was the highest Jewish ruling council. In Jewish law and order there were three tribunals. A town of fewer than 120 males (although some sources say 230) had the lowest tribunal consisting of 3 judges. Their jurisdiction was limited and didn't extend to capital causes. The next tribunal consisted of 23 judges. The highest was the Great Sanhedrin with 71 members. It was made up of elders, scribes and chief priests and met daily in the Temple to hold court except on the Sabbath and other holy days

The president of the Sanhedrin was the 'nasi' (prince) and the vice president was the Ab-beth-din (father of the court of laws). The Sanhedrin would sit in a semicircle. Sat facing these judges would sit 3 rows of 'the disciples' or students. Appointment to the highest tribunal or Great Sanhedrin was made by the Sanhedrin itself and was either made by promoting a member of the inferior tribunals or one of the students or disciples.

At least 23 members were required to form a 'quorum'. Two shorthand writers took notes of arguments for and against the accused. If one spoke in favour, then he couldn't speak against. Voting was from the youngest to the oldest so that the youngest could not be influenced by the older.

It is hard to know how much power the Sanhedrin had under Herod and Pilate. We know that forty years before the destruction of Temple the Sanhedrin ceased to pronounce capital sentences. The Romans would not want to abolish the Sanhedrin but would reserve to themselves final disposal in all cases. There is no doubt that if Pilate or Herod saw fit to interfere they would and especially would not have tolerated any attempt at jurisdiction over a Roman citizen. In short, the Sanhedrin would be accorded full jurisdiction in inferior and religious matters, with the greatest show, but without the least amount of real rule or supreme authority.

Significantly, both Herod and Pilate treated the High Priest as the real head and representative of the Jews. He was appointed by them and it would be their policy to appoint someone who would curtail the power of independent and fanatical rabbis. Therefore, in great criminal cases or important investigations, the High Priest would always preside not the 'Nasi'. In this the New Testament and Josephus (Maier, 1988) agree.

One thing is certain, in the light of all the strictness of the above, the Sanhedrin meeting that took place to judge the Lord

Jesus was no formal, regular meeting of the Sanhedrin. It was a gross violation of justice and law. It would not just be the friends of Jesus who would think this but all Jewish order and law would have been grossly infringed in almost every particular detail if this had been a formal meeting of the Sanhedrin.

The trial and sentence of Jesus in the palace of Caiaphas would have outraged every principle of Jewish criminal law and procedure. Such causes as this could only be tried and capital sentences pronounced in the regular meeting place of the Sanhedrin and could not could take place on Sabbaths or feast days.

This quick meeting was simply another attempt to make things legitimate and at least this early daytime meeting gave proceedings an air of legitimacy in which the essentials of the night meeting were repeated and confirmed.

It shows what religion thinks of Jesus

The Sanhedrin's judgement of Jesus shows exactly what religion thinks of him. Often those most opposed to Jesus are the religious, who've had their own man-made religion. Religion is man's attempt to be right with God. It relies on what we do and is geared to make us feel better. It is all about rules and rituals. Eat certain things, dress in a certain way, go on journeys. But none of it changes the heart. And the heart is the problem that really needs sorting. In fact, the heart of the problem is the problem of the heart!

But that is the one area that we don't want to be touched. We want something that makes us feel like we're doing something good but that doesn't impinge on what we are. If we can be seen to be good and get away with our badness, all the better. We choose a religion to fit around us; a religion that suits us, that makes us feel good about ourselves but doesn't cut across what we want to do. Once it does, it is too much, too fanatical, too extreme.

Church is great, particularly at certain times of the year. It can make us feel good and uplifts us. Being respectable and keeping the rules outwardly is what it is all about. But once the Bible says something we don't like, Christ has to be got rid of. Once the message offends our pride or is offensive to us morally or intellectually it has to go. Once it tells us we are sinners and need to be saved we can't cope with it and throw it out.

Christianity is about love for God but these men were all about the rules. They had to be seen to be keeping them and judged themselves on how well they kept them compared to others.

Jesus came and said, it is all about the heart. It is not what is on the outside. Not about the rules. It is about whether you love God in the first place and then about loving others as much as you love yourself (Luke 10:27). Keeping the commandments only because you think that is the right thing to do is no good. It is keeping the commandments out of love for God that matters. Jesus exposed these men for what they were. They liked status and having people look up to them. They enjoyed power and feeling better than others. But they had no love for God or others really, only themselves. It was all about them.

These men were relying on their morality, their pedigree and their spirituality to make them right with God. But the Lord Jesus Christ says it has got nothing to do with any of this. Jesus in effect says to them I don't care who you are, how moral you think you are or how religious and spiritual you seem. Do you see you are a sinner in desperate need of a Saviour and will you trust me as your Saviour? That is what it is all about.

Perhaps you are relying on being accepted by God on your church attendance, the fact you say your prayers, the fact you are outwardly very moral. Your position in life. Your status. You are outwardly very respectable. But none of these things can make you right with God. To get to Heaven the one thing you must have is Christ. You won't get there by trying your best and being worthy. Being worthy of heaven means perfect thoughts, perfect conversation, perfect actions 24/7, 52 weeks of the year, every year of your life! Just try it for one day!

This is why these men hated Jesus Christ because these were all the things they were relying on. And when they saw Jesus forgiving the sins of what they thought were really bad people, they hated it. They liked to think that there was a pecking order in society and they were on the top. When Jesus came and said you are all in the same boat, every one of you needs a Saviour, they hated it and had to get rid of him.

True Christianity isn't a religion but a relationship. A relationship with the living God. People like you and me can actually know God. We can have a real sense of fellowship with God; a deep consciousness of his love for us (John 17:26); someone we come to trust, love, pray to, serve, worship. We can know the Lord Jesus as a person, just as well as we get to know people well (wife, family, friends, colleagues, neighbours …). Jesus actually said, 'Behold, I stand at the door and knock. If anyone hears my voice and opens the door, I will come in to him and eat with him, and he with me' (Revelation 3:20). As our relationship with the Lord Jesus develops, we will think and act and talk in a way that Christ would. The Holy Spirit is within us affecting our minds, hearts, will, conscience and very character. This is what it is really all about and what these Jewish leaders knew nothing of.

They had no love for God which is really the heart and horror of sin. Maybe you don't get that. So what if we don't love God? How is that the worst thing?

A brilliant mathematician was interviewed on the radio. Her mother had also been brilliant but instead of pursuing a career she had sacrificed it all to bring up her children and give them the best possible start in life. The daughter said on the radio that she would be doing no such thing. She would be doing all she could to get to the top. She was not going to be making any sacrifices. There was no gratitude or comprehension that if her mother had adopted her attitude she wouldn't be where she is today! You and I may think this is ungrateful and selfish but that is exactly how so many treat God. Your gifts, talents, life, breath, everything apart from your sin, has been given to you by God but you ignore him. It is all about you. That was the Sanhedrin's problem and it is the age old problem. We love ourselves more than God.

Keep Sunday Special—But for the right reasons

This is why these leaders argued with Christ over the Sabbath. They were all about observing the rules externally but Christ came and said that the Sabbath was made for man and not man for the Sabbath (Mark 2:27). They didn't love the Sabbath day and want to keep it special out of love for God. They imposed rules upon rules to try and show how religious they were.

The Sabbath, or the Lord's Day is a contentious issue today. So let's be clear, the Sabbath is important. God created the world with a Sabbath principle (Genesis 2:3). The last command given to Moses before he came down from Mount Sinai instructed the people to 'keep the Sabbath, because it is holy for you' (Exodus 31:14). And in the New Testament Jesus upheld the Sabbath.

It is fitting and biblical, for one day in seven to be appointed a day set aside for worship (Leviticus 23:3; Luke 4:16; Acts 13:42–44; 15:21; 17:2; 18:4). After the resurrection Christians slide from Saturday to Sunday (Acts 20:7; 1 Corinthians 16:1–2) and the day of rest is called the Lord's Day (Revelation 1:10).

At the heart of this day is worship and rest. A day of sacred assembly (Leviticus 23:3) set apart from normal labours to be free to worship God. It is a weekly reminder that he is God and we are not. Sunday should be different from the other days of the week (Exodus 20:8).

But it is not all about rules. Jesus emphasised the spiritual significance of the Sabbath. While he certainly kept all the Mosaic Sabbath commands he did not hesitate to break the traditions and customs. For Jesus it was a day of freedom (Luke 13:10–17) a day for healing (Luke 14:1–6) and a day for doing good (Mark 3:1–6).

In the same way, Sunday should not be a day of rules and regulations for a Christian. It should be the best, most enjoyable day of the week. We should keep the Lord's Day special not because we don't want to break the rules but because we love God and want to spend the day worshipping him, resting, meeting with his people, reading and praying.

There are no set do's and don'ts about keeping the Lord's Day special. We are no longer bound to observe the Jewish Sabbath in a particular way. We need to still obey the fourth Commandment (Matthew 5:17) but we need to see how Christ transformed it. According to Luther (ed. Carson, 1999 p. 314) 'if anywhere the day is made holy for the mere day's sake—if anywhere anyone sets up its observance on a Jewish foundation, then I order you to work on it, to ride on it, to dance on it, to feast on it, to do anything that shall remove this encroachment on Christian liberty'.

Sunday is for our good and to be enjoyed. God made us with the need for rest. We trust in Christ enough to rest one day in seven. Sabbath was made for man not man for the Sabbath (Mark 2:23–28). But it is not just that we cease from work, switch off the lawn mower etc., but that we rest in Christ. Meditate on him and enjoy him.

If a Christian wants to only go to church once and then have the rest of the day to do whatever, it says a lot about how much they love God. If they would rather watch TV, play sport and do work and do whatever they do for the six other days of the week then there is something wrong. It should be a day that we want to spend with God's people, listen to preaching, read good Christian books, spend with family and turn aside from the world and work.

Stand up and be counted

To the Jews the Sanhedrin were a powerful group of men who wielded huge influence. They had the power to put you out of the Synagogue and exclude you from the Jewish community. Later on in this book we will meet two members of the Sanhedrin who became disciples of Jesus Christ but at first they had to be secret disciples because of fear of the Jews. It was hard for these men to stand up and stand out for what was right and what they could see was wrong because of the consequences; all they stood to lose.

I think that is becoming increasingly true today. As the ruling council for their day was the Sanhedrin, ours today is no doubt Political Correctness and none of us dare go against it.

The Church is too often more concerned with not upsetting the thinking of the day than being true to the Bible. So many people are scared not to bow down to the god of political correctness. While it is important to do things as winsomely as we can, we have to be true to God and his Word. Christian, take courage!

Privilege and Responsibility

These religious leaders were the principal agents in bringing about our Lord's death. Church leaders are not exempt from errors in doctrine and tremendous sin in practice. That is why it is important we judge even what the church says by the Word of God and pray for our ministers and leaders that they would be godly men. It is therefore important that ministers and religious leaders realise the responsibility they have (John 19:11).

But on the other hand, they need to realise how privileged they are. In fact there is no greater privilege. Levy (2015) says,

> I am paid to study the Bible, to read great books, to pray, to preach and care for people. I work long hours but I love it. I am protected from many of the stresses and strains of life. Being able to be a full time minister is an enormous privilege. There is no greater calling. Miserable, Moaning Ministers are a disgrace.

Reinforcing this point, the Rev. Geoff Thomas began his 2000 John Reed Miller Lectures at RTS Jackson in this way,

> The full-time gospel ministry is still a protected oasis. We are relieved of so many of the tensions and temptations that the men to whom we minister are meeting each day. They work with their minds and bodies in this evil world and give

their hard-earned money to us so generously that we may spend our days—think of it—in the quiet of our studies, in the Bible, in evangelism, and in pastoring God's people. I hope you will never join with those ministers who sit around grumbling in their fraternals about all the alleged hardships of being preachers. What a marvellously privileged life we lead. I trust that you earnestly believe that if it be God's will for you to spend the rest of your life caring for this particular congregation you will happily do so and thank the Lord at the end of each day for such blessings.

Hugely responsible. Enormously privileged.

Mockery

That night as Jesus was passed from Annas to Caiaphas and then to the guards, he had to endure so much from lying lips and mockery:

- Matthew says that 'Many' bore false witness against him (26:60)

- As Jesus stood before Annas, one of the officers, a minor official, stood up and slapped him in the face, saying 'do you speak to the High Priest like that?' (John 18:22)

- As soon as Caiaphas and the others agreed he was guilty of blasphemy they spat in his face and beat him and others struck him with the palms of their hands, blindfolded him and said 'prophesy to us Christ! Who is the one who struck you?' (Matthew 26:68; Mark 14:65; Luke 22:64).

- He was then put in the custody of Caiaphas' guards and servants until the meeting of the Sanhedrin at dawn, who took advantage of him, mocked and beat him (Luke 22:63–65).

Together that night, they had, as it were, all played blind man's buff with the Son of God and asked him to guess who hit him that time and then that time and then that time, as everyone else laughed. They spat in his face which was the depth of humiliation. As far as a Jew was concerned this was the grossest, most hateful form of personal insult (Numbers 12:14; Deuteronomy 25:9). The same face that had looked upon widows, children and the lame is now covered in saliva.

Perhaps some of you reading have been bullied at school or at work and know how awful it can be. That night, these men bullied the Son of God.

And most of these were university men, outstanding in the community. What a nice group! Dr Martyn Lloyd-Jones once spoke to a group of students at Oxford University. After he had spoken there was an opportunity for them to ask questions. One of the students stood up, and after thanking him for his well-structured and well-delivered message, said he was bemused because Dr Lloyd-Jones had addressed them in the same way as he no doubt would have spoken to a group of farm hands in West Wales. The other students agreed. Why talk to us like that? Don't you know we are well-educated people? Dr Lloyd-Jones pointed out that he spoke to them in the way he did because they were made from the same clay as the farm hands in West Wales. Inside, underneath we are all the same. Sinners! In desperate need of the same Saviour, who we all need to come to in the same way.

The mockery shows the hatred people have for Jesus Christ. That night all the enmity of man and the power of hell were unchained. The spitting, hitting, mocking, the High Priest tearing his clothes (Matthew 26:65) show you what hatred for Jesus can do and exposed the defiance of human beings towards God.

The world hates Jesus Christ. Maybe you are reading this book and are not sure you believe that. You think that the world is indifferent to him or is not particularly interested in him, but would not go as far as to say it hates him. But the fact that the Western world does not seem bothered by Jesus Christ has got everything to do with the Church's witness in these days. The Church doesn't seem that different to the world at the moment so why would the world hate the Church and her Lord and Saviour? However, when Christians live like they should and preach the true gospel clearly and faithfully, it is bound to offend the world and the church is persecuted.

The Church's message is that all have sinned. People hate to be told that they are sinners. There are sins the Bible condemns and commands people to repent of which would cut across many people's lifestyles and life choices. The Church's message is that unless people repent of their sins they will spend an eternity in Hell. The Church's message is that the only way a person can be saved is by trusting in Jesus Christ. He is the only way to get to God and go to Heaven; all other religions are false. If the Church preaches these truths and lives out these beliefs, she will face persecution.

Above all, Jesus Christ told people that they had to deny themselves if they were to follow him (Matthew 16:24). They have to give up living for themselves and doing what they like. They now have to seek to please and honour God. People hate being told to deny themselves. We all love ourselves and want to please ourselves. But the Church's message is that we are answerable to the one who made us and our chief aim is to glorify God.

Even though this world hates the Church and will persecute it, Christians should not go out of their way to be offensive and condemning; certainly never self-righteous! We should be as kind, winsome, loving and sociable as we can be, always remembering that we have been saved by grace and there is nothing in and of ourselves that has merited the love of God. By nature we are all the same.

The Bible says that Jesus grew in favour with all men. He loved people and was moved with compassion when he saw the crowds. We should be like him. It is our message that offends and we should never apologise for it or dilute it.

But as you look at the treatment Jesus endured that night,

it is exactly what you and your sin deserved. You know that the things you do, and say, and think, deserve to be spat at and slapped and mocked. But the Son of God took the shame, humiliation and blows that your sin deserves. The cruelty of sin and its consequences were on show that night.

He was majestically silent and despite being under great provocation he never lost his temper. Why? Because he was saying in effect, 'I know that this is what those I am representing deserve but I will take it for them.'

Handed him over

And when they had bound him they led him away and handed him over to Pontius Pilate (Matthew 27:1, 2). They had no power to sentence anyone to the death penalty. Caiaphas therefore needed to formulate a charge that would tell before the Roman procurator. Rome didn't care about Jewish law so they needed to now convince Pontius Pilate that Jesus was a fanatical seducer of the ignorant populace who might lead them to wild tumultuous acts.

We will take this up in Chapter 5 but before we do, in the next chapter, we will focus in on what was going on with Peter while all this had been going on.

For now, the Jews had put Jesus on trial and decided to hand him over. Will you? Before you decide, I urge you to at least give him a fair trial.

4

'I swear, I don't know him!'

Matthew 26:58, 69–75; Mark 14:54, 66–72;
Luke 22:55–62; John 18:15–18, 25–27

Setting the scene

PETER AND JOHN, AFTER INITIALLY FLEEING THE SCENE AT Gethsemane, roused themselves and tried to follow, at a distance, the procession that escorted Jesus to the High Priest.

The High Priest's palace was built on the slope of a hill. There was an outer court to the palace from which a door led into the inner court. John seems to have entered the inner court along with the guard (John 18:15). We can imagine that John hurried up to be in the palace and as near to Christ as he might. John could gain access quite easily as he was well 'known to the High Priest' (John 18:16). This word used can refer to a close friend or something of intimacy.

The courtyard had walls all around it which went up to a gallery above that ran all the way around. The gallery would have been lit up with lamps and lights

Below in the courtyard the guards had lit a charcoal fire. Once John had got Peter in, Peter joined these men around the fire. It is not hard to imagine the scene. Edersheim (2004, p.854) vividly paints the picture of that night. He says that the glow of the charcoal would have thrown a 'peculiar sheen on the bearded faces of the men as they crowded around it and talked of the events of that night', describing to those who had not been there what had happened in the garden of Gethsemane. As the night light 'glowed and flickered it threw the long shadows of these men across the inner court up the walls towards the gallery'. Along this gallery would have been apartments and corridors. From the courtyard, Peter would have looked up to those lighted windows where, in an inner audience-chamber, the prisoner, Jesus of Nazareth was being held.

Peter was there having ignored Christ's warning. He should have gone back to where he was staying but he could never have done that. It would have been even more cowardly. For all the bad press Peter has had over the centuries, at least he was there. Apart from John, all of the others had run off.

Seeming inconsistencies

It would appear at first that there are seeming inconsistencies in what the Gospel writers' record about the events surrounding Peter's denials.

According to the Greek text in Mark 14:68, the rooster crowing presents a problem. Some maintain that a rooster would not crow at such a time. But what is there to stop a rooster crowing between midnight and 3am?

Also, some see a problem in that Peter sat down by the fire in Matthew, Mark and Luke but stood up in John. But isn't that what we would expect from someone in Peter's position that night? He was restless and couldn't sit or stand still. The guards no doubt also stood and sat at various times throughout the night. It was a long time to be sat or stood for the whole time. (Matthew 26:69; Mark 14:54; Luke 22:55, John 18:18)

But the main problem surrounds the second denial. It appears at first that Matthew and Mark contradict each other. In Mark's Gospel there is one portress. The girl in Mark 14:66, 67 (first denial) is the same girl that is mentioned in v. 69 (second denial) and she asks the questions. However, in Matthew there are two girls, and a different girl asks the question in the second denial than the first. Furthermore, in Luke a man asks the question whereas in John a number of people question Peter.

However, it all fits together if we understand that the male servants were probably all gathered in the court. The slave girl in Matthew, Mark and Luke is the door keeper in John (John 18:17; Matthew 26:69; Mark 14:66; Luke 22:56). The fact there were two girls mentioned by Matthew (Matthew 26:69, 71) probably was due to the fact that the one relieved the other on the door for her to take a break. As the one took over from the other, she pointed Peter out to her. Moreover, it must be taken for granted that none of the gospels repeat all the words spoken by the girl, and a question that one person asked is likely to have been taken up by others around the fire.

How the events unfolded

So putting the four gospel accounts together, and with those apparent inconsistencies in mind, let's look at how the events unfolded that night and try to piece it all together.

First denial

John seems to have entered the courtyard along with the guard (John 18:15) while Peter remained outside until John spoke to the maid who kept the door and brought Peter in.

Once the servant girl let Peter in, he went to sit below in the courtyard (Mark 14:66). It was cold so the servants and officers made a charcoal fire in the middle of the courtyard where they stood warming themselves (John 18:18) and when it had kindled, they sat down together (Luke 22:55). These were the same guards whose custody Jesus would later be placed into. Peter also was with them, standing and warming himself.

From the very moment Peter had entered the palace the portress, or servant girl, viewing him from her nook in the doorway, had her suspicions about Peter. The way he behaved attracted her attention and the uneasiness on his face no doubt confirmed her suspicions. As she saw him by the fire she fixed her eyes on him, looked hard at him, stared at him (Luke 22:56) and she boldly charged him, though in a questioning tone (John 18:17).

The servant girl would never have confined her words to the short sentences reported by each of the evangelists so we need to put them all together to get the full picture. It would seem she said to him, 'You too were with Jesus of Nazareth, you surely are not also one of the man's disciples, are you? Why, I'm sure you were also with Jesus the Galilean' (Matthew 26:69; Mark 14:67; Luke 22:56; John 18:25).

But before everybody he denied it. He said 'Woman I do not know him' (Luke 22:57).

And it was at that point, Annas sent Jesus bound to Caiaphas the High Priest.

Second denial

Peter's second denial follows closely behind the first one. As Peter was denying the Lord for the second time, the Lord Jesus was being examined by Caiaphas along with some of the elders and scribes; the full Sanhedrin arrived immediately after the second betrayal.

The woman who first questioned Peter had either not made an impression on those around the fire or Peter's bold denial had satisfied them. Even so, it was getting too hot and uncomfortable for Peter so he goes out towards the gateway and tries to escape.

He walked down the porch (Matthew 26:71) which ran around and opened into the 'outer court' (Mark 14:68). It was while his feet sounded along the marble-paved porch, that a cock crowed (Mark 14:68).

But the portress was clearly unwilling to let him out (Mark 14:69). In putting Matthew and Mark's accounts together it would seem that there were two servant girls who saw Peter (Matthew 26:71 and Mark 14:69). Probably the one had come to relieve the first one of her duties so she could have a break. As she did, Peter was pointed out to her.

So having been refused exit Peter crossed the inner court to mingle again with the group around the fire (Luke 22:59). The girl, or girls, say to the people who were there, this fellow was with Jesus of Nazareth. At least one male bystander chimes in with the girls (Luke 22:58) but probably all of them around the fire turned on him with the same charge, that he was also one of the disciples of Jesus of Nazareth (John 18:25).

But to each of them separately and to all together, Peter gave the same denial. He was brief and to the point but determined and more emphatic. He said, 'Man I am not' (Luke 22:58). To reinforce it, he even swore with an oath that he did not know this man (Matthew 26:72).

This was enough to make the suspicion go away for a while or it could have been that attention was now elsewhere. Because just as the first faint streaks of grey light were lying on the sky, the maid now had to go and open the gate to let the leading chief priests, elders and members of the Sanhedrin in who had been summoned to the High Priest's palace. They must have been warned that the capture of Jesus would be attempted that night and to be ready.

Third denial

One hour passed (Luke 22:59) since Peter's second denial had, so to speak, been interrupted by the arrival of members of the Sanhedrin. There would have been great excitement surrounding the whole trial; lots of people coming and going and much chatter about all that was going on as people gathered around the fire warming themselves. The arrival of the Sanhedrin diverted attention away from Peter but now it turns once more to him and in the circumstances, is naturally more intense than before. News about Peter no doubt begun to spread. Furthermore, the chattering of Peter, whose conscience and self-consciousness made him nervously garrulous, betrayed him.

They began to say, 'He was with Jesus for he is a Galilean!' 'Surely you also are one of them for your speech betrays you. You are a Galilean' (Matthew 26:73; Mark 14:70). John says that one of them was a fellow servant and relative of Malchus whose ear Peter had cut off. He asserted that he actually recognised him and blurts out, 'didn't I see you in the garden?' (John 18:26).

With the heat turned up, Peter began to invoke a curse on himself and to swear, I do not know the man (Matthew 26:74); 'I don't know what you are talking about' (Luke 22:60). He vehemently denied with oaths to God and calls down curses on himself. He is saying in effect, 'May God do this or that to me if it be true that I am one or ever was a disciple of Jesus'.

Immediately the rooster crowed (Matthew 26:74) for a second time (Mark 14:72). And as Christ had predicted, Peter had denied him three times.

The look

At the very moment Peter denied the Lord Jesus the third time, as well as the rooster crowing, the Lord looked at Peter (Luke 22:61). But where was the Lord Jesus at this moment and how was he able to look at Peter?

While it is possible that Jesus was being led through that courtyard where Peter was warming himself, there is no indication in the text that at that moment Jesus was being led across the court. Nor indeed that until the morning he was removed at all from near the place where he had been examined.

It would seem to me that when Jesus looked at Peter he had been left alone in the covered gallery or at one of the windows that overlooked the courtyard. As soon as Peter denied the Lord Jesus for the third time, he looked up and saw the Lord who turned around and looked upon him; in all that assembly, at that very moment, upon Peter!

Jesus was by now waiting to be taken to Pilate and was in the custody of the soldiers. He had received so many beatings that he was black and blue and covered in spittle. And in that pitiful state, he looked at Peter.

The Lord Jesus' eyes searched down to the innermost depths of Peter's heart and broke him. It pierced through all his self-delusion, convicted him of his sin and shame. In that one look, Peter would have thought of all that he had received from Jesus. How kind he had been to him, the experiences and privileges he had shared with him that not even most of the other disciples had enjoyed. He would have remembered all his boasts that even if all the others abandoned Jesus, he never would (Mark 14:29). Peter was the spokesperson, the leader and yet in the face of remarks made by two weak women, he had denied ever knowing Jesus of Nazareth and had even sworn and taken oaths in God's name to that effect! Peter had sinned greatly. He had sinned against so much privilege. He had shown himself to be weak and pathetic. The shame he felt would have been huge. Imagine having to face the others after all he had said and all his boasts. Peter had messed up. Shamefully. And not just once.

But there were steps to Peter's denial that are important to trace. He was full of his own self-confidence. He thought he could stand for Jesus Christ in his own strength. But he couldn't. That is something we need to guard against. You and I will never be able to stand for him on our own. We need the help of the Holy Spirit.

The only way you will stand for him is in his strength. And to know that strength you need to be walking close to him by reading his Word and meditating upon it, listening to his Word preached and spending time in prayer.

Peter's problem that night was that he forsook him and then decided to try and follow at a distance. He was all over the place. He needed to be close to the Saviour. You cannot walk with Christ at a distance.

Instead of watching and praying, he slept. We need to be aware that we have an enemy of our soul who is out to destroy us (1 Peter 5:8). Unless we are on our guard and disciplined in our Christian life we will definitely fall. This means regularly reading the word. Times when we close ourselves in our room and pray. Meet with God's people to pray. Listen to good preaching. Get involved in, and be in the heart of the life of the local church. Partake of the Lord's Supper. Put sin to death. Fill our minds with good things. We cannot afford to take our eye off the ball. We are in a battle (Ephesians 6:12).

Peter wept

But the look the Lord Jesus gave Peter reached the man, the real Peter, the true disciple, the one who loved Jesus. He was so sorry and rushed out into the night. He broke down and began to weep bitterly.

He now remembered the words of warning; how Jesus had said to him, 'Before the rooster crows twice, you will deny me three times.' (Mark 14:30). Peter's sin caused him so much sorrow and pain.

Perhaps you can really empathise with Peter. You've messed up many times. Maybe God has been kind to you. You have been brought up in a Christian home and have read the Bible and been prayed with and learned about Jesus Christ all your life. You have attended a sound evangelical church. You may have even been actively involved in the life of the church. Spoke and read and prayed in public. You may have at times stood up for Jesus Christ and defended his cause. But now you have fallen into sin. Gross sin. Not just once or twice but many, many times. Maybe they are even sins that you once condemned in others. You feel dirty, embarrassed and a hypocrite. You say to yourself that you cannot imagine anyone else would behave or act the way you have. And there is no way Jesus Christ could forgive you and love you again. He must be sick of you. So many privileges. So much light. But such gross sin. That is exactly how Peter would have felt the early hours of that Friday morning.

There are sins we fall into and sins we just have to commit but afterwards we remember what Christ said and we feel dirty and sorry and sad.

The real Peter is the one weeping, broken down that has gone into the night. It shows us how deceitful our own hearts are. We can't trust our heart. It tells us certain things are so good and 'must haves' but they will ruin us, or certainly cause us pain and hurt. There may be a relationship that the Bible says is wrong but your emotions say you have to have it. There are things we feel we have to do. The pull and desire is so strong but they will destroy us. They are bad but they feel so good.

We cannot trust our hearts! The only thing that we can trust is the Lord Jesus and what he says in his Word. If we just do what he commands then we can be sure that all things will work for our good (Romans 8:28) and will relieve us of so much heartache and pain.

But however serious Peter's disowning of the Lord Jesus was, even greater was the grace that forgave him and restored him to fellowship and service. We shall look at this more closely in Chapter 21 of this book. But it is important to note at this point that someone can sin massively against God, can go so far from him and yet still there is a way back.

As Peter was down beneath in the courtyard, his suffering Saviour had prayed for him. Peter was a great sinner but Jesus Christ was an even greater Saviour. Where sin abounded, grace super-abounded (Romans 5:20).

According to Thomas Brooks,

> Christ looks more upon Peter's sorrow, than upon his sin; more upon his tears, than upon his oaths. The Lord will not cast away weak saints for their great unbelief, because there is a little faith in them. He will not throw them away for that hypocrisy that is in them, because of that little sincerity that is in them. He will not cast away weak saints for that pride that is in them, because of those rays of humility that shine in them. He will not despise his people for their passions, because of those grains of meekness that are in them. A wise man will not throw away a little gold because of a great deal of dirt that cleaves to it; neither, then, will God cast us away

More importantly, God himself says, 'a bruised reed he will not break, and a faintly burning wick he will not quench; he will faithfully bring forth justice'. (Isaiah 42:3). And John says in his first letter, 'And if anyone does sin, we have an advocate with the Father, Jesus Christ the righteous.' (1 John 2:1)

Perhaps you have messed up on the same scale as Peter. Maybe you think even worse. But can I tell you that there is forgiveness with God (Psalm 130:4).

Rabbi Duncan was administrating the Lord's Table when a woman came in late. She sat behind the elders because there was no other room. She had lived a notoriously bad life and felt too unworthy to take communion and wept as the cup came to her and let it pass her by. But Rabbi Duncan made her take it and insisted, 'Take it! It's for sinners'.

However bad you are. However much you have sinned against God. If you come to him he will abundantly pardon you.

There is a verse in the Bible that really troubles people. It is in Mark 3:28–29 and says, 'Truly, I say to you, all sins will be forgiven the children of man, and whatever blasphemies they utter, but whoever blasphemes against the Holy Spirit never has forgiveness, but is guilty of an eternal sin'. But if we look at the verse closely, it is actually a really encouraging verse. It says, 'all the sins and blasphemies of men will be forgiven them.' Everything you have done, (everything!) can be forgiven. Except one thing. And that one thing is to refuse to repent and believe on the Lord Jesus Christ. That, and that alone, is unforgiveable.

After Jesus rose from the dead, some women went to the tomb and found it empty. There were angels there who said to the women, 'Do not be alarmed. You seek Jesus of Nazareth, who was crucified. He has risen; he is not here. See the place where they laid him. But go tell his disciples and Peter' (Mark 16:6, 7). Why was Peter singled out? Because despite the fact that he had royally messed up, as the chorus says,

There is a way back to God from the dark paths of sin
There's a way that is open that all may go in
At Calvary's cross is where you begin
When you come as a sinner to Jesus

The Lord Jesus wanted Peter to know that. What is the difference between Judas and Peter? Both messed up. But Peter brought his sin to Jesus Christ. He loved Jesus Christ and trusted him. Judas, despite hating the mess he was in, never loved Jesus and never humbly came to him in repentance and faith. That is why today Peter is in Heaven and Judas is in Hell.

If you hear his voice, harden not your heart (Hebrews 3:15)

5

The question of the ages—what shall I do with Jesus?

John 18:28–19:16; Matthew 27:11–31;
Mark 15:1–20; Luke 23:1–25

Setting the scene

Real history

THE LORD JESUS CHRIST'S TRIAL BEFORE THE ROMAN GOVERNOR, Pontius Pilate really took place; it is a historic event. Some have cast doubt on the existence of Pontius Pilate but in 1961 Italian archaeologists discovered an inscription at Herod's amphitheatre in Caesarea that read 'Pontius Pilate, Prefect of Judea has dedicated to the people of Caesarea a temple in honour of Tiberius' (Bible History Online). They also discovered the stone pavement of the very platform where Jesus appeared before Pilate.

The sources of evidence concerning this trial could well have been some of Pilate's court attendants who may have become Christians and furnished the Gospel writers with information. Furthermore, there would have been some court records that were public and available to those wanting to research. John's sources no doubt would also have included his own testimony of the Lord Jesus who could have told him all about the trial after his resurrection.

Accurate history

This all took place early on a Friday morning. The earliness of it all is emphasised. It could have been as early as 6am. John says Pilate sat down on his judgement seat and it was about the 6th hour (19:14). John didn't have a wrist watch or clock but he guessed it was about 6.

However, some verses in John's account (John 18:28; 19:14) present a chronological challenge. In John 18:28 it would appear that the Jewish leaders hadn't eaten the Passover meal early on this Friday morning. John 19:14 states that Jesus' trial and crucifixion were on the day of preparation for the Passover and not after the eating of the Passover. However, Matthew, Mark and Luke (the Synoptic Gospels) portray Jesus and his disciples eating the Passover meal on Thursday evening. How can Jesus and His disciples already have eaten the Passover meal but the Jewish leaders haven't?

This has led some to conclude this is evidence that the Bible contradicts itself, and proves it cannot be the infallible (without error) word of God. But, even though this poses a difficulty, it by no means makes it impossible to reconcile the accounts and show that both John and the Synoptics are correct. That the Bible is without error does not mean it is without difficulties and it is our responsibility as good students of the Bible to work out these problems.

One possible solution is that the Passover Jesus celebrated

with his disciples does not refer to the actual Passover meal itself (the pinnacle of the festival) but to the continuing festivities of Passover which lasted for 7/8 days. There is ample evidence that 'the Passover' could not only refer to the Passover meal itself but to the whole festival of Passover in its entirety (e.g. Luke 22:1; Numbers 28:18–19). If the Jewish authorities wanted to continue full participation in the entire festival, they would have to avoid all ritual contamination. They would be conscious of their public position and be eager to avoid any uncleanness that would force them to withdraw from the feast, however temporary, which is why in John 18:28 they wouldn't enter into Pilate's headquarters. They didn't want to be defiled by going into Gentile premises at any time during the week of festivities.

However, according to John MacArthur, the most plausible solution would appear to lie in the way different Jews reckoned the beginning and ending of days. From Josephus, the Mishna and other ancient Jewish sources we learn that the Jews in northern Israel calculated days from sunrise to sunrise. That area included the region of Galilee where Jesus and all the disciples, except Judas, had grown up. Apparently most, if not all, of the Pharisees used that system of reckoning. But Jews in the southern part, which centred in Jerusalem, calculated days from sunset to sunset. Because all the priests lived in or near Jerusalem, as did most of the Sadducees, those groups followed the southern scheme.

Variations doubtless caused confusion at times but it also had some practical benefits. There were so many pilgrims in Jerusalem celebrating the Passover, maybe 100,000, that the Galileans killed their lambs on Thursday and ate them that evening while Judeans observed and celebrated one day later. Lambs for Passover had to be slaughtered in a two-hour window just before the Passover meal. The variations in time allowed the feast to be celebrated legitimately on two adjoining days and the sacrifices could be made over a total period of four hours rather than two. That separation of days may also have had the effect of reducing both regional and religious clashes between two groups.

Being Galileans, Jesus and his disciples considered Passover to be from sunset on Thursday to sunset on Friday which meant that Jesus could celebrate his last Passover with his disciples and yet still be killed/sacrificed on Passover day.

In fact, with the trial and crucifixion on Friday, Christ was actually sacrificed at the same time as the Passover lambs were being slain (19:14). I don't think it is stretching things too far to suggest that the variations in the way Jews reckoned the beginning and ending of days was all part of God's plan to highlight this watershed moment. In the last supper, Jesus is telling the disciples he is the fulfilment of the Passover, that he is the long awaited Lamb of God, and then on the Friday he is dying on the cross as the final and ultimate sacrifice at the very time the Passover lambs were being killed (cf. John 19:36; Exodus 12:46). Historically accurate, powerfully symbolic, planned to perfection.

Pontius Pilate

Pontius Pilate is probably the most troubled person ever to come into such close proximity to the Lord Jesus. The historian, Ann Wroe (2001), identifies the infamous governor as 'a symbol of ... all men facing, considering and ultimately rejecting the truth... [people] love to watch him ... In some sense, they feel they are watching themselves'.

He was the fifth governor of Judea, the Southern half of Palestine. He was appointed by the Emperor Tiberius in AD 26 and was governor for about 10 years. He was governor in the sense of being a procurator ruling over an imperial province and as such was directly responsible to the emperor. Although endowed with civil, criminal and military jurisdiction, he was under the authority of the legate of Syria. As a man, he cared about standing well with the emperor and hated the Jews who were under his jurisdiction. He was proud (John 19:10), cruel (Luke 13:1), self-seeking and shrewd (Matthew 27:18). He was also a coward and had a superstitious wife.

The Praetorium

The trial took place at the Praetorium which was the headquarters of the commanding officer of the Roman military camp or the Roman Military Governor i.e. Pilate. Pilate's actual headquarters were in Caesarea; however, he and his predecessors, in order to quell any potential riots, made it a point to be in Jerusalem during the feasts. In Jerusalem there were two such quarters: Fortress Antonia (named after Mark Anthony) north west of the temple complex and connected by steps to the temple's outer court (cf. Acts 21:35, 40) and the magnificent Palace of Herod on the western wall. Archaeologists differ as to which one is referred to here. Some maintain that as Pilate was accompanied by his wife he would have stayed in the truly royal abode of Herod's Temple as opposed to the fortified barracks of Antonia. There is also evidence (Edersheim, p. 864) that Roman governors took their seat in front of the palace on a raised platform to pronounce judgement. However, others think that from Luke 23:7 he was probably staying at Fortress Antonia because Herod would have been staying at his palace.

The Jews who brought Jesus to Pilate refused to enter the Praetorium because they didn't want to make themselves ritually unclean by entering the residence of a Gentile and consequently making themselves unable to participate fully in the Passover (18:28). So Pilate came out to them into the precinct of his palace. It would have been an easy task to order his servants to move his judgement seat outside. Jesus was held inside the Praetorium and Pilate spent the whole time in and out. The scene depicts the Roman Governor not able to sit down, up and down, in and out, not knowing what to do or where to go next.

The trial

What charges do you bring against this man?

The previous evening Pilate had sanctioned Roman soldiers to assist the Jews in the arrest of Jesus. These soldiers would have been part of a garrison of about 600 soldiers assigned to Pilate while he was in Jerusalem. After the arrest Jesus was tried by Caiaphas and some of the Jewish leaders and then held captive from about 3am until daybreak somewhere in Caiaphas' palace. As soon as it was daybreak they would have been keen to get him to Pilate before the crowds in Jerusalem knew what was going on. They would have made their way, with Jesus tied up, down the slope on the other side of the Temple mount where the palace of Caiaphas' stood and then made their way up the narrow streets of the upper city of Jerusalem to the Praetorium.

The same people who had spat at Jesus, punched him and asked him to prophesy who hit him, now arrive at Pilate's headquarters and won't enter because they don't want to be ceremonially unclean!

By now they would have got word around to many of the Sanhedrin (the Highest Jewish Council) and their number would have increased. They weren't interested in establishing Jesus' guilt; as far as they were concerned that had been proved during the night. They just wanted him dead. The Jews had no power to authorise capital punishment; only Rome could do this. In order for Jesus to die they needed to convince Pilate.

And so early on that Friday morning the wisest and most influential of the council, with their prisoner, stood outside the Praetorium in Jerusalem asking for an audience. The governor was no friend of the Jews especially so early in the morning and rather impatiently, came out and asked them, 'What accusation do you bring against this man?' (John 18:29).

Jews had been up all night asking themselves the same question, trying to work out what crime he had committed. The Pharisees were jealous of his popularity, saw him as a blasphemer and they smarted under his biting rebukes of their hypocrisy. The chief priests doubtless found their revenues hit when he cleansed the Temple (Matthew 21:12,13). During the Jewish 'trial' the night before they had accused him of threatening to destroy the Jewish Temple (Matthew 26:61) but Pilate would have no interest in a fine point of Jewish religious law. They had to draw up their accusations in terms that would seem serious to Rome and did it by accusing Jesus of being a king, a political revolutionary (Luke 23:2).

The real reason was that they just wanted to get rid of him. They didn't have time for Pilate's question and in effect say to him 'Governor if you know what is good for you stop asking such questions. You know very well that in nearly all matters we constitute the highest court in Israel. You should confirm our decision to do what we are about to ask you to.' (John 18:30).

Let me ask you the same question. What is your problem with Jesus Christ? Perhaps it is an intellectual one. It just doesn't seem believable to you. In our high tech, scientific, civilised, modern world can all this really be true? Are we really expected to believe what we read in the Bible?

Or maybe your problem is that it seems so irrelevant. Jesus Christ can't pay your mortgage. He doesn't entertain you. You don't see how he can repair your marriage, get you the girl/boy you want, pass your exams. It is all a bit pie in the sky.

Another reason could be that it all just seems all a bit embarrassing. Christianity is just so uncool.

But the real reason, like with these Jews, is you just don't want him ruling over you. There are sins you love too much and a way of life you just don't want to give up for Jesus Christ. Much easier and more convenient to kill him, shut him out.

But throughout the rest of this chapter as we listen in on the trial of Jesus before Pilate, let's do so with an open mind and at least give him a fair trial before deciding what we are going to do with Jesus.

(What) YOU(!) are a king?!

It was not going to be easy to get rid of an angry mob outside his palace, so in order to get to the bottom of it Pilate summoned Jesus to his palace and started to conduct his own investigation. Pilate goes back inside and asks Jesus if he is a king. Looking at him, the state he is in since his beating the night before, Pilate can't believe his eyes. The thought that this man is a king seemed incredulous. The way Pilate would have asked the question would have been along the lines of 'Seriously, YOU(!) are a king?!'

Christ says that he is a king but not the kind of King Pilate was used to (John 18:36). Neither is he a king simply of the Jews. Pilate had no time for this trial and wanted to get it over and done with. He saw this as a matter for the Jews and of no relevance to him. But the man that stood before Pilate that day was so much greater than he could ever have imagined. He wasn't going to lead a Jewish revolt against the Romans; He wasn't a rival king to Caesar. He was far bigger than that. He was the king of the whole earth. Pilate, even Caesar, were in his hand! The truth of the matter was that real power wasn't derived from this world but from another world (John 19:11).

Jesus is telling Pilate that things aren't how they seem. This world and all that is in it is transient and will one day come to an end. Christ's kingdom is not a realm but a rule. This rule is established in the lives of all those who follow and trust him; his kingdom crosses political boundaries and will grow and grow and grow through the ages. Rome would fall as would every other empire but Christ's kingdom will never end. All the governments and kingdoms of this world are in God's hand. Kingdoms rise and fall at his command. Daniel 5:21 says the 'Most High God rules the kingdom of mankind and sets over it who he will'. Kings, countries and world leaders are raised up and are struck down by the God of Heaven. World leaders and the kings and queens of the earth are full of their own importance and power and seldom do any of them acknowledge God. As they rule their countries and pass laws and make their plans and policies, almost never do they consider God. They seem to think that their power is in their own hands. However, an individual's, and even a country's, power is short lived. At the time of this trial Rome was the world super power. Before

Rome there were many world empires and since Rome other world empires have come and gone. L. James has written a brilliant book about the rise and fall of the British Empire. At the moment, America seems the world's dominant power with the biggest economy but one day it won't be.

What is truth?

Jesus tells Pilate what he is saying is the truth. When Christ talks about truth Pilate shrugs his shoulder and cynically asks, 'what is truth?' He doesn't want to hear it, is sceptical and didn't wait for an answer. He asked the question and then went out again to the Jews.

No one is interested in absolute truth today. According to Alistair Begg, 'plausibility is given to every idea, and certainty to none'. Furthermore, it is hard to know what or who to trust. Almost every advertisement is an exaggeration. We are told if we buy this make-up or that dress, go on that diet or do this work out, it will change our lives, but it hasn't. Politicians time and again have let us down, saying one thing but doing another. We can't really trust what we read in the newspapers. And it is not just 'them', it is us too. The one thing we do still all agree on is that lying is wrong and yet we all do it because it is so easy. We lie to each other, to the people we love. We've broken vows and promises too often. Parents split up and children get heartbroken. We are constantly being let, or letting others, down.

So who can we trust? What is truth? There are so many religions all claiming to be true. Not to offend any of them we try to say that none of them are completely true, but believe what you want as long as it doesn't hurt others.

But standing in front of Pilate was the one who said, 'I am the way, and the truth, and the life. No one comes to the Father except through me' (John 14:6). Jesus says that truth is not relative but absolute. What the Bible says about God and sin and judgement and the only way to be saved is the truth, the absolute truth.

But why should we believe him? Who can verify that what he is saying is true? He swears by the highest authority there is—himself (Genesis 22:16). There is no one higher to swear by. Jesus isn't just saying he speaks the truth, but that he is the truth. On that Friday morning, Truth was literally staring Pontius Pilate in the face.

We can believe it is true because this Truth has stood the test of time. In my job I have to investigate incidents between naughty boys. They will always say they haven't done it. So I cross-examine them, bring in witnesses, come at them from different angles and effectually the truth comes out. What they told me at first doesn't continue to be true. People over the last 2000 years have tried to prove the Bible to be wrong and the Truth that is found in Jesus Christ to be false. They have come at it from this way and that way and the other way but it keeps being true.

Barabbas or Jesus?

Pilate returns to the outer colonnade and yields his verdict to the Jews, that he can find no fault with Jesus. Time and again throughout the trial Pilate keep saying 'I find no fault in him', 'I do not find any crime in him' (John 18:38; 19:4; 19:6; Matthew 27:23; 27:24; Mark 15:14; Luke 23:4; 23:13–15; 23:22).

But the Jews kept insisting that he stirs up the people teaching throughout all Judea, from Galilee where he started even to here (Luke 23:5). At the mention of Galilee, Pilate tries to get him off his hands by sending him to Herod who had come to Jerusalem for the feast (Jesus before Herod is dealt with in the next chapter); anything not to have to deal with him (Luke 23:6–12). If Jesus is from Galilee then Pilate thought he would come under Herod's jurisdiction and he could deal with this problem. The problem was Herod could find no fault with him either and sent him straight back to Pilate. It was Pilate as the governor who had the real power and authority and it was down to him to make the decision. So Pilate tries another strategy.

It was a custom during Jewish Passover to release one prisoner.

It was similar to presidential pardons. By now a crowd was gathering to see what was going to happen and to see the release of another prisoner (Mark 15:8). Pilate standing on a gallery or porch over the pavement in front of them asked the crowd, 'Whom do you want me to release for you: Barabbas, or Jesus who is called Christ?' (Matthew 27:17). Pilate would have felt sure the crowd would choose Jesus. He would have known the crowd's reaction to Jesus as he entered Jerusalem the week before (Matthew 21:1–11).

Barabbas was a most notable prisoner. Matthew tells us he was actually notorious (Matthew 27:16). He was a terrorist from the Roman point of view and a guerrilla from the national perspective. Usually chief priests had nothing to do with zealots and others interested in armed rebellion. He had been involved in a rebellion and participated in a bloody insurrection (Mark 15:7). The murder (Acts 3:14) had taken place in connection with this uprising. He had committed murder in his struggle against Rome. His name was not taken out of a hat. Probably Barabbas was the leader of the two criminals that were crucified either side of Jesus. That middle cross was intended for Barabbas, their leader! Here Pilate is treating Jesus, the one he can find no fault with, in the same class as this dangerous criminal.

While he is giving the choice to the crowd, Pilate's wife sends a message to him, and as he is attending to what his wife has to say, the chief priests and elders work the crowd. (Matthew 27:19, 20). The chief priests knew how to manipulate the comparatively small number who would crowd around the Praetorium. Partisans of Barabbas would probably also have taken advantage of the opportunity to get their friend free. And so when Pilate asks them for their decision they cry out, 'we want Barabbas'. 'Loud cries' (Luke 23:18) give the impression that a riot was beginning to build up.

In the cold light of day, Barabbas would have been obnoxious to the crowd. But this is a picture of the choices all of us make. We would rather follow sin than Christ. We prefer Barabbas to Jesus.

But the greatest image of that day is the one of Barabbas walking free. He woke up with the prospect of his death and went to bed a free man. I wonder if Barabbas later that day walked down the road alongside the cross and thought, 'that should have been me'. Christ is bound that I may go free!

This is a wonderful picture of penal substitution; that is someone taking the penalty I deserve and being my substitute. It is a fulfilment of The Old Testament sacrifices that the priest brought to God to atone for sin. The animal dying instead of the sinner. Here Christ is dying instead of Barabbas. On the cross Jesus assumed Barabbas' identity. He was numbered with the transgressors (Luke 22:37; Isaiah 53:4–6).

Pilate in a strange way confirmed Jesus is the Saviour. No basis for a charge against him, nevertheless Pilate condemned him to die (Luke 23:14). Herod could also find no fault with him (Luke 23:15) and it was probably while Jesus was with Herod that Judas went into the chief priests and the elders and said, 'I have sinned by betraying innocent blood' (Matthew 27:4). Innocent, innocent, innocent and yet condemned! The picture is powerful: The innocent is condemned and the guilty go free.

Perhaps you are reading this book and you are plagued by your past. You've done things, hurt people, completely messed up your life. Maybe you are paralysed by guilt and the consequences of your actions. It keeps you awake at night. You would do anything to start again. Your sins have trapped you and you feel you cannot escape from your past. Your life is all knotted and tangled. Well let me encourage you to come to Jesus Christ. Confess your sins to him. Tell him everything, open up to him, be honest with him. Repent, that is turn away from your sin, and go free! He is ready, willing and able to forgive you and set you free. Wesley (*Christian Hymns,* 2005 no.509) put it brilliantly when he said,

> Long my imprisoned spirit lay
> Fast bound in sin and nature's night;
> Thine eye diffused a quickening ray,

I woke, the dungeon flamed with light;
My chains fell off, my heart was free,
I rose, went forth, and followed Thee
Charles Wesley, 1707–88

Behold the man!

Pilate is desperate not to crucify the Lord Jesus but he also fears the crowd. To satisfy their thirst for blood he orders that Jesus be flogged. He hoped that if Jesus was given a scourging it would avoid the necessity of crucifying him. Flogging could take three forms: less severe, brutal flogging and the most terrible scourging of all. In Roman law a light beating was sometime given together with a magisterial warning so that the accused might take greater care for the future

It is quite possible that Jesus endured two floggings. A lighter one in John 19:1 in Pilate's attempts to appease the crowd and the most severe one in Mark 15:5 after he had been sentenced to crucifixion.

These floggings were brutal. From the account in Mark it is clear that Jesus was badly beaten up and the soldiers had real fun at his expense. They get the whole battalion to get involved (up to 600 of them) and they take out on him their sadistic urges. Jesus would have been stripped naked, his hands would have been tied behind him, and he would have been bent over and attached to a pole in the centre of the Praetorium. The soldiers would have taken short wooden poles which had pieces of lead or brass or bone attached to the end of the leather straps and lashed his bare back. In some cases the beating was so severe the victim didn't go on to crucifixion.

After this the mockery began. They threw a discarded and faded soldier's cloak around him and gave him a sceptre made out of a reed to make him look like something from a dressing up box. They kept marching up to him, mock saluting him and as they did, giving him blows. They kept hitting him on the head with a reed and spitting on him, mocking him, paying him homage (Mark 15:16–19).

For what? Healing the sick? Bringing back to life the dead? Suffering the little children to come to him? He who spoke and a universe came into being; he who put the planets in their place; he who built every mountain and rolled out every sea; he of whom the disciples said, 'even the winds and the waves obey him'; he who was from the beginning God, subjected himself to this!

> Oh make me understand it
> help me to take it in
> what it meant to Thee, the Holy One,
> To bear away my sin   (Katherine Agnes May Kelly, 1869–1942)

As well as all this, they weave a crown of thorns and place it on his head. This would have been so painful and a great indignity. The soldiers just thought they were mocking him but what they were doing carried great significance. In Genesis 3:18 God says that thorns and thistles would grow as a result of sin entering the world. They would be symbols of God's curse on disobedience. Hebrews 6:8 says 'if it bears thorns and thistles, it is worthless and near to being cursed, and its end is to be burned'. The soldiers were doing something they didn't even realise. They were using the symbol of man's disobedience and turning it into a crown for the Lord Jesus to wear. He is crowned the sinners' king. He wears the crown we should have worn through all eternity.

The soldiers brought out Jesus battered and bloodied for Pilate to present to the crowd. Pointing at him he says, 'Behold the Man!' Look at him! A pathetic spectacle, pity him, not crucify him'. Pilate is saying to them, 'Look do you think this is a king?!' Look at the thorns, the reed, all dressed up, bleeding, swollen and bruised. Is this the man you find so dangerous and harmful? This is a man who cannot do anything for himself!

When you look at Christ what do you see? He is in this sorry state for you. The way Christ looks now, the way he's been 'dissed' is the treatment your sin deserves. This is the way sin should be treated; ridiculed for its folly.

As the crowd was beholding him, he was beholding them. In a few moments Pilate is going to take him back inside the Praetorium and be outraged that Jesus won't speak to him. He says 'what! You won't speak to me!' Christ would have been looking out onto the crowd, beholding them with the same compassion as he would have had looking out onto the crowds previously. As well as us beholding him, he is searching us out. All the noise and activity of the Jewish leaders, the crowds, the soldiers, Pilate; Christ permeates the whole scene silently and majestically.

Where are you from?

The more Pilate says he can find no fault in him, the more the crowd chant 'crucify him, crucify him, crucify him' (Luke 23:21, 23). Over and over these terrible words are yelled until they become a monotonous refrain, an eerie, ominous chant.

The chief priests and temple police remind Pilate that they have a law and according to that law he ought to die because he made himself the Son of God. Pilate had a duty to respect their laws. The Roman government left a considerable measure of freedom for the home nation to regulate its own affairs.

At the mention of 'son of God' Pilate, this superstitious governor is petrified and takes him back inside to question him one last time (John 19:8).

In front of Pilate stood the Son of God. As such he was a man but also God. He looked like a man. He got hungry (Matthew 4:2; 21:18; Mark 11:12, got thirsty (John 4:7), ate and drank (Matthew 9:10–13; 11:19), became tired (John 4:6), slept (Matthew 8:24), sweated (Luke 22:44), bled (John 19:34). He went through the same process of human development as all humans. He grew up and increased in wisdom and stature (Luke 2:52). He acquired knowledge like other boys of his day. But he was a proper man; what a man should be like. He was blameless. He was tempted in all ways like we are, but he never gave in and he remained immaculate (Matthew 4:1–11; Hebrews 4:15). Even his enemies said, 'we can find no fault in him'.

But this man is also God. He pre-existed. He said 'Before Abraham (who lived thousands of years before Christ) was, I am' (John 8:58). 'He was in the beginning with God' (John 1:2). He created the world. 'All things were made through him' (John 1:3). He was born of a virgin and had been placed in her womb by the Holy Spirit (Luke 2:35). On the one hand he was born in a tiny little place called Bethlehem, 'too little to be among the clans of Judah' (Micah 5:2), in a stable and his teenage mother wrapped him in cloths and laid him in a trough. (Luke 2:7). But when he grew up he stilled storms, fed 5000 people with just 5 loaves and 2 fish, made the blind see, the deaf hear, the lame walk, healed diseases and raised the dead. No wonder Pilate is so scared. In front of him is the man who is God.

Do you know how many things they have against you? (Matthew 27:13; Mark 15:4)

He is shaken to the bottom of his soul and trembling all over. He wants to know where Jesus is from, but Jesus gives him no response. Pilate is outraged that 'HE!' wouldn't answer 'HIM!' and reminds Jesus of all the accusations brought against him. But Jesus made no reply. As we picture it, all the while Christ stood near, perhaps behind Pilate, just within the portals of the Praetorium. To all these charges he made no reply. Pilate is used to people in this position cowering and begging, but Jesus is silent. Jesus made no reply, not even to a single charge (Matthew 27:12–14 cf. Isaiah 53:7; Luke 23:9; John 19:9). Later on Peter says when they hurled their insults at him he did not retaliate; when he suffered he made no threats (1 Peter 2:22–24).

Why? Why didn't he answer? Why didn't he speak up?

Why didn't he defend himself? Because in Roman law, silence was admission of guilt. Jesus Christ, the eternal Son of God, by remaining silent was saying, 'I'm guilty'. Not for crimes he committed but for the sins of all his people. Jesus was pleading guilty for all your sins. He is saying in effect all the charges against me should stand. I'm guilty of them all.

According to the famous trial lawyer Johnnie Cochran (June 29th 1998),

> Jesus is the person I would like to have defended. I would have relished the opportunity to defend someone who was completely innocent of all charges and a victim of religious persecution. However, because of his mission here, he would have undoubtedly declined.

What shall I do with Jesus?

The crowd

By the end of this trial Pilate is in a sorry state and totally frustrated. He says over and over that he can find no fault in him. He does everything he can to release him. His problem is that he feels he has to listen to the very crowd he hates, because he fears them. We feel like shouting back down the centuries, 'So let him go Pilate! Have the courage of your convictions man!' But before we are too hard on Pilate in some ways, watching him is like watching ourselves—we are pressured into making the wrong choice and face the same pressures of family, friends, general public and playing to the crowd. Edersheim (2004, p.867) says 'It was as if two powers were contending for the mastery of his heart, and it is the same two powers today.' You look at this Christ and then look at your friends, family, colleagues, fellow students, teachers, society; who do you fear most? Is it the crowd preventing you from believing in Jesus?

Loved his sin too much

The killer blow for Pilate is when the crowd says that if he releases him, he's no friend of Caesar. This was a threat that they'd report him to the emperor, Tiberius. They lodge a complaint against him about his softness towards rebels. He knew the Jews were liars and had no love whatsoever for Roman government. This was despicable hypocrisy but they had him cornered. He could lose his power, possessions and privileges.

What are you frightened about in following Jesus? What are you worried about giving up? Think about Pilate and where he is now. His power, possessions and privileges are no good to him now. As the Lord Jesus Christ said, 'what would it profit a man if he gained the whole world but lost his own soul? Or what can a man give in exchange for his soul?' The bottom line is this: is whatever you are clinging to worth going to Hell for?

Scared
But not only is Pilate scared of the crowd, he is also scared of Jesus. His wife warned him to have nothing to do with all this. She had dreamt about him which is not surprising as everyone knew about him. The dream had happened 'this very day' (Matthew 27:19). It would seem that after granting the garrison of soldiers, Pilate spoke to his wife.

The advice of his wife was fuelled it would seem by superstition. Beautiful stories about her are mere legends. According to Edersheim 'tradition has given her the name Procula and the Apocryphal Gospels describe her as a convert to Judaism, while the Greek church has actually placed her in the catalogue of the saints'.

The only thing we can be sure of is that God gave that dream. If a dream like this can cause so much fear, imagine what it will be like standing before him at the judgement? Imagine what it will be like when you leave this world and go out into eternity and face God.

Madness of sin
When Pilate brought Jesus out to the crowd he asked them, 'Shall I crucify your king?' The chief priests answered, 'We have no king but Caesar'. So he delivered him over to them to be crucified'. (John

19:15, 16). This reaction shows the total madness of sin. They would rather accept the political thraldom they earlier disavowed (John 8:33) than give up their sin and accept the kingship of Christ.

This is what sin does to you. You end up not thinking straight and selling your soul at a ridiculously high (or low!) price. All sense goes out of the window. You become so intoxicated by it that you do things that you know are wrong and senseless.

Consequences
The consequences of rejecting Jesus are catastrophic. They said to Pilate, 'his blood be on us and on our children!' (Matthew 27:25:) According to Edersheim (p.874)

> A few years more and 100s of crosses bore Jewish mangled bodies within sight of Jerusalem. And still have these wanderers seem to bear, from country to country and from land to land that burden of blood ... with this cry Judaism was in the person of its representatives guilty of denial of God, of blasphemy, of apostasy. It committed suicide and ever since has its dead body been carried in show from land to land and from century to century to be dead and to remain dead until he comes a second time.

It is very easy to condemn the Jews for their treatment of the Lord Jesus but today in the West in particular, on the whole, we have turned our back on God and his Son. We say we don't need him anymore, we'll do things our way. And the danger is that subsequent generations will grow up with no knowledge of the only true and living Saviour and no idea of the dangers of going into eternity without him.

Washed his hands
Pilate tries everything to get Jesus off his hands. In the end he takes a bowl and in front of the crowd says he is washing his hands of it all. He wants to evade the necessity of making a decision about Jesus. But you cannot remain neutral where Jesus Christ is concerned. You either accept or reject him.

Jesus is standing in Pilate's hall
Friendless and removed from all
Listen to the sorry call
What shall I do with Jesus?
What shall I do with Jesus, neutral I cannot be
And some day my heart will be asking what will he do with
me

What will you do with him?
And so as you have listened in on the trial the question remains, what will you do with him?

You cannot be passive or indifferent towards him. You either accept him or reject him. One day you will stand before God and he will ask you, 'What did you do with him?' How will you answer on that awesome day?

There is a famous nineteenth-century painting by Ciseri called 'Ecce Homo'. The painting which hangs in the Palazzo Pitti Gallery in Florence is based on Jesus' trial before Pilate. It takes its title from Pilate's words to the crowd: 'Behold the man!' or in Latin, 'Ecce Homo!' In the painting, Jesus stands on the terrace, stripped to the waist, his hands bound behind him; Pilate stands in the middle of the painting, with his back to the viewer. He is leaning forward, head bent over the railing, appealing to the masses gathered below him in the streets. With one hand he gestures toward Jesus, as if to ask, 'What will you do with him?'

It is the most important question you will ever answer. Your eternal destiny hangs on it!

Judgement passed

The moment for which the entire history of redemption had been waiting had come. As everyone knows the time and place they were when a famous event takes place—the murder of JFK, the death of Princess Diana—John recalls that it was the preparation for the Passover and about the 6th hour when Pilate sat in the judgement seat, a place called the Pavement which in Hebrew is Gabbatha. This was an area paved with stones, in area about 3000 square feet. He led Jesus out on his official chair which was standing on a platform reached by steps and delivered him over to the soldiers to take him away to be crucified.

6

The sound of silence

Luke 23:6–12

Passing the buck

As we saw in the last chapter, Pilate did not want to condemn Jesus to death. Time and time again he says that he can find no fault in him (John 18:38; 19:4; 19:6; Matthew 27:23; 27:24; Mark 15:14; Luke 23:4; 23:13–15; 23:22). But he can't release him because he is afraid of the crowd, led by the Jewish leaders, who are desperate for Jesus to be killed. However, something the Jews say gives Pilate what he thinks is the perfect opportunity to move this problem into somebody else's in tray.

Throughout the whole trial Pilate was up and down and in and out, not knowing what to do with himself. But on one of the occasions he goes out to the Jews he discovers that Jesus is a Galilean (Luke 23:5). If that is the case then Pilate thought he would come under Herod's jurisdiction and Herod could deal with the problem (Luke 23:7). A trial was usually carried out in the province where the offence was committed but could be referred to the province to which the accused belonged. It was a straw that

Pilate was desperate to clutch! And so Pilate tries to get him off his hands by sending him to Herod.

The only problem, as we shall see, was that Herod could find no fault with him either and sent him back. Whether he liked it or not, Pilate had to face up to the 'problem' of what to do with Jesus Christ. As we all do. On this matter of eternal significance, at the end, none of us can pass the buck.

Herod

Following the death of his father Herod the Great in 4BC, Herod Antipas became the tetrarch of Galilee and Perea (Luke 3:1) until AD 39.

Herod was crafty. Christ referred to him as 'that fox' (Luke 13:32). He loved pleasure and himself. While visiting his half-brother, Herod Phillip I, he became infatuated with his wife, Herodias, so Herod divorced his own wife and the two illicit lovers eloped.

Herod was probably in Jerusalem to observe the Feast, a tactic he no doubt thought would please his subjects. Up to this point he and Pilate didn't get on (Luke 23:12). Their feud had possibly turned on Pilate viewing Herod as just a tin pot ruler of a client state. Pilate had also, according to Luke 13:1, ordered some of Herod's subjects to be killed.

But this 'gesture' on Pilate's part was an almost ostentatious acknowledgement of the rights of the tetrarch. Despite it serving Pilate's own ends, Herod no doubt saw it as a compliment and from that moment on the two became friends (Luke 23:12).

So much noise

The scene of Jesus standing before Herod is a noisy one. In the background throughout are the chief priests and scribes loudly and vehemently accusing Jesus; no doubt repeating all the things they had said to Pilate. They are trying to give Herod as many reasons as they can as to why Jesus should be put to death and we can imagine them all talking at the same time, keen to put their points across, desperate to get what they want.

But the focus is really Herod who is plying Jesus with questions. He had wanted to see him for a long time. He was desperate to see Jesus 'perform' and so asked him many questions and kept on at him to do something miraculous (Luke 23:8).

Herod just wants to be entertained and when he doesn't get what he wants he loses interest and patience. He is disappointed and angry. While he can find no fault in him, before he sends him back to Pilate the real noise begins. He starts to have sadistic fun at his prisoner's expense. He and his soldiers begin mocking him, dressing him up, 'dissing' him and 'slapping him about'. In fact, just for fun, they send Jesus back to Pilate dressed up as a king.

But above all the noise—the accusations, the mocking, the repeated requests to be entertained, the rough handling—is the deafening sound of silence. Throughout it all, the Son of God was silent! (Luke 23:9).

We live in a noisy world. Everyone seems to have an opinion on everything, especially God. Rather than someone to be feared, God is a topic for discussion and debate. Governments and politicians; entertainers, commentators, journalists, 'experts', scientists, religious leaders; have all put themselves above God. They decide what is right and wrong. They announce whether they agree or disagree on what the Bible says; which bits to take out and leave in, which bits need modernising and sanitising for our era. The parts of Christianity that are acceptable and the bits to be dismissed as relics of a bygone era. They pass laws that oppose the Word of God and even dictate what children are taught in schools about these things. Some get angry with the bits that cut across what they want to do and think. Others just mock or dismiss it all as irrelevant in this day and age.

All the while the Son God is observing from Heaven, seemingly silent. But one day we will all stand before him and give an account of our lives.

Worthless!

It is frightening to think that with the Son of God before him Herod could only jest. Luke 23:11 says that Herod and his soldiers set him at nought. He had wanted to see Jesus to put his mind at rest that he wasn't John back from the dead. Once that had been established and his prisoner wasn't going to 'perform', Herod and his soldiers looked at him and thought he was nothing. Herod also wanted to see Jesus because he was threatened by him. Herod was a king and the thought that some people believed Jesus to be king bothered him. This was probably why he had previously wanted to kill him (Luke 13:31). But when he finally saw him, in the state he was in, he concluded he was nothing to worry about. This was no king. So unimpressive! A joke!

Herod took a superficial glance at Jesus and concluded, 'worthless'. Give me my sin and my pleasure any day over this. But in weighing him up he got his counting all wrong and we are in danger of doing the same. We look at the world today and in comparison, Jesus seems nothing. How can he possibly compete with all that is on offer in the modern world? He seems so old fashioned and unimpressive compared to the cool, trendy, powerful, rich and the famous of today. You look at this man from Galilee and think he's nothing!

But when I have to depart from this world, leave everything behind and stand before God, none of these things will be able to help me. Put all the powerful people together, the coolest, the richest, the smartest; they will be no good to me at all when I enter eternity. They can't forgive me for all the wrong I have done, put right all the hurt and pain I have caused. They can't ease my troubled conscience. They can't make me fit for Heaven. Only the one who Herod and his soldiers 'set at nought' (Luke 23:11, NKJV) will be able to help me on that day

Just do what I tell you

All Herod wanted was for Jesus to do what he wanted him to do. He was desperate for pleasure and to be entertained. Maybe that is you. All you care about is pleasing yourself. Sex, going out, popularity, your career, your family, friends, studies, job, getting on in life, mixing in the right circles, having influence, being well thought of, possessions, big house, expensive car, the right clothes, sport, fitness. It could be any number of things. It is all that matters.

Once Herod realised he wasn't going to get what he wanted, he got angry and impatient. So many people today are like Herod. They just want a religion that suits their purposes. That helps them through the bad times. Makes them feel good about themselves. Fits around their lives. Doesn't make demands. But when the Son of God doesn't do what they want him to do, they mock him, try to belittle the whole thing and even get angry.

Not now, maybe later

But the really frightening thing is that it wasn't always like this for Herod. At one stage he listened with interest to the preaching of John the Baptist (Mark 6:20).

John was the forerunner of Jesus Christ. He was the one who prepared the way for Jesus. He was like the herald proclaiming that the Messiah was about to come onto the scene. John was a no nonsense preacher who impressed upon his hearers the need to repent (Luke 3:1–18), that is turn away from their sin. John didn't pull any punches. He told it how it was. He put his finger on the part of Herod's life that was wrong; that everyone else also knew was wrong but just accepted or didn't say anything because it was Herod. John, however, repeatedly rebuked him (Luke 3:19, 20) but instead of repenting, Herod put John in prison. He didn't want to listen to what he knew was true. He probably thought 'I'll sort things out one day but not yet'. I'll put John in prison and at a more convenient time I'll listen to him again'.

But things didn't turn out like that. In his birthday party, Herodias' daughter danced seductively in front of Herod. Like so many men he clearly had a problem with sex. This man promised her whatever she asked for, up to a half of his kingdom. Prompted by her mother, she asks for the head of John the Baptist on a plate (Matthew 14:6–12; Mark 6:21–29; Luke 9:7–9).

You can imagine the party being in full swing. The drinks flowing, Herod the centre of attention, full of lust for his partner's daughter makes a rash promise and gets trapped. He can't go back on it and risk his pride, but is also too scared to kill the preacher. Something has to give though. This is not a life changing moment. It is an eternity changing one. Risk losing it all now to keep it later, or keep it all now and lose everything later.

From that moment on it would seem Herod tried to bury the truth. He didn't want to face up to it and just lived for the here and now. Whenever he was confronted or reminded about the things of God, he just tried to suppress it and get rid of it.

Herod had wanted to see Jesus for a long time. Jesus had come to his attention because news had reached him that Jesus had healed sick people, lepers had been cleansed, storms hushed, demons expelled and even the dead brought back to life. He was also performing miracles through his apostles. All this perplexed Herod because it was said by some that John had risen from the dead (Luke 9:7). But Herod said, 'John I beheaded, but who is this about whom I hear such things?' And he sought to see him (Luke 9:9). He was bothered by Jesus and worried it was John back from the dead (Matthew 14:1, 2). He wanted to see Jesus to put his mind at rest that John really was dead.

Perhaps this resonates with you. There was a time you went to church. Believed these things. Knew they were true. But Jesus Christ and his demands don't fit in with your lifestyle anymore. It bothers you a bit from time to time but the more you fill your life with things, the better it gets. You have spent your life suppressing the truth and it is working.

You have convinced yourself that you will be okay. You might have been troubled by your sin before but now your conscience is quieter. Hell can't be real can it? The judgement is too far-fetched isn't it? In this modern world God, his law, the Bible, the need for a Saviour are all a bit out of date. The culture of the day has well and truly seduced you. You now listen to the modern talking heads and ignore the Ancient of Days (Daniel 7:9). We are too sophisticated to be worried about these things. We have moved on. Besides, life is too short to think about eternity. Unless you can offer me something here and now then I am not interested and I'll just make fun of it or get angry.

That one sin

Herod made a big call. By choosing his sin the only option then was to put his conscience to death. He either had to kill sin or allow sin to kill him. Towards the close of Christ's ministry, certain Pharisees warned Jesus to get out from Jerusalem because Herod wants to kill him (Luke 13:31–33). Jesus reminded him too much of John. Herod was threatened by Jesus. Jesus was a king and Herod wasn't prepared to bow the knee to anyone. He didn't want anyone to tell him what to do. He just wanted to live for himself and do whatever he wanted. Anyone who challenged that, had to be got rid of.

Is that a choice you are confronted with as you read this book? There is a particular sin you really struggle with or a way of life or a relationship that you just can't give up. Maybe, probably, it is a sexual sin. I imagine nearly all men reading this book can relate to Herod's sex problem. When sex is involved most men stop thinking straight. Lust, pornography, adultery, flings, are all things men think they can control but end up being controlled by them. Every time you indulge in it you think it will be the last time, but you keep having to go back for more.

But while sexual sin is the focus here, sexual sin isn't the only sin or the worst sin. All sin—pride, covetousness, materialism, gossip, envy, selfishness, unkindness, malice, drunkenness, lying, foul language—are all equally abhorrent in God's sight.

You have to choose between your sin and Jesus Christ. You think that you can have it for a while and then sort out your eternal soul later. But there will never be a more convenient time than now. Every day you carry on in your sin it takes more and more of a hold of you. Every day you carry on in your sin you harden your heart until there comes that point of no return when God hardens it (Exodus 9:12).

Silence

When he finally got his moment with Jesus it was too late. His conscience was dead. Unless we silence sin, sin will silence our conscience.

You cannot play around with God. Hell is full of people who said, 'when I have done this and when I have done that I will sort things out'. But today is the only day promised as a day of salvation (2 Corinthians 6:2). You may die tonight. However, you may live another 70 years but have no interest in Christ at all after today. He may be calling to you now but tomorrow your heart may be hardened. He may never pass your way again. If you hear his voice harden not your heart (Hebrews 3:15).

Herod knew the truth. He just deliberately rejected it. Jesus had nothing more to say to him. I am sure many of you reading this book know what you need to do but you just don't want to do it. It is too hard right now to give things up. There is nothing else to say apart from repent and believe.

Jesus knew Herod's heart and said nothing to him. There was no point. Herod's conscience has gone to sleep because he had done so much violence to it. He was a man who had heard God's Word. Heard one of the best preachers of all time. He had been reasoned with time and time again (Mark 6:20) but rejected it.

Because of the way you are living you want Jesus Christ to be silent now. You don't want to hear what he has to say. But one day you will have a meeting with him. You can ignore him, mock him, be angry with him but eventually you have to meet him. You will stand before God and he will be there. At that moment you do not want him to be silent. As we saw in chapter 2 of this book, when your conscience, God's law, other people, your bad record are all screaming out, 'Guilty! Dirty! Send him to Hell!' you need Christ to speak up for you. If Christ is silent on that day you will be sent into everlasting torment (Matthew 25:46).

But you can meet him right now. If you come to him in repentance and faith he will receive you. Jesus never refused a sincere questioner but Herod wasn't in that class. Herod is the only person who Christ said nothing at all to. Today he will still speak to you if you come to him. 'Forgiven', 'Cleansed', 'Come unto me' (Matthew 11:28) are still words that can come to you from the Saviour's lips.

There was an article in *The Times* (18 October, 2010 p.28) about the 33 Chilean miners who spent 69 days afraid beneath the Chilean desert, certain they were going to die. With them was a Christian minister who read the Bible to them and prayed with them every day. The men prayed and believed God heard their prayers as all 33 of the men were saved. The title of the article was 'When a man screams to God then he will answer their prayer'. That is true today.

However, there will come a time when the day of salvation and grace will be over, when a man can scream and shout and beg and plead and do whatever he wants, but God will not hear his prayer. Mercy is over, judgement has come. 'Depart from me' will be the only words the un-repentant, unbelieving will hear.

The one who hung on that cross to save sinners is the same one who will one day send all those who rejected him to Hell. One of the Puritans, Thomas Boston, said, 'to be damned by Him who came to save sinners is to be doubly damned'. What an awesome, chilling thought! Pray, call out to him; 'scream' to him, while you can.

7

The walk of shame

Matthew 27:32–34; Mark 15:20–23;
Luke 23:26–32; John 19:17

In bad company

ONCE PILATE HAD PASSED THE DEATH SENTENCED (JOHN 19:14) the soldiers took the Lord Jesus Christ away and flogged him severely (Mark 15:5) and began getting him ready to be crucified.

The Lord Jesus was crucified with two criminals. Four soldiers would have been assigned to each cross and the whole operation was under the command of a centurion. According to tradition he was called Longinus but we don't know this for certain. By now they would have stripped Jesus of the purple robe they had dressed him up in, and put his own clothes back on him, only to take them off him again to gamble for them (John 19:23–24). Jesus had been abandoned by all his friends at this point and was now in the company of rough Roman soldiers, two thieves and a great rabble.

Walk of shame

A portion of the punishment imposed on the vilest criminals was that they should carry their own cross when they went to execution. Furthermore, when Christ carried his cross to Golgotha he would not have been taken on the shortest route but the longest way possible and would have had to walk step by step through the many crowded streets of Jerusalem. This was so that as many people as possible could see him. Crowds thronged and gathered to see it and criminals were made to do this to show everyone what would happen if you break the law. They would probably have gone past the Temple, through the first gate in the wall gate and into the busy business quarter of Acra.

In the fullest sense, the Lord Jesus was reckoned as a sinner, counted as a curse for our sake. The pain he was suffering was not just physical but psychological. He had to endure the shame of being viewed as a vile criminal. It would have been so embarrassing and humiliating.

When we think of him walking through those streets whipped to the bone, bloodied with a crown of thorns on his head, carrying his cross and doing the walk of shame, we must see that he was suffering the shame and guilt that our sin deserves. He was enduring our shame!

Guilt and shame paralyse us. Psychologists say that the biggest problem they deal with is guilt. So many of us live our lives worried we may get found out. Conan Doyle, apparently, sent a letter to famous people which just said, 'you've been found out' and over half of them fled the country. Every one of us has got guilty secrets. Some of them are so shameful. You may be quietly hoping and thinking you've got away with it. But you haven't. God has seen everything. If you are trusting in Jesus Christ, he bore the shame for you, but if you are not, you will one day suffer all the shame your sin deserves. You've been seen and one day it will all come to light.

I have a mate, let's say his name is Paul. Two friends called for him one afternoon. There was no answer but they could hear music in the house and knew he was in. He had a ground floor room at the back of the house so the two friends went around to it. They could see him in his room through the net curtains. He had Tina Turner, 'Simply the best' playing in the background. His top was off, he was flexing his muscles and saying to the mirror, 'No you're the best!' Being good friends the two boys just watched him for ten minutes before knocking on the window at which he groaned, 'oh no!'. He thought no one had been watching but his two friends had seen it all. Embarrassing, and we've never let him live it down! But not the end of the world. However, everything you have done has been seen and if you are not trusting Christ, one day you will do the walk of shame in front of the judge of all the earth.

In the Game of Thrones series 5 finale, the queen Cersei was forced to walk naked through the streets of Kings Landing as the screaming, hostile crowd threw food and the contents of their chamber pots at her. It turns out that Lena Headey who plays the vengeful queen had a body double to do the scene, Rebecca Van Cleave. As Jesus was walking through the streets of Jerusalem enduring all the shame, he was the 'body double' of all those who trust him.

Collapsed from exhaustion

Jesus started carrying the cross (John 19:17) but obviously weakened by scourging, falls under the weight of it and is unable to carry it any further. In all probability Jesus carried the cross as far as the last gate of the city which led from the suburb towards the place of execution. He then collapsed in weakness from pain and loss of blood. Mark also indicates Jesus needed help and uses an expression which conveys, though not necessarily, that the Saviour had to be carried, he had to be supported to Golgotha from the place where they met Simon (Mark 15:22). It is beyond comprehension that the one who was being supported by Roman soldiers was at the same time upholding the cosmos (Colossians 1:17).

It isn't really surprising that Jesus collapsed. He was no doubt dehydrated. He had had no food or drink since the Last Supper with his disciples and then he had gone through the agony in Gethsemane where he had actually sweat blood. He had then been arrested by a mob with torches, lanterns and swords; had stood trial before Annas and Caiaphas, Pilate then Herod then back to Pilate. He had been marched from one place to the other chained and bound; had been roughly handled, spat at, hit, mocked, beaten up, flogged and had a crown of thorns squeezed on his head. No wonder he collapsed from exhaustion!

Perfect timing

And so the soldiers, irritated and frustrated that Jesus was slowing down the procession laid hold of someone called Simon and forced him against his will to carry the cross behind Jesus (Luke 23:26).

Simon was from Cyrene which was a city in North Africa located 10 miles from the Mediterranean Sea in what is now Libya. He was probably from the large colony of Jews which had settled in Cyrene and was coming into Jerusalem to celebrate the Passover.

When the soldiers seized him he was going in the opposite direction to the procession, on his way from the country into the city. He could well have been staying somewhere north of Jerusalem for the Passover.

Before this day Simon was not a Christian but what happened next resulted in him becoming one. By the time Luke wrote his Gospel (probably AD 63) Simon of Cyrene was known in the early church. He was the father of Alexander and Rufus and subsequently he and his family lived in Rome (Mark 15:21; Romans 16:13).

Simon really wouldn't have wanted to carry the cross of Jesus. He was obviously on his way somewhere and this would have been a real imposition, a real pain. It would also have been a bit embarrassing to have to carry the cross of a criminal and be part of such a procession. The soldiers had to force him. He probably thought to himself 'of all the times to be coming into the city and get myself caught up in this!'

But can you imagine what that must have been like for Simon? He would have seen the difference between the way the Lord Jesus conducted himself and the other two criminals. By this stage Jesus would have been in a bad way from all the beatings, dehydration and loss of blood. He would have looked a sorry state. Weak and pathetic to an onlooker. And yet as he walks to Golgotha, needing support, he is majestic! The language from the soldiers and from these criminals would no doubt have been crude. As he carries his cross Simon must have begun to see that this man isn't an ordinary man. As he thought about it, at least reflected on it, did it start to dawn on him that the man who was so dependent on his help, had a job to put one foot in front of the other, is the God who created the Heavens and the earth. The cross Simon carried was the cross on which the Son of God died for his sins. The Saviour of the world, the promised Messiah, the fulfilment of the Passover Simon was about to celebrate, was right next to him!

Far from this being lousy timing, the time Simon came into Jerusalem on that Friday morning had been planned from before the world was made. It had been predestined and meticulously planned that he should meet Jesus and carry his cross. As the prisoner whose cross he carried looked into his eyes, Simon was conquered by his love for him.

You may be just like Simon. You are made to go to church by your parents or have been dragged along by your family, friends or spouse. Maybe you're reading this book under duress. But know this: You are actually reading these words, have listened to every sermon you have heard preached, ended up in church all the times you have because God has determined it. It has all been by Divine appointment.

You may think there are so many other more important or relevant or enjoyable things you could be doing than getting involved with this Christianity. It is all a bit inconvenient and actually quite embarrassing. But the Jesus of the Bible; that this book you are reading is all about, and you may have heard preached to you, died to be your Saviour. By trusting him he will forgive all your sins and make you clean.

Take up the Cross

But like Simon you have to take up the cross. The Bible talks about taking up your cross daily (Luke 9:23). This means you die to self. Christians no longer live for themselves but now submit their life to the Lord Jesus. This is the hardest thing in the world for anyone to do. We all love ourselves, want to please ourselves and don't want to deny ourselves anything. But let me ask you this, has living for you made you happy? Are you satisfied and content? The Radio 2 DJ, Chris Evans once said, 'happiness is just around the corner'. You can never quite get to it. The actor Jim Carey said, 'I wish all people could get rich and famous and have all they ever dreamed of so they would know it is not the answer'. If you gained the whole world, it would not make you happy. Jesus Christ isn't out to make you unhappy or to deny you things for the sake of it. He made us, knows how we are wired and what is best for us. The Lord Jesus is kind. I don't know about you but living for me, embracing the world's way of doing things has made me weary and heavy laden. But Jesus invites us to come to him and by putting his yoke upon us and learning from him, he will give us rest (Matthew 11:28).

The things he tells us in the Bible not to do, and the things he encourages us to do are all for our good. It is for my good that I read the Bible and submit myself to what it says.

Living for me, thinking all the time about me, worrying about me, trying to please me, is tiring and will always lead to discontentedness and messing up. The hardest thing to do is to deny 'me'. I love me. I live for me. It is all about me. But at the same time 'me' is my biggest problem. I am a slave to my lusts. I am self-conscious. I get stressed trying to keep up with my job. I am tired of keeping up with fashions and other people. My personality sometimes really gets on my nerves. Oh to be free from being me!

Dying to self is liberating. C.S. Lewis (1952) said, 'it is not thinking less of myself but thinking of myself less'.

Jesus Christ says, deny yourself, take up the cross and follow him. Whoever loses his life for Christ's sake will keep it, but whoever tries to hang on to it will lose it (Luke 17:33). By living for Jesus we find true peace and happiness.

Weep for yourselves

Luke 23:27 says that a great multitude, particularly women, followed him mourning and lamenting for him. It would have been a noisy demonstration of grief. The shops, bazaars and markets would have been closed on the holy feast day, but quite a crowd of people would come out to line the streets and to follow, especially women. They would have left their festive preparations and raised loud laments in pity and sympathy. The crowd would probably have been predominantly made up of people who lived in the city and not Galileans who had come to Jerusalem for the Feast.

The people, particularly the women, would have closed around the sufferer (Luke 23:27–31). There would be many in Jerusalem who would have admired Jesus and had sympathy for him. Those who clamoured for Jesus' execution were not necessarily a great number (it was possible for them all to congregate around the Judgement Hall). Not many would have openly hated Jesus and want him killed.

But Jesus tells them not to weep or feel sorry for him, but rather to weep for themselves and for their children. He tells them that days are coming when women who have been unable to have children will be glad and people will want the mountains and hills to fall on them and cover them (Luke 23:28–30).

What did he mean? Why should they be weeping for themselves and not feel sorry for a man in such a pathetic condition on his way to the cruellest form of execution? What would be so bad that people would want mountains to fall on them? Why would women wish they were childless? This would have sounded peculiar to the ears of a Jewish woman. To her it was always a disgrace to be childless.

Jesus is in fact prophesying the destruction of Jerusalem in AD 70: Ryle says that 'the Roman army brought on all the inhabitants of the city the most horrible sufferings from famine and pestilence that can be conceived. Women are reported to have actually eaten their own children during the siege for want of food'. It is reported that a frenzied mother roasted her own child. If the Romans were doing this to Jesus, what were they capable of doing to a rebellious Jewish nation? He uses a metaphor. If they do these things in the green tree, what will happen when it is dry? (Luke 23:31)

Furthermore, if Israel had put such a flame to its 'green tree'; the Lord Jesus, the perfect, spotless Son of God; the long awaited Messiah and their king, how terribly would God's judgement burn among the dry wood of an apostate and rebellious people that had so delivered Jesus up. It had pronounced sentence upon itself by pronouncing it upon him.

As well as prophesying the destruction of Jerusalem, the Lord Jesus is also referring to the judgement that awaits unrepentant sinners. What happened to Jerusalem is a picture of what will happen to all who reject God.

If you are not a Christian, perhaps you look at the Church, or particular Christians you know, and feel sorry for them. In the West, Christians today are viewed as a pitiably small group. In some places Christians are persecuted; in other places they are made fun of and left out of things. What Christians believe is seen as old fashioned, out of date and ridiculous. Christianity goes against the trend of society and is seen as completely unimportant to the overwhelming majority of twenty first century people. You think that our hi-tech, cool, trendy age has outgrown God and the need of Jesus Christ to be its Saviour and look down on and pity people who still think these things are important.

But in the same way the Lord Jesus said to these women not to weep for him but for themselves, if you are not a Christian he tells you to weep for yourself.

Whether you like it or not or believe it or not, one day you and I will stand before the judgement seat of God. Every great historical figure will stand before this throne. Every king, queen and world leader that has ever lived will stand before this throne. Film stars, pop stars, sports men and women will stand before this throne. Tramps, beggars, 'ordinary' people, Asians, Americans, Europeans, Africans, 'good people', terrorists, rapists, murderers, will all stand before this throne. You and I will stand before this throne.

As we are standing there, the books will be opened and the records of the life of every person will be read out. Those who have not trusted Christ will be condemned to Hell forever. Imagine it!

It is hard to take Hell seriously, but it is a real place. It is the final abode of those consigned to eternal punishment. It is a place of torment. A place of fire and darkness, where people are weeping and are in so much pain they gnash their teeth (Matthew 8:12; 13:42; 22:13; 25:30, 41; Mark 9:44). It is a place of distress and misery. All the things we enjoy on earth will be gone forever. It is impossible to imagine how awful it will be; never being able to hear music ever again; never tasting good food ever again; never having your thirst quenched; absolute darkness; horrible loneliness; never feeling loved or cared for. What a terrible plight to find yourself in for all eternity! (Revelation 18).

There are many successful, powerful, rich, famous and influential people in the world today. They are full of their own importance and consumed with their own success and wealth. They enjoy the power they have and the lavish lifestyles they lead. But one day these people, along with all people outside of Jesus Christ, will be terrified because this world they've lived for and whose pleasures they've indulged in, will come to an end. This will happen suddenly and before they can do anything about it, torment will be upon them. They will be terrified and amazed at the fact that judgement could fall so suddenly—'For in a single hour your judgment has come' (Revelation 18:10).

And worst of all, it will be forever. No chance of escape. No end to it all. Forever. Dante said that over the gates of Hell would be the words, 'Abandon hope, all ye who enter here'.

No wonder then that the Lord Jesus says to these daughters of Jerusalem, 'do not weep for me, but weep for yourselves and for your children' (Luke 23:28). And what he says to them he says to you as you read this book if you don't know him as your Saviour. Weep for yourself. He wants your repentance not your sympathy. He wants you to turn away from your sin and put your trust in him.

But today is still a day of mercy. If you call on him today, he will answer you and save you from this terrible wrath. The God who sends people to Hell is a God of love. The Saviour who told these women to weep for themselves is the same one who wept over Jerusalem as he entered it. As he left Jerusalem they wept over him but as he entered Jerusalem he wept over them. As he thinks about the consequences of the nation's sin it causes him to weep. He doesn't want them to face this end. He says, 'O Jerusalem, Jerusalem, the city that kills the prophets and stones those who are sent to it! How often would I have gathered your children together as a hen gathers her brood under her wings, and you were not willing!' (Matthew 23:37).

If you are not trusting Christ, you face eternal punishment. But you don't need to. Come to him now. Christ is pleading with these people as he walks to the cross, don't weep for me weep over your sin and repent because judgement is coming.

8

And they crucified him

Matthew 27:33–44; Mark 15:22–32;
Luke 23:32–38; John 19:16–25

Time

JOHN, USING THE ROMAN METHOD OF COMPUTING TIME (FROM midnight to midnight), says that Pontius Pilate passed the death sentence on Jesus at about the sixth hour (John 19:14). Mark, using the Jewish method of computing time (from 6am until 6pm), said it was the third hour when they crucified him. It was in the days before watches so, as John says, these times were approximate. We can assume therefore that Jesus was sentenced between 6am and 6:30ish and was crucified at 9am. All this seems very early but it would have had to have taken place in the relatively early hours before it got too hot.

Golgotha

The site of the crucifixion was a place called Golgotha, also known as Calvary. It means 'place of the skull' (Mark 15:22–23). Three possible reasons for such a name have been propounded: because skulls were found there; because it was a place of execution or because the site in some way resembled a skull. There is also a widely accepted legend supported by Origen, Athanasius and Epiphanies that the skull of Adam had been discovered there.

It is not possible to know with complete certainty where it was but there are a clues. We know that Golgotha was outside the city gate (John 19:17; Hebrews 13:12, 13) but near the city wall (John 19:20). It was situated near gardens (John 19:41) where there were tombs and close to the road or highway (Matthew 27:39). In the Old Testament the sin offering was taken outside the city (Leviticus 16:27; Hebrews 13:11). And so in the same way, the Lord Jesus Christ as the final, ultimate sin offering; the fulfilment of all the other sin offerings, must be sacrificed outside the city.

All of this points to the north of Jerusalem and two Jerusalem localities are today identified as the site. The traditional site is where the Church of the Holy Sepulchre now is. The other is Gordon's Calvary.

Gordon's Calvary was first pointed out in 1849 by the British General, Charles Gordon. It is 250 yards north east of the Damascus gate and is a rock formation which resembles a skull. Admittedly the site accords with biblical data. It resembles a skull, outside the city gate, near a highway and there are rock-hewn tombs and gardens nearby. However, there is no tradition or other data to support its claim.

A third of a mile to the south west of Gordon's Calvary and inside the walls of the modern city is the Church of the Holy Sepulchre. It has been confirmed by recent excavations to have been outside the city walls at the time of Christ. This site is supported by tradition but the church itself may indicate a tomb of slightly too late a date to be authentic.

Neither site can be proved but neither of these two favoured sites can be very far away from the actual spot

One thing we can be certain of. At Golgotha there was nothing pleasant, beautiful and refreshing to the senses but rather it was an ugly, atrocious and revolting place. Everything about the place had an odious look. Skulls and bones, tufts of hair and putrid flesh were probably scattered about. Jesus was crucified between two criminals and the three crosses that supported the three naked, blood stained bodies are in keeping with the dingy surroundings. The women who followed Jesus from Galilee (who we will meet in chapter 10) for most of the crucifixion stand afar off (Luke 23:49) cowering in horror.

Needed his wits about him

As Jesus arrived at Golgotha he was offered wine mixed with myrrh but he did not take it (Mark 15:22–23). This was a merciful Jewish practice, probably by an association of women in Jerusalem. At the end of a reed would have been a sponge with a draught of strong wine mixed with myrrh on it. It was given to those who were being crucified as a kind of anaesthetic to deaden consciousness.

But when he tasted it and realised what it was, Jesus pushed it away and would not drink it (Luke 23:36, 37). He was about to die for the sins of the world and take the eternal punishment of all those who trust him. He was going to face the wrath of God and needed to have a clear mind. It would be hard labour and require all his energy to pay off the debt of the sins of all his people. Besides, as we shall see in Chapter 9, one of the criminals who was crucified with Jesus was very glad the Saviour had his wits about him!

And they crucified him

Crucifixion is one of, if not the worst forms of punishment ever. The word 'excruciating' is the same root word from which we get crucifixion. Cicero the Roman writer declared crucifixion to be the most cruel and shameful of all punishments. He said, 'Let it never come near the body of a Roman citizen, nay not even his thoughts, his eyes or his ears'. The Romans devised crucifixion but it was intended to only be used on non-Romans.

It was reserved as a punishment for the grossest crimes and for slaves. It had the stigma of disgrace attached to it (Galatians 3:13; 5:11; Hebrews 12:2).

The soldiers would have laid Jesus on the cross and nailed him to it. They would have then lifted the cross up and dropped it into a prepared socket. Every bone in his body would have jolted and his nerves would have shivered with the excruciating pain.

Jesus would have been about 18 or 24 inches off the ground. He would not have been as high up as some pictures of the crucifixion suggest. As we shall see in the next few chapters, being only this far off the ground enabled him to communicate with those standing by the cross and allowed a soldier to moisten his mouth towards the end of the crucifixion.

On the cross, he was essentially forced to inflict upon himself a very slow death by suffocation. Grudem (2007, p.572) describes this in detail. 'The life would slowly drain and be squeezed out from him. When his arms were outstretched and fastened by nails to the cross, he had to support most of the weight of his body with his arms, the chest cavity would be pulled upward and outward, making it difficult to exhale in order to be able to draw fresh breath. But when his longing for oxygen became unbearable, he would push himself up with his feet, thus giving more natural support to the weight of his body, releasing some of the weight from his arms, and enabling his chest cavity to contract more normally. By pushing himself upward in this way the Lord Jesus could fend off suffocation, but it was extremely painful because it required putting the body's weight on the nails holding the feet, and bending the elbows and pulling upward on the nails driven through the wrists'. Even though the word hand is used (Luke 24:39–40; John 20:20), the word for hand can also be translated arm which was probably the case, as a nail through the hands would not have been able to support the weight of his body and would have torn.

To make matters even worse, his back, which had been torn repeatedly by previous floggings, would scrape against the wooden cross with each breath.

Jesus was also probably naked on the cross. Romans crucified people naked whereas Jews, for the sake of dignity, wanted the ones they put forward for crucifixion to be clothed. However, the fact that the soldiers gambled for Christ's clothes suggests he was naked.

On the cross Jesus was in a terrible state. People were astonished at him (Isaiah 52:14). They looked at him and were appalled at him (Isaiah 52:14). He was so disfigured that he was beyond human likeness (Isaiah 52:14). He no longer appeared human. He looked like a thing of horror; like a lump of flesh, unclear whether it was an animal or human. People hid their faces from him (Isaiah 53:3). He was crushed (to pieces), wounded and pierced (Isaiah 53:5)

But the accounts of the crucifixion showed marvellous restraint by the Gospel writers. All four of them simply say 'and they crucified him' (Matthew 27:32–35; Mark 15:21–25; Luke 23:26–33; John 19:17–18). They don't go into detail or dwell on the torment Jesus went through. They are good historians and avoid embellishing any of the details. They are not focusing on what it was like for him to suffer but why he suffered. The important thing is the significance of his death.

Who was there?

Soldiers

Different groups of people were present at the cross. The soldiers who crucified him were there. After nailing him to the cross, they sat down and kept watch over him (Matthew 27:36). They were there on surveillance, to make sure no one came to rescue those condemned to die. This is significant because it proves Jesus really did die and wasn't taken down from the cross by his disciples.

But they didn't just sit there watching. They had fun at Jesus' expense. After the exertion of nailing Jesus to the cross, the soldiers would have refreshed themselves with the cheap wine of the country. As they quaffed it they mockingly drank to him and brutally and coarsely came to him saying, 'If you are the king of the Jews, save yourself' (Luke 23:36, 37) 'he saved others; he cannot save himself' (Matthew 27:42).

As well as mocking him, they disrespectfully and callously divided his clothes between them. This was a perk of the job and an opportunity to add to their wardrobe or sell the clothes on the Jerusalem streets. John says they divided his garments into four parts (John 19:23), one for each soldier. One soldier would have got the head gear, another the outer cloak-like garment, another the girdle and another the sandals.

There was also his tunic or undergarment which was seamless, woven in one piece from top to bottom. This was by far the most expensive item and because it was expensive they didn't want to tear it, so they gambled over it by casting lots to see who gets it (John 19:23, 24). In doing this the soldiers had no idea that they were fulfilling Old Testament prophecy (John 19:24).

By-passers

As well as the soldiers, there were also people who were just passing by. The place of crucifixion was close to the great road which led from the north to Jerusalem. Many would pass it going in and out of the city and the crowd would naturally be arrested by the spectacle of the three crosses, especially the title over the cross of the Lord Jesus (Matthew 27:37; Mark 15:25; Luke 23:38; John 19:19). These people stopped and watched long enough to take it in (Luke 23:35).

'And those who passed by derided him, wagging their heads and saying, "Aha! You who would destroy the temple and rebuild it in three days, save yourself, and come down from the cross!"' (Mark 15:29–30). They were full of contempt and walked back and forward wagging their heads, saying as it were, 'so that's what you get for saying those things. Not much like a king now are you!'

They look at him and think, what a joke! Such a loser! They esteem him as nothing (Isaiah 53:3). Worthless!

Jewish leaders

The other group at Golgotha were the Jewish leaders. The fact they are there is very surprising. It was a very un-Jewish thing to be seen at such a place and they probably had no intention of going there. But, in all likelihood, after Pilate had passed judgement and condemned Jesus to death, they had gone from the Praetorium to the temple to take part in the Passover services. But they heard from some who had watched the procession on its way to Golgotha about the inscription Pilate had put above the cross.

Above each cross would have been an inscription stating the crime the person committed. It would have been carried in front of the criminal, or put around his neck, as they walked to the site of the crucifixion. If we put the gospel accounts together (Matthew 27:37; Mark 15:25; Luke 23:38; John 19:19), the inscription over Jesus' read, 'Jesus of Nazareth, the King of the Jews'. The crowd seeing this sign would have thought it strange. It was written in Aramaic, Latin and in Greek—the religious, social and intellectual languages. The whole world would have been able to read it.

When the Jewish leaders found out about this they hurried once more to the Praetorium to persuade Pilate not to allow it to be put up. They were afraid the many Jews who passed by might be influenced by the inscription. 'So the chief priests of the Jews said to Pilate, "Do not write, 'The King of the Jews,' but rather, 'This man said, I am King of the Jews.'"

But Pilate answered, "what I have written I have written'" (John 19:21–22), and so as he refused to change it they hurried to Golgotha and mingled with the crowd trying to incite their jeers.

They scoffed at the Lord Jesus, saying, 'He saved others; let him save himself, if he is the Christ of God, his Chosen One!' (Luke 23:35). They talked to each other saying, 'He saved others; he cannot save himself. Let the Christ, the king of Israel come down now from the cross that we may see and believe' (Mark 15:31–32). They mocked him by saying, 'He trusts in God; let God deliver him now, if he desires him. For he said, "I am the Son of God"' (Matthew 27:43).

Two criminals and some women
There were also two criminals crucified with him who we will meet in chapter 9, and some faithful women who we shall look more closely at in chapter 10

King

But what was going on at Calvary? What was really taking place? What does it all mean? Why is this crucifixion so important that history is divided between before and after the coming of the man hanging on this Roman cross (BC and AD)?

The inscription above his cross gives a big clue. Pilate wrote it maliciously but never has a truer word been written! The one who hung on that cross isn't just the king of the Jews; isn't just a powerful earthly monarch. He is the king of kings! (Revelation 19:16) The one nailed to that Roman cross created the world and upholds the universe by his power (Colossians 1:17).

As the Son of God hung on the cross the soldiers, passers-by and religious leaders had no idea who he was. He didn't look like a king or Saviour. The Jews were expecting a king like their greatest kings of the past, David or Solomon. Isaiah said that he had no form or majesty that we should look at him (Isaiah 53:2b). He was born in a stable not in a palace. Not to royalty but a working class family. He was reared in a notoriously shabby country village, the back of beyond (John 1:46).

But despite appearances, his kingdom is huge and his power infinite. He is the king of heaven and earth, and not only does he rule over it, he made it. In his poem, '*Maker of the Universe*' F.W. Pitt says,

He died upon a cross of wood,
    yet made the hill on which it stood.
The sky that darkened o'er His head,
    by Him above the earth was spread.
The sun that hid from Him its face,
    by His decree was poised in space.

The reality is that at 186,000 miles a second or 5:88 trillion miles a year, the mangled one hanging on this cross breathed out light. He built every mountain and rolled out every sea. He made the whole cosmos.

He put the sun in its place, which the planet we live on orbits. It is some 93 million miles away and a million times the size of the earth. Imagine you wanted to travel to the sun and went in a very fast car. You travel at 150 miles per hour and you never stop for fuel, food or rest. At 150 miles per hour, 24 hours a day, 365 days a year, it would take you 70 years to reach the sun! Our sun belongs to a galaxy called the Milky Way which contains about 100,000 million other stars. So having been on the Sun a while you decide to head off for the next nearest star, Alpha Centauri, some four light years away. You travel at the same speed of 150 miles per hour and 15 million years later you are approaching the outskirts of Alpha Centauri! (Christofides, 2002 p.13)

And our galaxy is not alone in the universe but is just one of 100,000 million other galaxies.

He who hung on the cross made all this and more without lifting a finger! (Psalm 33:6–7, 9). It is over this kingdom he rules. Kings and empires rise and fall at his command (Daniel 5:21). And while we condemn unbelievers for mocking and ridiculing and dismissing this great God, as Christians we can be guilty as we pray to him, of advising him, correcting him, questioning, suggesting things to him and counselling him. We have such little comprehension of the greatness and majesty of the God we are coming to!

During the first performance of Handel's Messiah in London, attended by King George II, as the first notes of the triumphant Hallelujah Chorus rang out, the king rose to his feet and remained standing until the end of the chorus. The exact reason why the king stood is lost to history but as well as clearly being moved by the performance, one of the most popular explanations is that, it was, and is, custom that one stands in the presence of royalty as a sign of respect. The Hallelujah chorus clearly places Christ as the king of kings. In standing, King George II accepts that he too is subject to the Lord of lords.

But those at Calvary had no idea who he was. He came to his own people and his own received him not (John 1:11). The one the Jews had been waiting for throughout the ages, the one spoken of by the prophets, the longed for Messiah, their king, their God, was among them and they didn't recognise him.

In 2007, the famous violinist Joshua Bell was part of an experiment conducted by the *Washington Post*. He packs out concert halls and people pay $100 for a ticket. But on a stradivarius violin made in 1713 and reportedly worth $3.5 million he played all day in L'Enfant Plaza Metro Station incognito and made $32.17! They didn't have a clue who he was. As Jesus hung on the cross, they had no idea he was the king of heaven and earth!

The good and the great of this world may well shake their fist at God. They may well mock him and dismiss him. They may think that we have outgrown God and are now bigger than him. But to him the nations of the world are like a drop in a bucket (Isaiah 40:15). The nations may well rage, the people can plot and plan, the kings of the earth can set themselves and the rulers take counsel together against the Lord. But he who sits in the heavens laughs; the Lord holds them in derision. (Psalm 2).

When the Titanic set sail she was the largest moveable object ever made by man and said to be so well built that 'God himself couldn't sink the ship'. However, on her maiden voyage she struck an iceberg in the North Atlantic and sank.

God's power and authority is over all things. Nations are under God's control (Psalm 2:1–4; 33:10). As is nature (Mark 4:41; Psalms 135:7; 147:18; 148:8). God does what he pleases and his purposes cannot be thwarted (Isaiah 46:9–10; Daniel 4:34–35). God controls everything.

Forgiveness

So if he was a king why did he take such mockery from his subjects? Why was the Son of God naked and the object of shame on a Roman cross? Why didn't he come down from the cross, save himself, prove he was the Son of God and shut them all up?

During the six hours the Lord Jesus was on the cross, he made seven utterances. To help us understand what was happening on the cross we will look at each of these in the next few chapters. The first is a prayer to God the Father. He says, 'Father forgive them for they know not what they do' (Luke 23:34). The Greek can be translated, 'Jesus kept on praying'. This gives us a big clue as to why he was on the cross.

He wasn't on the cross for himself. He was on the cross to bring forgiveness to people who didn't deserve it. Hell-deservers like me and you. Golgotha showed people doing their worst but the love and compassion of Jesus at its best. The overwhelming majority of people at the cross were cruel, angry, rude, mocking and dismissive towards the Son of God. But as the murderers, bigoted religious leaders who hated him, the howling mob lusting for his blood, the soldiers completing their awful task, were doing their worst, he kept praying, 'forgive them, forgive them, forgive them'.

He says of the soldiers, 'forgive them because they do not know what they are doing' (Luke 23:34). While they were totally responsible for what they were doing, at the same time they had no idea of what was really going on. They were responsible for mockery and cruelty but they didn't understand the eternal ramifications of what was really taking place; that this seeming 'laughing stock' was in fact the Son of God who was dying to be their Saviour. They had no idea that the wind of Hell was about to blow over Golgotha. That the Son of God was going to face the wrath of God as the representative of all who place their trust in him; and that Satan himself, with all the forces and power of darkness, was going to be there to try and destroy the work he was doing.

It illustrates the mixture of ignorance and knowledge when we sin. We know that what we are doing is wrong but don't fully comprehend the seriousness or consequences of our sin. We don't properly think about all the damage and heartache it could cause; how much it is messing up our own lives and consciences and the devastation it will have on others. We know it is wrong but don't grasp that the sin we are indulging in is dragging us to Hell.

But on the cross Jesus was dying for all this sin. All our mess, tangled up lives and iniquities were laid on him (Isaiah 53:5). He was there so that our iniquities could be forgiven. These are all the things we do that are wrong. We do them because our natures are corrupt, perverted, twisted, dark and devious; unclean, ugly and distorted. You may find that offensive but think about what you are like when you are on your own; what you would naturally do left to your own devices. Think about how angry and jealous you get, how gossipy you can be, how dirty your mind is, how shameful some of the things you have done are (or would have done given half the chance and you could have got away with it!). Think about your past. Think about your internet history. Think about your language, your pride, how nasty you can be, how you look down on others. Think about how lazy you are, things you've stolen. All of this was laid on him!

But none of these things are the worst thing about my sin. Yes, sin has messed up my life and the lives of others. But the real horror and heart of sin is that it is against God. I don't love him. I hate the thought of being told what to do by him. I get angry with him.

Maybe you think, 'No I don't. I don't particularly love him but neither do I hate him. I'm just indifferent'. But think about how kind he is to you. All the good things you have come from his hand (James 1:17). He made you; sent his Son to die for you and you don't give him a second thought. Imagine if my wife said to me tonight, 'Alun I don't love you anymore. You're okay but I just prefer being with other people. I'll do some chores for you and I'm happy to give you a bit of time over Christmas and Easter but I don't really love you!' I'd be devastated. And yet that is how we treat God.

But despite all of this he wants to forgive us, and died to do so. Our indifference and even hatred towards him, was laid on him.

All my sin of every kind
All the thoughts that stain the mind
All the evil I designed
Laid on him

All that sinks me in the mire
All the times of base desire
All that needs a cleansing fire
Laid on him

All the times I've grieved the spirit
All the nature I inherit
All the punishment I merit
Laid on him

Laid on him, God's own dear son
Laid on him the holy one
Blotting out the noonday sun
When laid on him   *Lance Pibworth*

When they hammered him onto that cross, he was taking the hammering our sins deserve. On the cross he was saying to God in effect, 'don't punish them, don't be angry with them, take it all out on me!' I find it amazing, mind-blowing, that a holy God who had every legitimate reason to judge me and be angry with me actually loved me and is willing to forgive me. I deserved to be punished but he took the punishment for me. And on the cross he showed the lengths he was willing to go to.

In 1964 Kitty Genovese was murdered in Kew Gardens in New York. It was witnessed by thirty-eight people who saw the killer come into the park and carry out the attack. They shouted from the windows for him to stop and even though he did leave the park, he came back and killed her. When the police asked the witnesses why they didn't come down to help the lady when they saw the danger she was in, they said that they didn't want to get involved. But Jesus Christ, when he saw the mess we had made of our lives and the danger we were in didn't just shout down from Heaven, he came down, right down. He rolled his sleeves up, put on human flesh, became one of us and took on himself all our sin.

An Indian philosopher in explaining the difference between Islam and Christianity said that Allah was too majestic to lie in a dirty manger, hang on a shameful cross and enter filthy hearts. His adherents have to get to him. But I am so glad that the Son of God, this great king, was on the cross so that I could be forgiven and saved from the wrath of the only true and living God.

Archibald Alexander said that his whole theology comes down to this, 'Christ Jesus came into the world to save sinners' (1 Timothy 1:15)

But to know this forgiveness, you have to come to him in

repentance and faith. You have to be sorry for your sin and turn away from them and trust in what Jesus did on the cross. Whatever you have done. However tangled up and messed up your life is. However full of pride and scornful and hateful towards God you have been, you can come to him now. Meet him at the cross. Jesus doesn't meet people in offices behind big desks; the only place he keeps appointment is at the cross.

Blanchard (2012, p.50) said that on one occasion when he was leading a tour to the Holy Land, he left Jerusalem by the Damascus Gate and turned right by the bus station. As he looked at the buses for the destination sign he needed, his eyes caught sight of a little hill just behind the bus station. It was 'Gordon's Calvary'. He thought that he might actually be looking at the place of the skull, Golgotha, Calvary (Matthew 27:33) the very spot where 2000 years ago the Lord Jesus Christ bore the penalty for every sin that was to stain and scar his life. Mr Blanchard said that he stood looking at it with tears of gratitude running down his face.

We were there

When we look at the scene we want to detach ourselves. But we were all there. We all had a part.

I wonder if any of the reactions of the groups of people resonates with you. When you look at this crucified Saviour how do you react? Maybe you just think it is a big joke. You just make fun. You have no fear or respect for God. You think it all seems ridiculous.

As you look at the solders you cannot help being struck with their cruel, callous hatred. We live in different times to these soldiers and may frown on their behaviour. But while we may not display such cruel, callous hatred we can show cruel, callous indifference.

Or maybe like the passers-by you look down on it. When you think about the Bible and what it says you wag your head in disdain. You can't believe people still take it seriously. You cannot believe that in the 21st century there are still people who believe in a God who created the heavens and the earth; that the Bible is the inerrant word of God. You dismiss the notion of standing before the judgement seat of God and of there being a Heaven and a Hell. You bunch all religions together and think that none of them are right and none of them are wrong and certainly no one should take any of them too seriously. Anyone who says they believe the Bible to be true and says that Jesus is the only Saviour, is to be pitied and looked down on.

But perhaps you are a moral, church goer. You like going to church because it makes you feel good. It is the upstanding, right and proper thing to do. But like these religious leaders, you hate it when the claims of Jesus Christ cut across your way of life. You get angry with it and say, 'How dare you tell me I am a sinner! How dare you tell me I need to come to this Saviour for forgiveness! I'm a respectable, upstanding member of society. I do my best. He is not the Lord of my life. No one tells me what to do.'

But it was for these people he prayed. The question is, was his prayer answered? Were these soldiers and other people at the cross forgiven?

Well, seven and a half weeks later on the day of Pentecost (see Chapter 23 of this book), Peter preached in Jerusalem. He charged the people with the death of Christ and in one day 3,000 were converted (Acts 2). No doubt many of those who were converted were present at Calvary (Luke 23:48).

Think about how hateful, mocking and dismissive these people were and they are all in Heaven now.

If these could be forgiven, there is hope for you too if you will only repent and come to him.

One last thought

If the Lord Jesus could show such love towards us while we were his enemies, then we should love our enemies. Furthermore, as Christians, it is right and proper we feel angry at sin. We should be concerned when God's laws are broken and trampled on. But we should not be self-righteous and adopt a 'holier than thou' attitude. We should pray earnestly, thanking God he has been gracious to us and that he will gracious to others too.

9

A bad man who went to Heaven

Luke 23:39–43

Close to the action

THE SECOND WORDS JESUS UTTERS WHEN HE IS ON THE CROSS IS to one of the criminals hanging next to him. He says, 'Today you will be with me in paradise' (Luke 23:43). He tells a bad man he is going to heaven!

All four gospel writers draw attention to the fact Jesus was crucified between two thieves, but it is Luke who provides the most detail (Matthew 27:44; Mark 15:32; Luke 23:33–43; John 19:18). John simply mentions he was crucified between two thieves while Mark and Matthew talk in general that the two thieves joined in with the derision of the Sanhedrin. Luke, however, focuses in on the thieves, particularly the one. He leaves the impression that his account has come from one who had stood quite close to the cross; probably even took official part in the crucifixion. Quite possibly the centurion.

Numbered with the transgressors

Jesus crucified in such company isn't insignificant. Isaiah prophesied that Jesus would be numbered with the transgressors (Isaiah 53:12). He was identifying himself with sinners. As he hung on the cross in the eyes of God he was one of us, the worst of us. The one who had never sinned was becoming sin for us (2 Corinthians 5:21). He took upon himself all the sin of his people, including all the wrong this dying thief had ever done.

On the television programme Crime Watch they show 'wanted faces'. These are people the police would like to speak to in relation to different crimes. They show pictures of them or CCTV clips. It is a real gallery of rogues. Well Christ was in such a line up. He was counted as one of them.

A really bad man

It is important to note that the dying thief wasn't just a thief. He must have committed far more heinous crimes than robbery. Crucifixion was reserved for the very worst criminals not just common thieves. This man was as hard as nails, heartless; a really nasty piece of work. He was probably a terrorist who would have hated the Romans with every fibre of his being. He would have loathed the intolerable taxes imposed upon the Jews by the Romans and detested the slimy little taxman. He would have got frustrated watching all the money that was poured into the Temple coffers and viewed the Jewish leaders and priesthood as totally irrelevant and incompetent in getting Israel the independence he so desperately wanted. He would have to take things into his own hands, do whatever it takes and hurt and kill whoever got in the way. He was a rebel and hated the system and the way things were done. He refused to conform and raged against all the perceived injustices that surrounded him. He was bitter and angry and full of hate.

In all probability he was part of Barabbas' gang and the centre cross on which the Lord Jesus died was meant by the Romans to be for Barabbas.

Consider Christ

The thief would have woken up on that Friday morning a condemned man. A hardened criminal. Even on the cross with Jesus he was full of insults and sarcasm to begin with. At first he, along with the other thief, derided Christ (Mark 15:32) and sarcastically asked him, 'Are you not the Christ?' But by 6 o'clock that evening he was in Paradise (Luke 23:43). What changed?

No doubt how the Lord Jesus conducted himself as they walked to Golgotha carrying their crosses would have made an impression. The difference in how Jesus behaved to all those around him would have been stark.

Hanging on the cross next to Jesus for all those hours would also have had an effect on him. Even being in the state he was, Jesus was calm and majestic. The thief would have seen the impact he had had on the lives of others. He would have compared the way those who put him on the cross were behaving, all his enemies, the religious leaders, to the way Jesus conducted himself. Why had these religious leaders come to taunt him at a place they would not normally have set foot in? Why did they go out of their way to hate him so much? What had he ever done? But he never responded to their jibes and nastiness.

He could see that Christ was perfect and had done nothing to deserve death whereas he was guilty.

No doubt listening to Jesus pray that the soldiers would be forgiven for what they were doing to him (Luke 23:34) had a profound impact on this dying villain. He must have thought, if he can forgive these men who mock him, have stood on his hands and driven nails into his hands and feet, could he possibly forgive me?

The words and taunts of some of the crowd, including himself, would have played over in his mind, 'he saved others, he saved others, he saved others'. He no doubt started to think, even in my helpless, awful plight, with all that I have done, could he possibly save me?

Maybe he thought back to his childhood and remembered what he had learned as a Jewish child from Psalm 22, 'they pierced his hands and feet'; as he heard the shouts and jeers of the crowds did he remember the words, 'all they that see me laugh me to scorn' (AV). He would have known that Psalm 22 was a Messianic Psalm, which is a Psalm written about the promised Messiah or Saviour that God would one day send. The thief would have seen the inscription over the cross, 'Jesus of Nazareth, the king of the Jews' and begun to think, could it really be? His heart would have begun to throb with the reality that prophetic scripture was being fulfilled at that very moment.

He wouldn't have been able to explain the theology of the atonement by substitution nor the incarnation nor the resurrection that was yet to come but he displayed great faith. He was hoping in one that seemed to be in the same condition as himself. But despite appearances, he could see Christ was a king (Luke 23:42).

It was when the thief considered Jesus Christ that everything changed. Let me invite you to do the same. Read the gospels and think about his character. What he was like. No one ever spoke like this man (John 7:46). He had compassion on people. He went around doing good. Children were drawn to him. He always had time for people. He was strong and always did what was right.

And this man came into the world to save sinners. He saved this thief and he can save you. In fact, whoever calls on the name of the Lord shall be saved (Acts 2:21). The 19th-century preacher, Charles Spurgeon, said that no one will be able to say on judgement day I called out to him and he didn't come to me.

King

But you must acknowledge like this thief that Jesus is a king.

The thief says to Jesus, 'Remember me when you come into your kingdom' (Luke 23:42). He acknowledged that Jesus was a king.

But that is so hard and the reason why these religious leaders turned up at the cross so full of venom and hate. They would not bow the knee to him. They wanted to do things their way. It is the same today. No one has a problem with religion or Christianity providing it lets you live like you want. It is only when you have to deny yourself and bow to the kingship of Jesus. When I hear men like Richard Dawkins (2007) and Stephen Fry (RTE One, 2015) talk it is clear that it is not that these men don't believe in God; it is that they hate him. And whatever we say, that is our problem with Jesus Christ too. We don't want him touching parts of our life that we don't want to give up.

It was hard for the thief to see Jesus was a king. At that point he had been badly beaten up, whipped to the bone. He didn't really look like a human being, just a lump of flesh. He was nailed to a Roman cross and laughed and mocked at by the crowd and mourned over by a group of fearful women. Maybe you find it hard to believe he is a king. He seems irrelevant and not real compared to the kings and presidents of our day. You compare him to pop stars, movie stars and sportsmen and he just seems embarrassing. But look closely and see that the one hanging on this tree holds the whole world in his hands. The breath the good and the great take is given to them by him. Their empires rise and fall at his command. One day we will stand before him and he will no longer be a cursed bloodied lump of flesh but he'll be clothed in majesty. He's the king of kings!

Sinner

Like this thief you also need to see your sin (Luke 23:41) Maybe you have found it difficult to admit you are a sinner. You compare yourself to others and feel quite good. But the problem is you think of yourself when you are at your best. But what are you like at your worst, when you're left to be yourself? What would you be like if you could do what you really want? Stop protesting your innocence. Own up to God. Nothing is hidden from him. Stop trying to convince yourself otherwise; he has seen the lot!

I once caught a Year 7 boy called Kieron smoking behind the Technology block. When I asked him he denied it completely. I remember him looking at me in total consternation that I should even think or suggest that he would do such a thing. I remember him saying to me, 'Mr Ebenezer I am so hurt you think I could do such a thing!' So I marched him by the scruff of the neck to watch the CCTV recording which showed him puffing away to his heart's content! He looked at it and said, 'You're right sir, it does look a bit like me!' One day God will take you to his CCTV that has been on you throughout your life. It has seen everything you have done, heard everything you've said and even knows your every thought and intention.

Trust him

Having considered Christ, the thief asked Jesus to remember him when he came into his kingdom' (Luke 23:42). He had nothing to offer Jesus but trusted solely in his power to save. He just rested on the Saviour. He never took communion. Wasn't baptised. He just put his trust in the one hanging on the cross next to him. He had committed terrible crimes. He was a vile man. Moments before he had been blaspheming against Christ. He could do nothing to make amends for his past or put things right.

This thief's only hope was in Christ. He had absolutely nothing else to offer. He could say with the hymnist,

Upon a life I did not live,
Upon a death I did not die;
Another's life, another's death,
I stake my whole eternity.

We find that so hard to do. The problem with me is that a bit of my faith is in Alun Ebenezer. The fact that when I sin I feel like I should earn my repentance before I come back to God, tells me that. But you cannot trust Christ truly unless you trust Christ alone.

A story is told of a young Irish boy who went along to a mission to hear a famous evangelist preach about Hell and sin and judgement and the need to be saved. The mission lasted a week and as the week went on the boy became more and more troubled. After the last meeting he went home and couldn't sleep. Over and over in his mind went the question 'what must I do to be saved? What must I do?' The following morning he got up straight away and ran back to the field where the mission had been held. The organisers were taking the tents down and packing up. After looking frantically, the young boy finally found the evangelist. He said to him, 'Sir, what must I do to be saved? What must I do?' The evangelist said to him, 'You're too late son. You're too late! In fact you're two thousand years too late. It's all been done for you. Trust in a finished work!'

When Christ cried out with a loud voice, 'It is finished' (John 19:30 cf. Luke 23:46), all the thief's sins, his terrorist acts, his rebellion, his theft, his murder, Christ had finished paying for.

The puritan, John Bunyan, started off by praying, 'forgive me my sins I'll try harder tomorrow' but ended up praying, 'I can't be any better please save me.'

Amazing grace

Christ promised him that that very day he would be with him in Paradise (Luke 23:43). The first person to enter heaven after the Lord Jesus was probably this terrible man. This shows amazing grace. Grace is undeserved favour, which means in essence, that God is for us even though we are against Him. This grace, or as John Newton put it this, 'amazing grace' is absolutely free and available to all. However bad you are or have been; whatever secrets you are hiding, God will be gracious to you. It is what makes Christianity different to all the other religions of this world.

One day a meeting took place in London where the topic of religion was being discussed. C.S. Lewis, the Narnia author, arrived at the meeting late and one of the men said to him, 'what makes Christianity different to all other religions'. 'That's easy', Lewis responded, 'grace!'

Tender mercy

This incident also shows the great love and compassion of the Saviour. He was at his weakest, suffering agony, undergoing the pain of Hell in his soul but even then he had compassion on a terrible sinner.

This man had lived a terrible life. He deserved what he was getting. He should have died on that cross and woken up in Hell. But Jesus was merciful to him. We need mercy when our resources are non-existent and our only hope is evoking someone's pity. We need mercy for past failures that we can't put right.

If Jesus can show grace to this man, there is hope for anyone. My dad was a minister in Pontypridd in South Wales. An Irish navvy would come in every Sunday night and listen to him preach. He would be stinking of drink and very unkempt. All of a sudden he stopped coming. One evening my dad was driving through Pontypridd, past the bus station and saw Frank waiting for a bus. He swung the car around and told him to get in. He asked him where he'd been and that he'd missed him. Frank said that some of the deacons had told him not to come until he'd cleaned up his life a bit and was not smelling of drink. Thank God, the Saviour is nothing like those deacons! He says, come as you are. Whoever comes to him, in whatever condition—a dying thief or an alcohol fuelled tramp—he will never turn away. He will save whoever calls out to him.

The mercy Christ shows is a tender mercy. He does not show mercy with a grudge. My parents broke down one evening in Cardiff and called me to go and help them. I was really busy doing the school timetable and up to my eyes in work. I went to help them but boy did I do it grudgingly and let them know how much I was putting myself out! But Christ is nothing like me. He didn't say to this thief, 'Okay! Okay! but can't you see how much pain I'm in? I've got my own problems at the moment!' He just had compassion on him. He delights to be merciful time and time again.

Paradise

Christ says to him, 'today you will be with me in paradise' (Luke 23:43). This shows clearly that there is life after death. Heaven is real and a place of paradise. It is referred to as a country (Hebrews 11:16) and a city (Hebrews 11:10).

The word used here is the Persian word for garden. The Garden of Eden, the paradise that Adam and Eve lived in before sin entered the world, is in mind. Only this time there is no chance of sin ever spoiling it.

It is beyond our comprehension to imagine the splendour of this Paradise. The eighteenth century Welsh hymn writer, William Williams, thought Heaven was too far away to see clearly. He said,

The lenses lack the power, the distance is too vast.
I comprehend but dimly the glorious life to last.

We know that in heaven there will be no more sin, no sorrow, no pain, no night, no death (Revelation 21:4, 27; 22:5). It will be a place of breath-taking beauty. It is also worth saying in this day and age that there will be no more stress. We were on holiday in West Wales a few years ago. It was a lovely spring evening. We were in middle of nowhere surrounded by beautiful scenery. It was totally peaceful. Then my wife said, as only my wife can, 'make the most of this we'll be back in work and the real world next week and the busyness of everyday life'. But one day I will be in Paradise, the real world, and it will be forever and I will never have to go back (Revelation 22:5).

We all enjoy going out for a nice meal with our family and

friends. It is one of the most enjoyable things in life. Very often in the Bible, this Paradise is described as a place where there will be eating and drinking. We will eat and drink at the marriage supper of the Lamb (Revelation 19:9). The poor beggar Lazarus is pictured being carried to Abraham's bosom and there reclining and feasting along with Abraham. When this thief got to Heaven that evening he sat down for supper.

It is the eternal home of everyone who trusts in Jesus Christ (John 14:2). It has many mansions (John 14:2). As our home it is a place we can feel safe, can relax, feel loved, cared for, welcomed and wanted. There is no place like home and as this thief entered heaven God would, as it were, say to him 'Make yourself at home'.

The old Negro Spirituals sung that, despite being slaves, they had a 'home in glory land that outshines the sun'. Likewise, the group of coalminers from Kingswood near Bristol in the 18th century. These men lived in some of the most wretched living conditions in England at that time. They lived in hovels, dens and holes in the earth (Dallimore 2001, p.256). They spent their days burrowing in the hills and were covered in coal dust and were black as soot. They were violent people and outcasts in society. When Wesley and Whitefield were preaching to them the first signs they were being affected by the gospel were the white streaks on their faces where the tears ran down their cheeks. John Wesley wrote a hymn for these filthy men to sing as they came out of their holes in the ground. The last verse says:

> With him we walk in white
> We in his image shine
> Our robes are robes of glorious light
> Our righteousness divine
> On all the kings of earth
> With pity we look down
> And claim in virtue of our birth
> A never ending crown

These 18th century miners are no longer in filthy holes in the earth but they are in Paradise, the same paradise the dying thief would enter with Jesus that very day.

Jesus says to him 'you will be with me' (Luke 23:43). That is what really makes paradise, paradise. We will actually see his face (Revelation 22:4). According to Hendriksen (1971, p.211)

> Christ's loving presence will be that which makes the father's house a real home and a real heaven for the children of God'.

We will enjoy the company of the God the Father, Son and Holy Spirit.

In Paradise, we will associate with the angels. They will be fascinated to learn about our redemption (1 Peter 1:12) and we will find out about their earthly ministry on our behalf (Hebrews 1:14).

We will be with all God's people from throughout history—the Old Testament, New Testament, Church history, present and future. You may be in a small little church now and find it hard. You may enjoy going to large Christian conferences to meet up with thousands of other Christians. They are your favourite times of the year to be surrounded by so many other believers. Well in Heaven there will be millions and millions of Christians. It will be a great multitude which no one could number, of all nations, tribes, peoples and tongues (Revelation 7:9). And we will all be united (Psalm 133:1, 3; John 17:21). No falling out or churches splitting.

'Names and sects and parties fall,
Thou, O Christ, art All in all'

Maybe someone you love has recently died. Well if they were a Christian, one day you will be re-united. In 2 Samuel 12:23, King David is mourning the death of his baby. He says, 'you cannot come to me, but one day I will come to you'. Christians are those who do not sorrow as those with no hope (1 Thessalonians 4:13, 14) and while relationships will not be the same, everything we enjoy here will be so much better there.

And while we will rest (Hebrews 4:9; Revelation 14:13) we will not be idle or in any danger of getting bored. We will have so much of the new heaven and new earth to discover, other Christians to meet and get to know and so much of God to enjoy. We will be active. We will be stewards of the reconstructed universe and use our God given talents to serve and reign with Christ (Revelation 7:15; 22:3; Matthew 13:12; 19:28; 25:21).

The Garden of Eden required keeping and tilling and there is no reason to think that the new creation will be any different. Eden offered scope for art, science and technology. We will have opportunities to be creative, enjoy music and athletics and we will be there for all eternity (Revelation 22:5). We will know fullness of joy (Psalm 16:8–9, 11). Above all we will worship God as we should in wonder, love and praise.

Bunyan in *Pilgrim's Progress* (1997) describes Christian and Hopeful about to enter Heaven. He says,

> The two pilgrims were told, 'You are going now to the paradise of God ... you shall have white robes given you, and your walk and talk shall be every day with the King, even all the days of eternity ... you shall not see again such things as ... sorrow, sickness, affliction and death ... There your eyes shall be delighted with seeing, and your ears hearing the pleasant voice of the Mighty One ... enjoy your friends again ...'

Bunyan's description of Heaven and Christian's entry to that glorious place is only an allegory, but it is firmly grounded in, and full of references from, the Bible.

Imagine the thief's last few moments on earth. The Jewish Sabbath went from Friday sunset to Saturday sunset. On the Sabbath, a body must not hang on a tree. Romans had no interest in Jewish laws but cared about public order and that meant showing sensitivity to the laws and traditions of the people. The next day was Sabbath, and a particularly special one as it was

Passover. So as 6 o clock approached, soldiers would have come towards him with their clubs. They would have slammed their clubs into his legs. His body would have sagged and without the support of his legs he would no longer have strength to lift his body and breathe. Unbearable pain would go through his aching hands and in just a matter of minutes he would have died. His body would then have been thrown on a garbage heap outside of the city. A bad man thrown on a rubbish tip, job done. But while all this was going on his soul was entering Paradise! Let me describe it by adapting Pilgrim's Progress slightly.

The dying thief and his Saviour had arrived in close proximity of the Celestial City. The Saviour struggled to keep his brother's head above the water. 'Brother, I see the gate, and men standing by to receive us', were the Saviour's comforting words to his companion. 'Be of good cheer, Jesus Christ maketh thee whole.' They were escorted up a hill, left their 'mortal garments' behind and heard about the glories of the city they were entering. The city's beauty was inexpressible, the conditions perfect and the privileges unimaginable.

Several of the King's trumpeters arrived who gave them ten thousand, thousand welcomes.'

He would think, 'after all I've done, I don't deserve this!'

Today

And all this is certain. Jesus says 'verily' or 'truly' (Luke 23:43). Most assuredly, absolutely definitely. You will be with me in Paradise today. It shows that believers do not sleep until the Second Coming of the Lord Jesus Christ. Right now they are with God in Paradise. Heaven is where God dwells now. When Jesus taught his disciples to pray he said 'Our Father in heaven' (Matthew 6:9).

According to Grudem (p.1160) 'Heaven is even now a place— though one whose location is now unknown to us and whose existence is now unable to be perceived by our natural senses'. This thief was in Heaven by 6 o clock that evening.

However, it is important to note that even though this thief went to Paradise that very day, he, like all the other Christians who have died are in what theologians call the 'intermediate state'. Currently, they are the 'spirits of the righteous made perfect' (Hebrews 12:23). They, like us, are still waiting for the final judgement when Christ will come again and there will be a new heaven and a new earth, and they will have new resurrection bodies. The whole cosmos will be reconstructed and the earth will be renovated (2 Peter 3:13; Revelation 21:1; Isaiah 11:6; 35:1; 65:17; Psalm 96:11–13). The present creation will be renewed. The world now is very beautiful but it is also marred by sin and the fall. But one day God will renew it (Psalm 102:26, 27; Hebrews 1:10–12; 12:26–28). He won't give up on it and when his Son returns to this world to judge it and put everything right, there will be a new heaven and a new earth. For this reason the whole of creation is on tiptoes eagerly waiting his return (Romans 8:19, 21). We may not remember it as our previous home, 'the former things shall not be remembered or come into mind' (Isaiah 65:17)

It also shows there is no such place as purgatory. Purgatory is the place Roman Catholics believe people go to until all sin is purged away, after which they are translated to Heaven. The sufferings vary greatly in intensity and duration depending on the person. If ever there was a man who needed to go purgatory, and for quite a long time, it was this thief! And yet the Lord Jesus says to him, 'today you shall be with me in paradise' (Luke 23:43). The moment the thief closed his eyes in death he was welcomed into paradise. He was Jesus' last companion on earth and his first in Heaven.

The other thief

It is important to remember though there were two thieves not just one. The other didn't call to him. He didn't go to be with

Christ when he died but instead went to Hell where he still is. Just because you face death doesn't mean you will want Jesus or automatically seek after God. If you don't want God now there is nothing to say you will want God nearer the end. Every time you hear the gospel and reject it you harden your heart until eventually God hardens your heart. Imagine being that thief right now. Going through his mind all the time is how close he was to one who could have saved him but he didn't call out to him.

On Judgement day the Lord Jesus Christ will divide human beings into two groups. All the important figures from history will be there, sports people, pop stars and movie stars, world leaders; all the good and the great. You'll be there and I'll be there.

All of us however famous or insignificant, however rich or poor, however educated or uneducated, will be judged by God and put into two groups. One group will be consigned to everlasting torment in Hell and the other will enter eternal paradise in Heaven. On that day all that matters will be what you did with Jesus Christ; did you accept him or reject him? There will be some people on that awful day whose shoes I would not want to be in. Imagine being Hitler, Jimmy Savile or Saddam Hussain or another person who has been guilty of heinous crimes, standing before a just God!

But the people who will be the saddest on that day will be those who heard the gospel and were almost persuaded. They read books like this, heard sermons, went to youth groups and on Christian camps and almost put their faith in the Lord Jesus Christ but something, some person, some fear or some sin, held them back. They will spend eternity regretting it over and over and over again! Like this thief they were so close …

He serves as a warning against presumption. One thief was saved at the very end that no one should despair, but only one that none should presume.

10

Take care of my mother

John 19:26, 27

Introduction

As we saw in chapter 8, by the cross were soldiers, Jewish leaders, passers-by and a group of faithful women. Luke also says there were some of Jesus' acquaintances. In this chapter we will look more closely at the group of women; particularly Jesus' mother, and consider the third words he uttered from the cross.

The women

How many women and who were they?
We know there were at least four women who stood by the cross.

Luke simply says 'the women who had followed him from Galilee stood at a distance watching these things' (Luke 23:49).

Matthew names three: (1) Mary Magdalene, (2) Mary the

mother of James and Joseph, and (3) the mother of Zebedee's sons. But he indicates there were many women there (Matthew 27:55, 56).

Mark also names three: (1) Mary Magdalene, (2) Mary the mother of James the Less and of Joses, and (3) Salome (Mark 15:40) and says there were also many other women who came up with him to Jerusalem.

Whereas John selects four for special consideration: (1) Mary, the mother of Jesus, (2) his mother's sister, (3) Mary, the wife of Clopas and (4) Mary Magdalene (John 19:25).

Putting Matthew, Mark and John's accounts together we see that three of the women are probably the same.

One of them was a lady called Mary Magdalene. We will consider her more closely in Chapter 18 of this book.

Christ's mother's sister (in John's account) was Salome (in Mark's account) who is also the mother of Zebedee's sons, James and John (in Matthew's account). This would make James and John, as the sons of Zebedee (Mark 10:35), cousins to the Lord Jesus and nephews to Mary which would explain why Jesus entrusted her to John's care.

Mary the wife of Clopas (John's account) is also the mother of James the Less and of Joses (Mathew and Mark's accounts).

As well as Salome, it is possible that Mary the wife of Clopas had family ties with Jesus. According to Edersheim (2004, p.889), Hegesippus in Eusebius' *Ecclesiastical History*. H.E. 3:11 and 4:22, describes Clopas, which is the same name as Alphaeus as the brother of Joseph, the husband of Mary the mother of Jesus. This would make Mary the wife of Clopas an aunt to the Lord Jesus and her sons, his cousins. If this is the case, John had gone into the city to get his mother and those closest to her.

The reason Mark and Matthew omit the mother of the Lord Jesus from their list is probably because they refer to these women at the end of their crucifixion accounts. By which time John, as we shall see in this chapter, had taken Mary, the Lord's mother to his home.

There were other women there too. Some of the women had followed Jesus from Galilee to care for his needs (Matthew 27:55). Some were there who had come up with him to Jerusalem. These women had been present when Jesus entered Jerusalem.

The ones mentioned are no doubt those who had particularly supported Jesus and the disciples on their preaching tours and in Jerusalem (Luke 8:1–3). They would have been well known in the early church and a point of reference. They were real people in a real time in history.

Where were they stood?

Those determined to disprove the Bible believe there is a problem in where these ladies were placed. In John 19:25–27 the women, and John, are standing near. However, Matthew, Mark and Luke say they were watching from afar or from a distance (Matthew 27:55; Mark 15:40; Luke 23:49).

But surely over the course of the six-hour crucifixion both were no doubt true. Maybe the women stood at a distance at first but came near when they realised the soldiers wouldn't harm them. Matthew, Mark and Luke say they are standing afar and they are introduced only after Jesus has died (Matthew 27:55–56; Mark 15:40; Luke 23:49). Maybe they ventured close for a time but were repulsed and being unable to watch, withdrew again. Perhaps when they heard Jesus say he was thirsty they hastened forward to help him.

All of this is not only possible but would make more sense than them being rooted to the same spot the whole time. As we shall see again and again throughout this book, the witnesses to these events didn't cook all this up together, and make sure it was all slick and polished before it went to the publisher. They were ordinary first century people who just told it as it was.

The weaker sex doesn't look so weak by the cross!

One thing we can be certain of is that there was a group of loyal women at the cross. Apart from John, none of the disciples put in an appearance. They had all deserted their master in his moment of desperate need.

The importance and strength of character of women comes through clearly on the pages of the New Testament. They are given honourable mention and play an important role in the ministry of the Lord Jesus. Jesus and his twelve disciples weren't a self-contained little group but they relied on the help and support of women (Luke 8:1–3). It would have been impossible for Jesus and his disciples to have done what they did without the vital role of these women.

As well as the picture of devoted women here at the cross and by the tomb, (see chapters 17 and 18), they are to be found in the upper room on the Day of Pentecost (see chapter 23) and at the heart of churches in New Testament letters.

This is in stark contrast with the thinking of their day. During these times rabbis refused to teach women and generally assigned them a very inferior place. They were of the opinion it was better to burn the law than teach it to a woman. Women were not trusted to give testimony in a court of law. Aristotle and Socrates also held women in low esteem. But Jesus freely admitted them into his fellowship and assigned them a place of high honour. While the Bible recognises that men and women are different and have specific and particular roles to play within the church, far from being sexist and chauvinistic, nothing has done more for the dignity of women than this great faith! But it is important we don't swap the roles of women and men and try to give women significance by doing a man's role. The role both men and women have been given is different but equally vital and significant.

Tender care

Mary arrives at the cross and stands near her dying son. She had nursed him on her lap, fed him, clothed him and brought him up. She loved him and must have been heartbroken to see him nailed to a Roman cross barely recognisable as a human being!

When Jesus saw his mother and the disciple whom he loved standing by he said to his mother, 'Woman, behold your son!' Then he said to the disciple, 'Behold your mother!' And from that hour that disciple took her to his own home (John 19:26–28)

It is almost certain that Joseph, his father, had died when Jesus was young. His request to John to look after his mother implies that Jesus was the breadwinner. None of his four brothers or sisters were there (Matthew 13:55, 56). Maybe there was an estrangement in the family? We know they were unsympathetic to his ministry (John 7:5). Furthermore, Jesus' brothers were probably not even in Jerusalem at this time but in Capernaum. It would seem that by the time of Jesus' public ministry the family had moved from Nazareth to Capernaum (Matthew 4:13; Luke 4:31; John 2:12).

Whatever the reason, Jesus hands her over to John. However, it would seem that John didn't need to look after her for long at all. In Acts 1:14 when the early Christians were gathered together in the upper room all Jesus' brothers were there, and Mary.

At that very hour John took Mary to his house (John 19:27). This would explain why John doesn't include in his Gospel the three hours of darkness and the Lord Jesus crying out 'My God My God why have you forsaken me' (Matthew 27:46; Mark 15:34). He wasn't there. It also seems that this way Mary was spared seeing her son going through what he did from noon until 3pm.

Jesus' words show how much he cared for his mother. When we read it in our Bibles in the twenty-first century, Jesus referring to his mother as 'Woman' can sometimes sound cold and disrespectful. But it should really read, 'dear woman'. It is the same as lady or madam in our culture. It is a title of deference, honour and respect.

As he hung on the cross in agony, he tenderly thought about

his mother. He wanted to make practical arrangements to make sure his mother would be looked after. But this care wasn't just reserved for his mother. Throughout the gospels, the care of the Saviour is seen time and time again. He was busy and often needed to withdraw to 'recharge his batteries' (Luke 5:16) but even when he was shattered he always had time for people. When he saw crowds of people he had compassion on them. Let me give you two examples.

In Mark 7:31–37 there is an account of when Jesus healed a deaf man. Verse 34 says 'Looking up to heaven he (Jesus) sighed'. He is saying in effect, 'I'm so sorry. I'm sorry you live in a fallen world and have suffered like this. And then he takes him aside from the crowd privately. He is going to make this man hear for the first time. The man had never heard a noise and Jesus doesn't want it to be too noisy for him the first time he can hear, so he takes him away from the crowd. He doesn't want him to be alarmed so he uses sign language to explain what he is about to do by putting his fingers in his ears and after spitting touched his tongue. Such tender care!

Another example is in Mark 9:14–29: Jesus heals a boy with an unclean spirit. Jesus asked the father, 'How long has this been happening to him?' (v.21). He is interested. He says to this heartbroken, beside-himself father, 'tell me your story; tell me all about it'.

And he cares for you. He wants to look after you. In 1 Peter 5:7 you are invited to 'Cast all your care upon him because he cares for you'.

Honour your father and mother

As the Saviour of the world was dying for the sins of the world, in physical agony; about to experience abandonment by his Father and feel the full onslaught of the wrath of a sin hating God, he was mindful of his responsibilities and obeyed the fifth Commandment to the end: 'Honour your father and mother' (Exodus 20:12)

Honouring our parents is not an option just for those who like mam and dad. We don't just listen to them when it suits us or when we agree with what they say. Independence, thinking for yourself, trying and failing are all part of growing up. However, stubbornness, rebellion and disobedience are not.

In our culture it is almost a given that teenagers rebel. But none of us have the right to break the fifth commandment no matter what our friends or hormones tell us.

In choosing a marriage partner, it is important to seek our parents' blessing and listen to their advice.

As we get older and set up our own homes we should visit them, listen to them, appreciate them, see they are well cared for and be patient with them!

Of course obedience has its limits. Acts 5:29 teaches that we should obey God rather than men. If your parents command of you what God forbids then we should obey God but even then we should do it sensitively and as respectfully as possible.

But honour for our father and mother can also extend to our attitude to all in positions of authority. Younger men to older men (1 Peter 5:5). We should not think our generation knows it all. In our day and age, we seldom think, 'this person is older and probably has something to teach me' but rather 'this person is older and out of date'. Students in Christian Unions, young ministers, Bible college students (and me!) too often think that the last 2000 years of Church History has just been treading water for our arrival on the scene! I mean, what were Augustine, the Reformers, the Puritans, Whitefield, the Wesleys, Spurgeon, Lloyd-Jones etc. playing at all those years!

We are also to obey and work hard for our bosses (Ephesians 6:5) and while there is nothing wrong with disagreeing and working for change we should obey the government (Romans 13:1ff) and honour the king (1 Peter 2:17).

Jesus was subject to his parents when they were imperfect and he was perfect (Luke 2:51). We should definitely do the same.

No special treatment

We have seen that Jesus referred to his mother respectfully by saying dear woman or lady or madam, but why not call her mother?

It would seem that the human relationship of son and mother is about to be superseded. While he loved his mother and honoured and obeyed her to the end, he was now severing their relationship. It was no longer son and mother but Saviour and saved.

Even though she was highly favoured among women (Luke 1:28) Mary should not be exalted or elevated in the Christian Church. Praying to Mary will do you no good at all. In fact, it is expressly forbidden (1 Timothy 2:5; Exodus 20:4; Revelation 19:10).

Furthermore, Christ makes it clear that family ties and friendships are not as important or as lasting as being part of the real family of God (Mark 3:31–35). In Acts 1:14 Mary is pictured as just a believer among other believers; all members together of the same family.

There is a way back to the Cross

The only one of Jesus' disciples who was present at the cross was John. It would seem that even he wasn't there the whole time. He records very little detail of what happened between Pilate passing sentence and Jesus telling him to take care of his mother, so it can be fairly assumed that he wasn't present the whole time. The silence suggests his absence from the cross.

John was the disciple who loved Jesus best. From a young man, he had followed Jesus Christ. He was one of the twelve disciples and among those twelve disciples one of the three Jesus was closest to. John had spent three years in close proximity with Jesus and was an eyewitness of all that Jesus said and did on earth. He heard his parables and saw his miracles; he listened to his sermons, observed his character and watched his life. No one knew Jesus better than he did. The night Jesus had his last supper with his disciples, John leaned on his chest (John 13:25). He went to the High Priest's palace when Jesus was on trial, here he stands by his cross and in Chapter 19 of this book he entered his tomb. He saw him after he had risen from the dead and watched him ascend back up into Heaven (Chapter 23). John knew and experienced that Jesus Christ was God and had come to this world to save anyone and everyone who would trust him. Knowing this, he was compelled to tell and write to people about these things. He wrote the Gospel according to John, 'so that you may believe that Jesus is the Christ, the Son of God, and that believing you may have life in his name' (John 20:31). He also wrote three letters in the New Testament (1, 2 and 3 John) and the book of Revelation. He was one of the leaders of the early church and an elder in the churches of Asia Minor (2 John 1; 3 John 1). The Romans persecuted anyone who acknowledged Jesus Christ, and not Caesar, as Lord and therefore John, even though he outlived all the other disciples, spent his last years exiled on a prison island called Patmos. He refers to himself throughout his Gospel as 'the disciple who Jesus loved' (John 13:23) because he can't believe Jesus loved him.

Despite John's love for the Lord Jesus, he no doubt fled with all the others at first (Matthew 26:56) but he came back. As the final sentence was pronounced maybe he hurried into the city to find as many of the disciples as possible and those faithful women, especially Mary his mother. Then he returned to Golgotha. But it is also likely that along with the others he fled at first, too

This should encourage us to think that cowardice can overtake even the very best. Some of you reading this book may have really let the Saviour down. Denied him by your words or actions and let the side down badly. The devil will tell you there is no way back. Your conscience will convince you that he is sick of you. But listen to John himself when he says, 'whenever our heart condemns us, God is greater than our heart' (1 John 3:20). There is a way back to the cross. Apparently the American evangelist, Billy Graham, once spoke to Winston Churchill about the Saviour but Churchill replied by saying, 'it is too late for me'. Today it is not too late. It is still the day of salvation. Backsliders can be healed (Hosea 14:4).

11

God forsaken by God

Matthew 27:46–48; Mark 15:33–35; Luke 23:44, 45

Darkness

IT NOW IS 12 O CLOCK. JESUS HAS BEEN ON THE CROSS FOR THREE hours. It was midday so the sun should have been blazing at its zenith of heat and light. But for three hours, at the brightest time of the day, everything goes black. According to Webster (1957, p.46) 'At the birth of the Son of God there was brightness at midnight; at the death of the Son of God there was darkness at noon.'

As well as this phenomenon being recorded by the gospel writers, it was also documented elsewhere. The early Christian apologist Tertullian, cited in Sanders (1971 p.203), referred to this darkness when he reminded his heathen readers that the 'wonder is related in your own annals and is preserved in your archives to this day'.

As we have seen time and time again, Matthew, Mark and Luke are good historians and their treatment of this darkness enhances their reputations as such. They did not embellish what happened, just reported it. Luke simply says, 'It was now about the sixth hour, and there was darkness over the whole land until the ninth hour while the sun's light failed.' (Luke 23:44–45). Before the darkness we hear the taunting of the Jewish leaders, the disdain of the crowds and the mockery and callousness of the soldiers, but during these three hours of darkness, no one speaks. The jeering and laughter is replaced by silence and fear. Shock and fear overwhelms everyone at Calvary. It is an eerie, silent darkness.

This darkness was not a natural darkness. It was Passover so there would have been a full moon, which means there could not have been an eclipse of the sun. So why did it turn so dark?

In the Old Testament darkness is a sign of God's judgement (Deuteronomy 28; Amos 8). In Exodus 10 God sent a plague of darkness as a sign of his judgement. It lasted three days and it was a darkness that could be felt. The darkness that came over Calvary was a symbol of a much deeper, more frightening darkness, an 'outer darkness' (Matthew 8:12; 22:13; 25:30). On the cross Christ was going through eternal Hell for all those who would trust him.

For the first three hours, the Lord Jesus has suffered intense physical pain. But the remaining three hours he is on the cross he suffered incredible internal pain; pain in his soul. Calvin said 'his soul shared in the punishment'. Such pain, that darkness descended on Calvary. The heavens go black and the Lord Jesus goes into the darkness alone.

If you are not a Christian this darkness should scare you. Death, standing before God at the judgement, Hell, eternity are all terrifying. You may try to convince yourself that after death there is nothing, but you know that is just not true. If that was the case, why do we fear death? An animal just finds a corner, curls up and dies. But we know death is not the end. We go into eternity via the judgement. We try not to think about it, trivialise it or come up with our own ideas about what happens. At funerals or wakes we tell ourselves, 'another one has gone next door', 'he's on the golf course in the sky'. The most frequently requested music at funerals according to Co-operative Funeralcare is 'Always look on the bright side of life'. It goes on to say,

Life is quite absurd and death's the final word
You must always face the curtain with a bow
Forget about your sin—give the audience a grin
Enjoy it, it's your last chance anyway

But we know this is total madness! After death is the judgement (Hebrews 9:27). And sinners going to this judgement alone will be condemned to an eternal Hell. They will go out into an eternal darkness.

In his poem, Bertram Shaddock described the petrifying scene on judgement day for all those outside of Jesus Christ

I dreamed the great judgement morning had dawned and the
    trumpet had blown
I dreamed that the nations had gathered for judgement
before
    the white throne
From the throne came a bright shining angel who stood on
the
    land and the sea
And swore with his hand raised to heaven, time was no
longer
    to be
And oh what a weeping and wailing as the lost were told of
    their fate
They cried for the rocks and the mountains, they prayed but
    their prayer was too late

But during the three hours of darkness on Calvary, if your faith is in the Lord Jesus Christ you have nothing to fear. He endured eternal Hell for you. In World War I it was said that the trenches were Hell on earth. While being in those trenches was unimaginably awful, there has only been once when there has actually been Hell on earth. That is when millions of sins of millions of people were laid on one man, Jesus Christ, and he went through Hell on earth.

During these hours of darkness Christ was in torment. He had to endure the pain of bearing the sin of many (Isaiah 53:12; Hebrews 9:28). He bore our sins in his body on the tree (1 Peter 2:24). In fact he was made sin for us (2 Corinthians 5:21). He feels on the cross the fact that he is the cursed one who is vile, foul and repulsive. We all know what it is to feel guilty. It is an awful feeling to be wracked by guilt. So we cannot begin to imagine how Christ must have felt when he was taking the blame for the sins of millions and God thought of these sins as belonging to Christ.

On the cross he went through Hell. But you may ask how on the cross for six hours did Jesus suffer an eternal Hell? How could the millions of sins of millions of people, each one deserving eternal Hell, be paid for in a few hours on a cross, however painful those hours may have been?

I don't know, but maybe it was something like Narnia. In the Lion the Witch and the Wardrobe (Lewis, 1950), the children go through the wardrobe and enter Narnia. They feel like they are there for thousands of years but when they come back through the wardrobe into England again they have only been away a few seconds. In Narnia, time is not the same. I think this is what happened on Calvary. On earth it was hours but as Christ went into the darkness he left time and entered eternity and suffered an eternal Hell.

That Hell is eternal is what makes it so awful; there is no end to the pain. I once had to go to hospital to have an endoscopy. It was the worst experience of my life so far. I knew I was in trouble when one person held my arms and another held my legs down! A nurse kept telling me to keep calm as a doctor pushed a tube with a camera on the end of it down my throat. For twenty minutes I retched as with two hands on the tube the doctor pushed and shoved it around my stomach. It was awful. But after twenty minutes it was over. Hell is torment but it won't be over after twenty minutes. It won't be over after twenty years. It won't be over after 20 million years. In fact, for those there it won't be over at all! That is why I urge you to trust in the one who suffered an eternal Hell on Calvary. If you don't, you will enter the darkness he went through on Calvary for all eternity.

Abandoned

After three hours of this darkness came the fourth words Jesus spoke from the cross. It is the only one of the seven sayings that Mark records.

He says, 'at the ninth hour Jesus cried with a loud voice, "Eloi, Eloi, lema sabachthani?" which means, "My God, my God, why have you forsaken me?" And some of the bystanders hearing it said, "Behold, he is calling Elijah."'(Mark 15:34, 35).

In attempting to understand these words, it is important to appreciate that we can only wade in the shallows of these verses. John Murray (cited in Reymond, 1998) said that this was 'the most mysterious utterance that ever ascended from earth to Heaven'. When Martin Luther, the 16th century reformer, set himself to study these verses, he fasted and spoke to no one. For several hours he did not move, then he got up from his chair to walk around the room. He was overheard saying, 'God forsaken of God? Who can understand that?'

The Lord Jesus was quoting these words from Psalm 22 which is a Messianic Psalm; that is, a Psalm which talks about the promised Messiah. He doesn't quote it in the Hebrew but in the vernacular Aramaic, his native tongue. Most of the Jews present at the cross would have been more familiar with Hebrew and so misunderstood what he said. They mistook 'Eli' for Elijah and assumed he was calling for Elijah, one of the greatest Old Testament prophets, to come and help him.

In the Garden of Gethsemane he cries out to God, 'Abba Father'. He is intimate; a son calling out to his 'dad'. But here in contrast, he calls out, 'My God, my God'. It was a cry of desperation.

Apparently at Jewish abattoirs the sound and screams that the animals made when the blood was let out of them as they were being prepared for sacrifice was like no sound on earth! But these were just pictures of the reality of what was happening at Calvary. As the Son of God is being sacrificed in the place of millions of sinners, under so much stress, he screams out, 'My God, my God, why have you forsaken me?' The Puritan, John Flavel comments,

> It is as much as if Christ had said, O my God, no words can express my anguish: I will not speak, but roar, howl out my complaint; pour it out in volleys of groans: I roar as a lion.

On the cross for three hours Jesus was forsaken by God. There is no sadder word than 'forsaken'. Think of a widow coming home from the funeral of her husband, or a child whose parents have been killed in a car accident. If a child is in trouble, need or pain, they call out 'Dad, Dad'. But imagine dad doesn't come. Forsaken, abandoned, alone!

But not even these compare with being forsaken by God in your hour of need. Jesus knew what it was like to be forsaken by men, even his disciples, but now it's God (see John 16:32). He was totally alone. He faced the weight of the guilt of millions of sins alone. He now feels so guilty, under so much wrath, in agony, with no one for support or comfort. Satan whispers in his ear, 'despair and die. God has abandoned you!' He is now going through Hell, in the hands of his adversaries, feeling the full weight of the powers of evil and God leaves him. He feels no love or care. Just wrath and anger.

I wonder if this cry of abandonment frightens you. Today you may be surrounded by family and friends. You've got your job and your home. You've got hundreds of TV channels to watch, theatres, cinemas, shops, sports matches to go to. After a long day at the office, heartbreak, tough times, you've got a husband or wife or friends and family to rally round and support you.

Even though we live in a fallen world, there is still so much of this world that is good. God's general goodness is still evident. The sun shines, people show kindness, love, happiness, laughter, crunching through snow, crusty bread. But imagine none of these. Just you and your guilt and shame. God's goodness has been withdrawn and it is just his white hot anger. This is what Christ experienced during these hours. The wrath of God, feeling the guilt of millions of sins. Totally abandoned!

It is important to say that even when he had been abandoned, the Lord Jesus still has complete trust in God. In Psalm 22, the Psalmist is rescued (v. 22–31), and by quoting this Psalm, Jesus is showing that he has faith in God that he will ultimately rescue him. But the suffering had gone on so long and there was no release in sight. Hour after hour it went on and on. To bear the guilt of millions of sins even for a moment would cause the greatest anguish of soul. To face the all-out wrath of an infinite God, even briefly, would cause the most intense fear. When he cries out 'My God, My God why have you forsaken me' (Matthew 27:46), it is if he is saying 'Oh God, my God will you ever bring it to an end? Why have you left me for so long?'

But for everyone who dies without Christ they will go into eternal Hell and God will never come to them. It won't be that God will leave them for a long time. It will be that God will has left them forever. Abandoned in Hell forever!

Trinity

While it is impossible to really grasp what these words mean, it is important that we guard against saying anything erroneous. These words do not diminish the Lord Jesus' deity. At no point on the cross does he stop being God. He is and always will be, fully God and fully man.

Neither does the Trinity stop being united. There is one God who cannot be divided (Deuteronomy 6:4; Colossians 2:9). These words do not mean that the Trinity was destroyed, not even for a second! God the Father does not forsake the Son as God. The Father and Son are still one in their being and attributes. The Son is still full of the Spirit.

When Christ cried out 'My God My God why have you forsaken me?' he experienced complete desertion in his human nature. The love of God had abandoned him because on that cross he was standing in the sinner's place. All that he felt was the anger and wrath of a Holy God instead of the love of his Father.

This would have been so awful for the Lord Jesus. Between the Father, Son and the Holy Spirit there had always existed a perfect loving relationship. Proverbs 8 pictures this relationship of the Son before the Father. He says, 'I was daily his delight, rejoicing always before him' (Proverbs 8:30 NASB). There has never been a more loving Father and Son relationship.

God didn't create humans to love and be loved. Rather, he created humans so that the love the Father, Son and Holy Spirit enjoyed from all eternity could overflow to us.

All of this makes this cry of, 'My God my God, why have you forsaken me', all the more incredible. In his hour of utmost need Jesus felt himself bereft of the love and fellowship he had enjoyed from all eternity. During his extremest need he was forsaken.

Propitiation

So how does all of this affect us?

Because the Lord Jesus was abandoned for us. The wrath that God should pour out on us, was poured out on him. When he cried out 'My God My God why have you forsaken me?' God's answer in effect was, 'because in the twenty first century there will be people who will need a Saviour. You are abandoned so they don't have to be'.

On the cross Jesus was paying the wages of sin. He had no personal sin of his own but as a representative bore so much sin. He paid the price of the sins of everyone who will trust him. He assumed the liabilities and responsibilities of all his clients.

Our sin has made us enemies of God, and it was while we were God's enemies that Christ died for us. God is so angry with sin. It isn't the sort of anger where someone flies off the handle, but a just, steady, constant burning anger. During these hours Jesus was turning away this anger. He was extinguishing the wrath of God. According to Reymond (1998, p.639)

> When we look at Calvary and behold the Saviour dying for us we should see in his death not first our salvation but our damnation being borne and carried away by him

The Bible uses the word 'propitiation' for this (1 John 2:2) but we must distinguish between the pagan idea of propitiation and what the Bible teaches about how the Lord Jesus is our propitiation. In pagan rituals the sacrifice was the means by which people placated an offended deity. But the God of the Bible is not capricious or easily angered.

The Lord Jesus Christ is the fulfilment of all the sacrifices that were offered in the Old Testament. These sacrifices weren't some kind of bribe. These sacrifices didn't make God gracious but were provided by a gracious God. God took the initiative. Out of great love God acted to propitiate his own wrath and thereby save us. On the cross Christ pacified the wrath of God. He bore the wrath of God so that God becomes 'propitious', or favourably disposed, towards us. It isn't just that he stops God being angry towards us, but that we can know God's favour.

Neither did the Old Testament sacrifices take away or atone for a single sin. They were pictures and pointers to what Christ would do on Calvary. In the Old Testament the sins of a multitude of people were forgiven on the grounds of what Christ would one day accomplish on Calvary (Romans 3:25). God's wrath had been stored up over the centuries and was now poured out on Jesus Christ. But it is not only the sins of these Old Testament people, but the sins of every person from the very beginning of time to the very end who will put their trust in him. Jesus was putting out the wrath of God against millions and millions and millions of sinners

It is important to note that forgiving our sins isn't just a legal dilemma for God. It isn't only a case that his justice needs to be satisfied; that is, the law says that sin must be punished and therefore someone has to pay that punishment. But sin is also against the very character and being of God. He is offended by it and is angry with us, and if we are to be friends with God and at peace with him, this anger needs to be turned away, quenched.

If we are trusting in Christ, not only has God stopped being angry towards us but he is now happy and pleased with us.

Love

What happened on the cross shows how much God loves sinners. He was prepared to put his own Son through this awful pain and abandon him. He loved us so much that he would do this to his own Son. Isaiah says that it pleased the Lord to bruise him (Isaiah 53:10).

Because of what was achieved by the Lord Jesus on Calvary, God was so pleased with his Son. Thomas Goodwin said, 'God was never more happy with his Son than when he was most angry'.

It also shows the love of the Lord Jesus. Despite all that he went through to save you, he has no regrets. Isaiah says that he sees the travail of his soul and is satisfied (Isaiah 53:11). He thinks back to being born in that stable in Bethlehem, growing up in Nazareth, pouring out his soul in Gethsemane and suffering such pain on Calvary and says, 'no regrets'. Not the slightest grudge about the terrible price he paid. Were it still to be accomplished he would do it all over again. When we see him he will look at us and say 'you were worth it'.

12

Thirsty work

John 19:28, 29; Matthew 27:48, 49; Mark 15:36

A thirsty man

As the end nears, the fifth word Jesus utters from the cross is, 'I thirst' (John 19:28). Jesus had been on the cross six hours. Crucifixion is probably the most painful and cruel form of death ever invented. It was excruciating and prolonged. Blood gradually drained from the body, causing dehydration and increasing thirst.

The last time the Lord Jesus would have had anything to drink was at the Passover meal with his disciples in the Upper Room. That was Thursday evening and it was now about 3 o clock on Friday afternoon. In that time he had walked to Gethsemane where he had spent several hours in prayer. He had been in agony and had sweated great drops of blood. He had been betrayed by one of his disciples and then arrested by a 300 strong mob armed with torches, lanterns, clubs and swords. They had then taken him to the house of Annas, then Caiaphas where he had to endure a mock trial where he had been hit, blind folded, mocked and spat at. He was then taken early in the morning to stand trial before Pilate and then Herod and then back to Pilate. He received probably two floggings; one really severe one. A crown of thorns had been squeezed on his head, he'd been stripped and dressed up as some kind of king from a dressing up box and then made to carry his cross through the streets of Jerusalem to Golgotha. He had collapsed with exhaustion and needed help to get there. On arrival soldiers stood on his hands and hammered nails into his hands and feet. Hanging on the cross he endured more mocking and shame as well as being in the most unimaginable physical pain. Soldiers had taken his clothes off him and gambled for them. And then at noon, for three hours on earth, but an eternity really, he had been abandoned by, and endured the wrath of, God. He had been to Hell and back!

He had done all of this without anything to drink. He had refused the wine mixed with myrrh that was given to those led to execution to deaden consciousness. He needed his wits about him. The one consuming concern of the Lord Jesus on the cross was the redemption of the world. He had to face the full blast and onslaught of physical and spiritual agony with as clear and lucid a mind as possible.

But now as the work nears completion he is aware of his own sufferings. He is almost coming to the end and realises the pain he's in. He had endured burning thirst and a headache. He would not face death without restoring the physical balance he needed to cry out in a loud voice to death, sin and the devil, 'It is finished'. Mission accomplished. Job done!

This shows the humanity of Jesus. On that cross was no superman but a real man. On the one hand, on the cross we see God as he pardons a criminal, but on the other a man who thirsts. And this man got thirsty like we get thirsty. Headaches would have caused him as much pain as it causes us. And he went through all of this for us! He must so love me and you!

Two different reactions

When the Lord Jesus said 'I thirst' one of the men standing nearby brought some sour wine in a sponge, and lifted it up on a rod to the mouth of the Lord, and the Lord accepted it from the sponge. The sour wine would have essentially been vinegar for soldiers to quench their thirst at the foot of the cross. The centurion ordered the sponge. He, and maybe others, who had for the first three hours taunted Jesus by coming to him offering vinegar (Luke 23:36), are now possibly more sympathetic. The soldier who passed the sponge was doing it sincerely. Matthew suggests he pressed the sponge to his lips again and again. Maybe grace had begun to work in his heart. It was the only act of kindness shown by the crowds.

The rest of the crowd still mocked. They said, 'let him alone; let us see if Elijah will come to save him' (Matthew 27:49 NKJV).

What is your reaction to Jesus as you see him so thirsty in such a state? Are you moved at the thought he was enduring all of this to save you? More importantly are you moved enough to turn from the sins that caused him to thirst like this and put your trust in him? Or do you still think, what a joke? Does he still have no effect on you whatsoever?

Your word is truth

The last thing that we need to note in this chapter is the Lord Jesus' high regard for scripture. John says, 'After this, Jesus knowing that all things were now accomplished that the scripture might be fulfilled said, "I thirst"' (John 19:28 NKJV). This was a fulfilment of Psalm 69:21.

Christ's great respect for scripture was also seen in the Garden of Gethsemane when he tells Peter to put his sword away because if he wanted to he could call down 12 legion of angels, but then how would the scriptures be fulfilled (Matthew 26:53,54). There are also numerous other examples of events that happen throughout the death and resurrection of Jesus which are a fulfilment of the scriptures: The soldiers dividing his garments among them and casting lots for his clothes (John 19:24); that none of his bones were broken (John 19:36).

To the Lord Jesus the scripture is the highest authority and cannot be broken. It is the inerrant, infallible, trustworthy, authoritative, perfect Word of God.

The Word of God (The Bible) was written by over 40 people spanning a period of 1500 years and yet there is a remarkable unity and coherence because it is really the activity of a single divine author. All of the Old Testament prophecies have been fulfilled in the New Testament even though they were prophesied hundreds of years before they took place. The Bible continues to be as relevant as it was when it was first written because it is a living book through which the living God still speaks today. And the power the Bible has can been seen in human lives today and throughout history.

It has stood the test of time. It is no novelty. For thirty years after Christ's death it was passed on by word of mouth and embraced and lived. It has been subject to persecution and ridicule and yet it still survives today. Despite continued attempts, no one has successfully disproved or discredited it. In fact, archaeological findings just support its claims.

The Word of God must therefore be more important than the traditions of the church, our own human reason and any feelings or leadings we may have. According to Dr Lloyd-Jones (cited Jeffrey 1988, p.21)

> The church is built upon the foundation of the apostles and prophets. We must therefore reject every supposed new revelation, every addition to doctrine. We must assert that all teaching and all truth and all doctrine must be tested in the light of the Scriptures. We can build only upon this one, unique, authority.

The message of the Bible could not be more important. Today

people spend their time emailing, texting and tweeting online 'friends' about such effluvium as what they ate for lunch in ever more abbreviated language. Neal Gabler in the *Los Angeles Times* (*The Week*, 11th December 2010 p.17) described the future as 'one in which words are abundant but exist mainly to express the trivial and the transitory'. The Bible is far from trivial and transitory and so much more important and exciting than a message from an online 'friend'. It is from Almighty God.

The biggest problem is when I want to do things that God's Word forbids. God gets to make the rules, and we don't like it. But we need to trust God's Word. He knows best. Even when it cuts across our plans or way of life we must 'Trust in the LORD with all your heart, and do not lean on your own understanding; In all your ways acknowledge him, and he will make straight your paths' (Proverbs 3:5, 6).

Paul Williams, who was the Bishop of Kensington at the time, came to The Fulham Boys School to take an assembly. He told a story about when he once set out to climb a mountain. He begun bounding up it and passed a man in his 70s. The man was slow and doddery and he thought to himself that a man like that shouldn't be on such a mountain. But the weather changed and Paul Williams began to slow down and become hesitant and unsure. He saw the same man coming slowly alongside him. The man said to him that he had been climbing this mountain for 50 years and told Paul to follow in his footprints. Every now and then he would point his stick and say 'watch here, be careful over there'. He knew the mountain. We think we know best how to climb life's mountain but we need to trust the Word of the One who hasn't been climbing the mountain for the last fifty years but who built it!

I urge you to read it. Trust it. Obey it and live off it. If the Lord Jesus held it in such high regard, surely we should. And importantly, think about it yourself and don't rely or follow blindly any one particular commentary or interpretation.

Read it daily and meditate (think deeply) on it. See if there is a sin it is telling you about and then repent of it and avoid it. Look for a promise it is giving then claim it. Find an example it is setting and then follow it. Think about how the chapter or portion you are reading increases your knowledge and understanding of God and how it points to the Lord Jesus Christ.

It is the truth and it is this truth that will set you free (John 8:32).

13

Tetelestai!

John 19:30

Tetelestai!

THE LORD JESUS CHRIST HAD BEEN ON THE CROSS FOR SIX HOURS.

For the first three hours, from 9am until noon, he had endured the mockery, disdain and taunting of the crowds. During this time he made sure his mother would be taken care of after his death, promised a really bad man he would be with him in Paradise that very day, and prayed that those nailing him to the cross and mocking him would be forgiven.

But then from noon until 3pm everything went dark. The sun stopped shining, the crowd were silenced as the Lord Jesus Christ faced the eternal wrath of a sin hating God. This torment went on and on and on; so much so that he cries out, 'My God, my God, why have you forsaken me' (Mark 15:34). How much longer will you leave me like this!

But now he realises the end is in sight and he becomes aware of the physical pain he is in. His head must have been throbbing and his throat parched. He wants to die triumphantly so he asks for a drink and after receiving the drink, he calls out with a loud voice, 'Tetelestai'.

'Tetelestai' literally means, 'It is finished'. When the Lord Jesus cried out 'it is finished' he was saying, 'it has been and will for ever more remain finished'. The Lord Jesus said it with a loud voice so that everyone could hear. Not only was this loud voice to be heard at Calvary but was so loud that it would ring out down through the corridors of time. He wants us to hear it today. Everyone must know that 'it is finished!' There is nothing more to add. Everything that needed to be done to make us right with God has been done. Tetelestai!

Accomplished

So let's consider six things this finished work has accomplished.

1. Full atonement

My sins have put me in debt with God. A debt that I would spend eternity in Hell paying off. But when Jesus cried out 'It is finished' he made full atonement for these sins.

Atonement means 'a making at one' and points to a process of bringing those who are estranged into unity. In Theology (the study of God) it denotes the work of Christ in dealing with the problem of our sin and in bringing sinners into a right relationship with God.

The atonement he made was vicarious, that is, he made atonement in the place of others. On the cross he was putting right, making up, paying a debt on behalf of all those who trust him. All our sins were laid on Christ (Isaiah 53:6, 12; John 1:29; 2 Corinthians 5:21; Galatians 3:13; Hebrews 9:28; 1 Peter 2:24). He took upon himself all my sins and paid for them all. He paid off every last one of them. The secret ones, the 'little' ones, the shameful ones, the ones I commit time and time and time again.

The ones I have forgotten. The wilful ones. All paid for. God thought of our sins as belonging to Christ (2 Corinthians 5:21; Isaiah 53:6). He 'bore our sins in his body on the tree' (1 Peter 2:24). Finished! There is no more debt to pay.

There was once a chief of a tribe who was just and good. Someone in the tribe had been stealing and the chief said that whoever it was must be beaten. The thief turned out to be his elderly, frail mother. But justice had to be done. They tied her to the pole and were just about to beat her when the chief cried out, 'stop!' He got up and walked towards the pole and took off his shirt. He wrapped himself around her and said, 'Proceed'. On Calvary justice had to be done. A price had to be paid. A debt had to be settled. Someone had to take a beating. But for every man and woman, boy and girl who trusts in Jesus Christ, he wrapped himself around you on Calvary and said to God, 'Proceed'. The beating is over. The debt we owe has been fully paid. The wrath has been expended. It is finished!

According to the hymn writer Phillip Paul Bliss (1838–76),

Guilty, vile and helpless, we;
Spotless Lamb of God was He:
Full atonement!—can it be?
Hallelujah! What a Saviour!

2. Evil defeated

We live in a bad world. It is a world full of evil, pain and sadness. Marriages and families break up, addiction takes hold of people, pornography dominates the internet, paedophilia, rape, murder, lies, deceit, theft, terrorism, greed are all around us. People get ill, depressed, suffer pain and heartache; natural disasters leave countries and peoples devastated. And all of this because we live in a fallen world. As a result of the fall fear entered the world (Genesis 3:10). Blame entered the world (3:11–13). Pain entered the world (3:16). Relationships break down (3:16), shame is felt

(3:7). Just making it through life is a chore (3:17). Christians are marginalised, made fun of and persecuted.

And behind all of this evil is Satan. According to Lloyd-Jones (2002, p.176)

> We all know something about persecution. We know what it is to be confronted by people who are unbelievers and anti-Christian, and how difficult they can make life for us at times. Yes, we know all that, but that is not the whole story. We need to be made aware of the fact that these men and women, these individuals, are but instruments of the great powers behind our world. The Bible impresses upon us the truth that it is the devil who is fighting God. So often we fail to remember that and, therefore, become confused and cannot understand things. What you and I see with our physical eyes is simply the visible part of a great spiritual war that is going on in another realm, in which we are being used, as it were, as the instruments.

He has many different names and titles. The Devil which means accuser (of God's people, Revelation 12:9–10); Apollyon (Revelation 9:11) which means destroyer. He is also known as the tempter (Matthew 4:3; 1 Thessalonians 3:5) and the evil one (1 John 5:18–19). He is called the 'prince' and 'god' of this world which point to him presiding over mankind's anti-God lifestyles (John 12:31; 14:30; 16:11; 2 Corinthians 4:4 cf. Ephesians 2:2; 1 John 5:19; Revelation 12:9).

But at the cross Jesus disarmed and triumphed over Satan and all the principalities and powers at his command. Even though the devil was thrown out of Heaven before the world was made (Revelation 12:7–10), he was defeated once and for all when Christ died on Calvary. In Luke 10 the Lord Jesus Christ said 'I saw Satan fall from Heaven'. This actually happened when the Lord Jesus Christ died on the cross and rose again.

Satan knew that if Christ died and rose again he would be

defeated, so all the time Christ was on earth he tried to do all that he could to stop Jesus going to the cross. At his birth King Herod is used by him to try and kill all boys in Bethlehem aged two or under (Matthew 2:16). He tempted Christ in the wilderness for forty days trying to get him to give into him (Matthew 4:1–11). When Jesus tells his disciples that he must suffer and die, Peter tries to stop him to which Jesus says to Peter, 'Get behind me Satan' (Matthew 16:23). As we saw in Chapter 2 of this book, it was Satan who was really behind Judas' betrayal. On the cross Satan thought he had him but he had to concede defeat. Christ decisively won victory on the cross. According to Bruce (1984, p.239)

> As he was suspended there, bound hand and foot to the wood in apparent weakness, they imagined they had him at their mercy, and flung themselves upon him with hostile intent ... But he grappled with them and mastered them

But even though Satan was defeated he has not yet conceded defeat. He is overthrown but not yet eliminated. He is like a roaring lion (1 Peter 5:8) and a dragon (Revelation 12:9). He is deceitful and can disguise evil as good (2 Corinthians 11:14). He hates Christians and is always probing for weaknesses and undermining faith and hope.

He realises that he now has no chance of overcoming the Lord Jesus so he turns all of his vengeance on Christians. He is wicked and frustrated. He is mean, furious, malicious and cruel towards all those who trust in God. He is filled with rage because he knows his time is short and so he aims to do as much damage as possible. Though he is defeated, he will not be cast into Hell until the very end of time and meanwhile is determined to cause as much havoc as possible.

As the accuser, he reminds people of their sin and whispers to them that there is no way they can be right with God. He brings to their memory all their failures and haunts them with their past. But after Christ's victory on Calvary his accusations lose every semblance of justice.

As the hymn writer Charitie Lees De Chenez puts it

When Satan tempts me to despair
And tells me of the guilt within
Upward I look, and see Him there
Who made an end of all my sin.

While Satan should be taken seriously, we need to remember that he is a beaten enemy. Satan is stronger than we are but Christ has beaten him (Matthew 12:29) and Christians will triumph over him, too, if they resist him with the resources Christ supplies (Ephesians 6:10–13; James 4:7; 1 Peter 5:9–10). Satan is a creature, superhuman but not divine. He has a lot of knowledge and power but he is not all knowing or all powerful. He can move around in ways humans can't, but he is not omnipresent (everywhere at once). We must remember he is beaten and destined for the lake of fire (Revelation 20:10).

But it is hard to remember that Christ was victorious on Calvary because we live in a world that is so godless. The church is ridiculed and persecuted. Laws are passed that are against the Bible and Christians are marginalised and pitied in society. What we believe is seen as ridiculous and society would make us feel that Christianity is outdated, archaic and wrong. Even as Christians we can doubt what the Bible says and the Church can get infiltrated by the standards and values of the world. The world is hostile to the Church. We have made God answerable to us, and if what he says cuts across our way of thinking and living we get rid of it and write it off. The world is in charge.

But Jesus tells his follower to take heart because he has overcome the world (John 16:33). As evil rages and the devil tries to cause as much havoc as possible, we need to remember, even though it doesn't seem like it at times, he's chained. This is illustrated in Pilgrims Progress. Christian was afraid when he saw two lions on his way to the Promised Land. Bunyan says, 'the lions were chained' and then adds, 'but he saw not the chains'. That is true today. The devil at times can torment and trouble us and get us down but we need to remember he's chained!

Revelation 12:11 gives three ways that Christians can overcome the rage of Satan.

Firstly, we overcome him by the blood of the Lamb. When the devil accuses us and makes us feel guilty, we'll never beat him by saying, 'I'm not that bad'. The only way we can ever beat Satan is on the grounds of the blood of the Lamb. As Christians we can have good days and bad days; days we feel like Christians and days we don't. Days we really fail him and days we feel close to God. But our feelings are not what save us. The only way to overcome accusations is on the grounds of the blood of the Lamb. One day I will stand before God. There will be many people who know me who could present a case as to why I should not be allowed into Heaven. People I grew up with, went to school with, went to university with, worked with, my family, friends who could all point to my sins and say there's no way he should be allowed into Heaven. Then there is my conscience that can bring to mind the things I've thought and done that no one else knows. That will definitely condemn me! On top of all that, God's law shows me I've failed on every point. The devil through all of these things will accuse me. But on that awesome day when I stand before the judge of all the earth, Jesus Christ will plead for me. He will stand with me and when the devil, the law, my conscience, my past and everyone who knows me will condemn me, he will say as it were: 'look back to before the sun, the moon and all the stars were made, that is when I set my love upon you. Look at those three crosses. On the middle one, I took all your sins upon myself and paid for every one of them! When you confessed your sins to me I was faithful and just and forgave you. When you called upon me I saved you. My blood covers all your iniquities.' Don't look at yourself; trust in Christ's finished work!

Secondly, we overcome him by the word of our testimony. How do we fight the Devil and attempt to transform society by the gospel? By the word of our testimony. As Christians we will never beat the world by trying to be like the world. We'll never win people for the gospel by trying to be cool or trendy. God has promised to bless just two things: prayer and preaching. Never lose faith in them!

Thirdly, we are willing to die. A Christian realises that death has lost its sting. The apostle Paul said, 'For me to live is Christ and to die is gain'. Death for a Christian means to be with God so it holds no fear over him. Witnesses say that the Christian martyrs embraced the flames like a stream on a hot summer's day. As he was about to die, William Haslam said, 'I am just beginning to live'.

3: Redemption

When he cried out 'it is finished', it meant that Christ fully paid the price for our redemption.

By nature we are slaves to sin (Hebrews 2:15; Colossians 1:13). We think we may do what we want and no one tells us what to do but the reality is we are slaves to our sinful lusts. We are in bondage to sin and Satan and to free us from this, a ransom had to be paid. Christ's death as a ransom was paid to God whose holiness and justice had been offended

Man's original state was sinless but since the fall sin has a hold on us. In the ancient world there were three ways in which a person could become a slave—born into slavery; fall into slavery through conquest; become a slave through debt. The Bible speaks of sin in these three ways.

We are born into sin; my nature is sinful and corrupt (Psalm 51:5; Ecclesiastes 7:20; Jeremiah 17:9; Romans 3:10; 1 John 1:10). I am captivated by sin. I am a slave to my lusts. And my sin has put me in such a debt with God that I cannot pay it back. But on the cross Christ was buying us back, he was redeeming us.

Through his death we have been freed from bondage to the guilt of sin and from its ruling power in our lives (Romans 6:11, 14). By redeeming us Jesus has delivered us from the power of sin and paid the price for our forgiveness (Matthew 20:28; Mark 10:45; 1 Peter 1:18, 19; Hebrews 9:12; Romans 3:24–27; Ephesians 1:7; Colossians 1:14).

The debt I owe has been paid in full. Christ has finished paying it off so I can be free. He paid a 'ransom for many' (Mark 10:45). His death liberates us from all the ravages of the fall.

At the moment we still live in a fallen world but when we become a Christian the Holy Spirit is our seal or guarantee of our redemption (Luke 21:28; Ephesians 1:14; 4:30; Romans 8:18–23).

We were enslaved by all kinds of passions and pleasures; sexual immorality, idolatry, hatred, jealousy and anger, selfish ambition, drunkenness. But on the cross Jesus redeemed us from these things so while at the moment we have to contend with the world, the flesh and the devil we no longer are mastered by them (John 8:23–24; Romans 8:7–8; 1 John 5:19). They have no longer got any claims on me or can hold anything over me.

4: Reconciliation

When he cried out 'it is finished' the curtain in the temple tore in two from top to bottom (Mark 15:38). This means that the barrier between us and God has been removed. We can be friends with him; get close to him and have direct access to him.

The curtain was 80 foot high. No human could tear it. When Christ cried out 'It is finished', it was God himself who tore the curtain.

Curtain can be translated veil and it was a means to hide or cover. The temple area was designed as a series of courts. In the centre was the temple building itself which was divided into two parts.

Boice (www.alliancenet.org/tab/the-death-of-jesus-christ-part-two) helps us to picture it. He says that:

the first and larger part was the holy place. The other and smaller part was called the most holy place. Separating the two parts, or rooms, was the veil or curtain. In the early days of Israel's history, before the destruction of the Temple by the Babylonians, this innermost room contained the Ark of the Covenant with its necessary seal where God was understood to dwell in a symbolic sense. The presence of God above the ark in the most holy place showed the presence of God with his people. This veil therefore pointed to the enormous gulf between God in his holiness and us in our depravity. The veil said in effect, 'Come this far but no farther'.

'There was only one day in the whole year when the veil could be passed and that was on the Day of Atonement. This was the day when the High Priest alone took the blood of an animal that had been killed moments before in the courtyard into the temple, carried it past the veil and then sprinkled it in the mercy seat of the ark.

'The mercy seat was the ark's cover or lid. On it were figures of two angels who faced each other and whose wings stretched backward and upward and almost touched the top. That made a space in which God was understood to dwell in a symbolic way. Within the ark, below the space where God was thought to dwell, were the two tables of the law. The Ark of the Covenant was for Israel a picture of judgement.

The righteous, holy God of the universe looked down on the law, knowing that it had been broken, and that he must punish the people for their sin. This dramatic illustration was a constant reminder of God's verdict against his people's sins.

But when the High Priest sprinkled blood on the mercy seat, the blood came between God and the broken law. This act indicated that atonement had been made for sin. An innocent victim (the sacrificial animal) had died in the people's place, so that rather than pouring forth wrath, God could shower his people with grace and mercy.

All of this pointed forward to the final atonement that Jesus would make by dying on the cross. None of it, in and of itself, took away a single sin. The ceremony, sacrifices and priesthood acted as types and pictures of what the Lord Jesus would do on Calvary. God dramatically tearing this curtain from top to bottom marked the completion of all the Old Testament sacrifices. Everything to which the Old Testament sacrifices pointed was fulfilled. There was no more need for any sacrifice for sin.

As well as there being no more need for sacrifices, the priests that offered these sacrifices were also made obsolete. Jesus Christ is our Great High priest (Hebrews 4:14–16) and once he cried out, 'it is finished' we no longer need these priests to offer sacrifices on our behalf. We can come to God directly on the grounds of Jesus' finished work. I don't need to have a priest to get me access to God. I can go to him directly. Wherever I am I can pray to him on the grounds of Christ's finished work. All Christians are now priests and can come directly to God through Christ (1 Peter 2:5). There is no longer anything between God and those who are trusting in his Son.

Significantly, the veil was torn at 3pm, which was the time for the evening sacrifice. Priests would have been in the temple, engaged in their duties when the veil was torn. They should have realised that the age in which they had served was now over and a new age of God dealing directly with his people, and pouring out his Holy Spirit, had begun. This is maybe why in Acts 6:7 the number of disciples in Jerusalem increased rapidly and a large number of priests trusted Christ.

It is hard to imagine how many sacrifices must have been made. The offering of blood that the High Priest made on the Day of Atonement was only one of many sacrifices. In the book of Leviticus there are various offerings. There was the burnt offerings which was an offering for sin. This is when a large animal like a sheep or a goat or a small animal like a pigeon was totally consumed on the altar. Then there was the fellowship offering. Part of it was burnt and the other part the worshipper and family ate together as a fellowship offering.

But when Christ cried out, 'It is finished', all of these sacrifices were ended. Through the death of Christ we are reconciled to God.1 Peter 3:18 says that 'Christ suffered once for sins, the righteous for the unrighteous that he might bring us to God'. God was in Christ reconciling the world to himself. We can be friends with God. More than that, we have been adopted into his family and he calls us his son and we enjoy all the privileges of being his son (Ephesians 1:5). We are heirs of God and joint heirs with Jesus Christ. Everything God has is mine! Cornishman Billy Bray (1794–1868) the one-time miner and drunkard who after he was converted became a preacher would ask people, 'I be the king's son, who be ye?'

This reconciliation could only be brought about by the Lord Jesus Christ, the one who is man and God. Anselm said that only man should make reparation for his sins since it is he who has defaulted and only God could make the necessary reparation since it is he who has demanded it. Jesus Christ, the one who is man and God, is therefore the only Saviour since he is the only person who should and could bring about reconciliation.

When Christ cried out 'It is finished' all the wrong and grievance was put right and we can be accepted by God.

Acceptance is the thing that worries young people the most. They worry whether their friend request will be accepted on social media. Well can I tell you that if you sent God a friend request he will accept you. In fact he is waiting for you to send it. And all because of Christ's finished work.

Imagine the cross of Christ as like a wedding between God and sinners. The question is asked to God 'will you take her to be your lawful wedded wife'. He looks at the finished work of Christ and, with a loud voice, says 'I will!' The question is, what will you say back?

5: Justification

When Jesus cried out 'It is finished' it meant that everything that needed to be done to put us right with God had been done. The Bible calls this 'justification'. Justification frees a person from the guilt of sin and its condemnation. It is a judicial act of God where he pardons sinners. He declares the sinner righteous; perfect in his sight.

For me to be right with God I must keep God's law perfectly—in thought, word and deed. But it is impossible. I break it every day and there is nothing I can do to atone for all the sins I have committed. All I can offer God is a bad record. Far from putting me right with God, the law and my attempts at keeping it confirm I am guilty and deserve God's wrath.

It is impossible for me to be justified before God by the law. But based on what Christ did on Calvary, God is able to justify me.

Justification makes no actual change in me. It is a declaration by God concerning me. It is not something I get from what I do but rather something that is done for me. I have only been made righteous in the sense that God regards me as righteous and pronounces me righteous. As soon as I am justified I am right with God.

On the cross Jesus Christ was my substitute and took my place. In a legal sense, in God's eyes, he became me and I became him. According to Brunner (1934, p.524), 'Justification means this miracle: that Christ takes our place and we take his.'

Jesus lived a perfect life. This is called his active obedience. By trusting him the life he lived becomes mine; his righteousness becomes mine. I take off the sinful life I have lived and put it on Jesus and he clothes me with his righteousness. When you stand before God, whose lifelong record would you rather rely on, yours or Christ's? I am accepted by God in Christ (Ephesians 1:6).

Maybe you are a Christian and are worried about standing before God at the judgement. But if you are trusting in Jesus Christ you have nothing to fear. You will stand before him clothed in his righteousness as if you've done nothing wrong.

I taught a boy whose father was a bit of a small time crook. He and his mate once broke into a factory in Cwmbran in South Wales and stole a load of materials. They were caught red handed. However, they managed to get a hot-shot lawyer to represent them. They went to court and stood in the dock and the lawyer made the case for their defence. He said that there was no way his clients could have been in the factory on that particular night and no way could they have taken the materials they were accused of taking. His case was so powerful and convincing that the boy's father turned to his mate and said, 'perhaps we didn't do it!'

On judgement day, when everyone will stand before God's judgement throne, Christians will have someone far greater pleading their eternal cause for them. The elect will turn to each other and say, 'it's like we didn't do it'.

6: No condemnation

All of this sounds amazing yet so many of us who are Christians still feel condemned. We live with this horrible sense of shame and guilt. We feel there is still unfinished business between me and God. We still worry that we'll be found out, something will come to light and it is only a matter of time. So we do this or that to ease the guilt. We never feel totally safe with God.

But there is no more condemnation for those who are in Christ Jesus. (Romans 8:1). 'It is finished' means that the Lord Jesus took all the condemnation we deserve so now 'there is no more condemnation'!

If you are trusting in Jesus Christ then you are 'in him', and what is true of him is true of you. God says in effect, 'In Christ, I nailed you to a cross and punished you for your sins. You deserved to die and in Christ I put you to death. You deserved to go to Hell and on the cross I sent you there because you were in Christ. I exhausted all my condemnation on Christ'.

It isn't that your sin hasn't been dealt with or that it has been swept under the carpet and may crop up again at any time. God the Son took the condemnation instead of you. Tetelestai!

At Calvary, God's mercy, truth, righteousness and peace all met. In Psalm 85 these four are personified. It is as if Truth turned up and said 'the soul that sins must die' (Ezekiel 18:20). Mercy turned up and said 'forgive them'. Righteousness said 'all of this must be put right. The guilty verdict cannot stand'. Peace said, 'is there any way we can sort all this out?' Through Christ's death on the cross all their hearts desires met. There was no compromise. Christ became sin for us, which means that in a legal sense the soul that sinned did die. Things were put right because all transgressions, sin and iniquity were laid on him. He took the blame and suffered the wrath that it all deserved. Christ put it all right and therefore he can show mercy to us and we can be at peace with him.

The Son of God suffered in our place. Tertullian used the startling expression, 'a crucified God'. Our sin has caused suffering; it does deserve to be punished eternally, but incomprehensibly, God suffered for you! Barth (1956–57, p.446) said 'God's own heart suffered on the cross.'

In Christ we have nothing to fear. The law no longer condemns us. We are no longer under its tyranny. Everything that we should be afraid of has been dealt with by Jesus (Romans 8:15; 2 Timothy 1:7). Tetelestai!

Applied

So how can all that Christ finished or accomplished on the cross come to me?

By grace alone through faith alone

This finished work is ours by grace through faith (Ephesians 2:8). It is undeserved kindness. You benefit from what someone else did and someone else takes the blame and faces the punishment you deserve. Grace! You can't earn it or deserve it. You get the complete opposite to what you should get. Your sin and your conscience will make you feel unworthy. They tell you God will never accept you. You're too bad. You will want to put things right yourself, try harder, be better. But it is all of grace.

You are a rotten sinner. Like me I am sure many of you have committed awful sins, wilful sins, shameful sins. But God is gracious. The Bible says that where sin abounds, grace abounds all the more. God is more gracious than you are sinful. I remember when my son was very little and being by the sea with him. He started to run down the jetty towards the sea. As he ran he got faster and faster and faster and couldn't stop. But I ran down the jetty after him and being quicker caught up with him and stopped him. Your sin is fast. It abounds quickly, it may have already run away with you. But God's grace abounds even faster and can outrun your sin.

However bad a sinner you are, he is a better saviour than you are a sinner. He is more gracious than you are sinful.

And you receive this by faith. The apostle Paul says, 'the righteous shall live by faith' (Galatians 3:11). But what is faith?

It really means to take God at his word. It is believing what he promised and trusting in what he has done. You have to know certain things and believe them to be true. That you are a sinner and need to be saved. That you cannot save yourself and that Jesus Christ is the Son of God and the only Saviour. You then have to trust your whole life to him. Throw your whole self upon him. Your past, your present and your future. You stop trusting yourself and trust him.

Every religion in the world says that to be right with God you must do something. Keep certain food laws, wear certain clothes, follow certain rules, fast for one month of the year during sunlight, go on pilgrimages, bathe in a particular river, confess your sins to a priest, 'do, do, do'. And even then you can't be certain. But Christianity says with a loud voice, 'Done!' Everything's been done for you. Trust in a finished work.

Maybe you've been trying to save yourself. You've tried turning over a new leaf, giving up some bad habits, started going to church, reading your Bible, even trying to pray, but none of it seems to be working. You keep wondering if you've done enough and are always worried about that one dreadful thing I did in my past. Like Lady Macbeth in Shakespeare's play, you have cried out in despair, 'Will all great Neptune's ocean wash this blood clean from my hand?' Well let me urge you, as Staupitz urged Martin Luther, to 'Look at the wounds of Jesus Christ, to the blood He has shed for you. Instead of torturing yourself on account of your sins, throw yourself into the Redeemer's arms' (Leahy, 1999 p.15).

Putting your faith in Jesus Christ is to put your whole weight onto him. You need to trust him in a sitting down kind of way. Hebrews says that after Christ had made purification for sins he sat down at the right hand of the Majesty on high (Hebrews 1:3). Hebrews 10:11, 12 says, 'Every priest stands daily at his service, offering repeatedly the same sacrifices which can never take away sins. But when Christ had offered for all time a single sacrifice for sins, he sat down at the right hand of God'. A person sits down when the work is complete. The Old Testament priests could never sit down because their work was never done. But when Christ cried out 'It is finished', he sat down. Everything to make us right with God has been accomplished. There is nothing else to do. I can add nothing more to it. I don't have to do anything else. I don't have to perform certain rituals, eat certain foods, wear certain clothes, visit a priest. 'It is finished!' But some of you feel you are too bad. That the cross didn't quite cover everything. There is that one sin that haunts you. But it is finished! Everyone is happy with his work except you. You won't sit down.

But real faith is inextricably linked to repentance. If I have real faith in Jesus Christ and totally trust in him then I will repent. That means I will turn away from my sin and my old way of life. According to Packer (1993, p.162)

> The New Testament word for repentance means changing one's mind so that one's views, values, goals and ways are changed and one's whole life is lived differently. The change is radical, both inwardly and outwardly; mind and judgement, will and affections, behaviour and life style, motives and purposes, are all involved. Repentance means starting to live a new life.

If you say you are a Christian, do you love him? Those who do, cannot go after Christ and go after sin. They are in opposite directions. You cannot love and indulge in sin and have Christ. That is not to say you will never sin, but your attitude towards it has changed. You turn your back on it and run away from it. The Bible calls it repentance. You never want to sin and when you do you hate it. William Gurnall said, 'to forsake sin is to leave it without any thought reserved of returning to it again'. Positively you grow to be like Christ more and more. You are gentle, patient, loving, kind, honest, self-controlled and content.

True faith will also lead to good works. If you trust him as your Lord and Saviour, you will want to please him and submit to his Lordship. Our good works don't justify us but if we are really justified I will want to do good works. James 2:14–26: Good works are evidence that we have true faith. As James says, 'faith without works is dead'

14

Bowed his head and died

Matthew 27:50–56; Mark 15:37–41;
Luke 23:45–49; John 19:30–37)

Last words

A<small>T THE FOOT OF THE CROSS WERE THE SOLDIERS, THE TWO</small>
thieves still hung on their crosses, the faithful women by now stood
at a distance and a crowd were still gathered (Luke 23:48, 49).

And so, after he had said, 'It is finished!' (John 19:30) with a
loud voice Jesus said, 'Father into your hands I commit my spirit'
(Luke 23:46) and then bowed his head and gave up His spirit (John
19:30).

Bows his head and hands himself to God

For the first three hours the Lord Jesus was at Golgotha he was
subject to the taunting and ridicule of the soldiers, the Jewish
leaders, and the crowd. Then from 12 noon until 3pm the suffering

deepens at the hands of God and he entered the realms of outer darkness. In those three hours he suffered an eternal Hell in the place of all those who have and will trust in him.

Then the darkness dissolved and he knew he was in touching distance of accomplishing the salvation of all his people. A salvation that had been planned from before the world was made (Ephesians 1:4; 1 Peter 1:20), promised from the very beginning (Genesis 3:15), prophesied throughout the centuries and had hung over the Saviour like a spectre throughout his life. The 'hour' had almost passed. Forgiveness of sins, peace with God and a home in Heaven were all about to be secured for all those who will trust him!

As we have seen, he now becomes aware of the physical pain he is in, and particularly how thirsty he is. His throat would have been parched and, determined to die triumphantly, he asks for a drink. Having received a drink, he shouts out with a loud voice, 'It is finished!' and knowing that it is mission accomplished, he commits his spirit to his Father's care, bows his head and dies.

A dying man normally lifts his head as the final act of self-preservation to get as much air as possible into his lungs and of course after death his head droops down. But Jesus voluntarily bowed his head. In every account of his death in the gospels it is made clear that the Lord Jesus' death was voluntary. He decided the precise moment at which his death should come. He wasn't a victim of circumstances or a martyr to the cause. He laid his own life down in the place of sinners (John 10:18; 15:13; 1 John 3:16).

Once he had paid the price in full for the sins of all his people and turned away the wrath of God, he trusted his spirit into the hands of his father. The fellowship they had enjoyed since before the world begun was re-established. God's countenance turned again in love towards his Son. He totally trusted his Father to receive his spirit.

This should really encourage and comfort any anxious soul

that is wondering whether God will accept them at the end. Many people spend their lives worrying whether God will accept them; whether he has really forgiven them for all their sins. They cannot forgive themselves and fear dying and standing before God. If that is you, stop worrying and looking to yourself. If your faith is in Jesus Christ then it is no longer about whether you are good enough before God, but whether his death on Calvary was accepted by God on your behalf. The fact he cried out 'It is finished' and entrusted his spirit to his Father shows it was.

He was the firstborn from the dead and everyone who trusts in him has the same victory over death and can face it without fear or dread. The Apostle Paul, who wrote many of the books in the New Testament, could say 'O death, where is your victory? O death, where is your sting?' (1 Corinthians 15:55). Christians can face death with confidence because Jesus Christ has conquered it.

Christians can therefore die well. Luther Rees, who was a famous preacher in Wales in the 1950s and 1960s, was dying and losing consciousness. His wife was holding his hand and his daughter-in-law said to him, 'Dad, you don't know who's holding your hand do you?' 'Yes', he said, 'and he'll never let it go!'

Death, judgement, eternity are all awesome. But these are things Christians should look forward to. To fall into the hands of the living God is a terrifying thing (Hebrews 10:31) but if we are in Christ we have nothing to fear. We can bow our heads and confidently trust our souls to God.

The White House is closed to the American public and protected by the United States Secret Service. Every road within a 300-yard radius is closed, a ten feet high gate circles the grounds, snipers are posted on most roofs, and it is one of the only buildings in the whole world to have its very own paramilitary army protecting it.

Not only this but if you wanted to try and land a helicopter there or jump the gate, surface to air missile launchers stationed around the site would shoot you down—if you were an unauthorised guest.

One day, a little boy, walked through the gates, smiled at the security guards and carried on across the grass. As he walked he saluted the army officers and skipped towards the west wing doors. When he reached the door, he knocked, then flung open the doors impatiently.

Running straight past the registration desk he began to quicken his pace towards the president's private office. He went past guard after guard after guard until he reached the door to the President of the United States main office door.

Outside stood two guards six feet four inches of muscle and gun with sun glasses to match. They looked at the boy, the boy looked back …

In a hurry with no time to waste, he pushed open the doors, and there before him stood the president of the United States, John F Kennedy. The president looked up from his desk and said …

'Son! Where have you been? I've been looking forward to seeing you.'

The little boys name was Jack Kennedy, the son of J.F. Kennedy the president.

One day, unless Jesus comes back first, I will die. I will leave this life and enter eternity and stand before a holy God. As a sinner with a bad record it could be, should be, a terrifying prospect. But because I am in Christ, when I breathe my last I can totally trust God, as my Father, to receive my spirit. When I close my eyes for the last time in this world and open them in the world to come, I will see God and he will say, 'Son, I have been looking forward to seeing you!'

An earthquake

Christ's death was accompanied by miracles. One of these was an earthquake and the rocks split. This caused the centurion and the other soldiers to be afraid (Matthew 27:54).

But this was just a taster of what will be like when Christ comes to the earth for a second time—known as the Second Coming. The first time he came Jesus came to be the Saviour and came quietly to humble surroundings. The second time he will come as the judge of the whole world (Acts 17:31). 1 Thessalonians 4:16 says, 'the Lord himself will descend from heaven with a cry of command, with the voice of an archangel, and with the sound of the trumpet of God'.

When Jesus comes a second time he will come with his angels in great glory (Matthew 24:30, 31). The trumpet will blast and summon everyone to judgement. Every eye will see him (Revelation 1:7). People will be separated into two groups. Those who trust Christ and those who do not. Those who trust him will be taken into Heaven whereas those who don't will be condemned to Hell forever.

Following the Lord Jesus Christ's return to this world, he will be sat on a great white throne. All the dead, the great and the small, will stand before this throne (Revelation 20:12).

As we are standing there, the books will be opened and the records of the life of every person will be read out. The book of life will also be opened containing the names of all believers.

Imagine a person on that day who has not trusted Christ. They stand before this great white throne and everything in their lives has been recorded.

The person's turn will come and God will say, 'review his life'. It will start from when he was a baby 'For nothing is hidden except to be made manifest' (Mark 4:22). It will show him as a teenager and then as a man. He will have to give an account of every word he's spoken (Matthew 12:36). The gossip he indulged in, the lies he told and lived, angry outbursts, unkind words and foul language. Every impure or lustful thought he's had will be shown (Matthew 5:28). 'For nothing is covered that will not be revealed, or hidden that will not be known' (Matthew 10:26). This person has heard the gospel and has been offered Jesus Christ as his saviour but he rejected him because he wasn't interested. He was too busy. The cost was too great and he didn't want to give up his sin. As he stands before this great white throne, he realises he must have been insane and it dawns upon him that it's all too late, and he's guilty, without Christ and damned forever! God commands the book of life to be opened and an angel says, 'his name does not appear, Lord'. Then he hears the most chilling words anybody will ever hear, 'Depart from me, you cursed, into the eternal fire prepared for the devil and his angels' (Matthew 25:41). And he shall go away into everlasting punishment (Matthew 25:46). Visualise it! Imagine it! Sent to Hell forever!

If the earthquake on Golgotha frightened these hardy soldiers, it is unimaginable the fear people will experience when that trumpet is blasted and Christ returns to judge the world. Christ says the sun will be darkened, and the moon will not give its light; the stars will fall from heaven and the powers of the heavens will be shaken. Men's hearts will fail them for fear (Luke 21:26) and people will run to the hills and want the mountains to cover them (Luke 23:30).

Dead people walk around Jerusalem

Another miracle that took place at Calvary was the bodies of some of the saints (Christians) who had fallen asleep were raised. They were raised the moment of Christ's death and appeared to people in Jerusalem on the Sunday morning. Where they went in between we don't know. But they appeared to many on that first Easter morning (Matthew 27:53). Nothing more is said about these people other than what is said here. Evidently they were given glorified bodies, like that of the Lord Jesus after he had risen from the dead (see Chapter 18 of this book). It would be unlikely they remained on earth for long, just enough to establish the reality of the miracle and then no doubt they ascended to glory. It was a kind of foretaste of what will happen when Christ returns to this world for a second time (1 Thessalonians 4:16).

These bodies being brought back to life and appearing to many in Jerusalem was a powerful sign that Christ's death guarantees the resurrection of the dead and our eternal life in heaven with him (see Chapter 9 of this book).

We considered a moment ago a person who has not trusted Christ. Now consider a person who has. Just as much of a sinner as the first one but he repented of his sin and put his trust in the Lord Jesus Christ. He would say, 'For me to live is Christ and to die is gain' (Philippians 1:21). As he stands before this great white throne he has got nothing to answer for because Jesus Christ has taken all his sin and guilt and clothed him with his own righteousness. He stands there as if he's never done a thing wrong. More than that, he stands before that throne as if he was as good as Christ himself! He's got nothing to fear. The book of life is opened and his name is found. It is unimaginable, the eternal, never-ending joy he is about to enter. 'As it is written, eye hath not seen, nor ear heard, neither have entered into the heart of man, the things which God hath prepared for them that love him' (1 Corinthians 2:9 AV).

Confirmed dead

The normal Roman practice was to leave crucified men and women on the cross until they died. Their bodies could have been hanging there to rot for days and for the vultures to eat.

In contrast, Jewish law insisted that no one should be left hanging over night (Deuteronomy 21:22, 23) especially on a Sabbath, even more so on a special Sabbath. The Jews had no interest in shortening Jesus' pain or time on the cross. They did not want to mitigate the punishment in the slightest. But at 6pm the Sabbath would begin and the Jews did not want the bodies hanging on the crosses when Sabbath began so they go to Pilate to ask if their legs could be broken and the bodies be taken away (John 19:31).

The soldiers would have come and with a hammer or club smashed the victims' legs. It was incredibly inhuman. Apart from the loss of blood and shock this prevented the victim from pushing with his legs to keep his chest cavity open. Strength from the arms was soon insufficient and asphyxia followed.

But when the soldiers came to Jesus they saw that he was already dead so they did not break his legs (John 19:33). He was confirmed dead. This again was a fulfilment of scripture that not one of his bones shall be broken (Exodus 12:46; Numbers 9:12). Christ was the Lamb of God that takes away the sin of the world (John 1:29). He was the lamb that all the Passover lambs were types and pictures of. In the same way that not one of the bones of the Passover lambs were broken, none of Christ's bones were broken either.

Blood and water

When they saw he was already dead they didn't break his legs but one of the soldiers pierced his side with a spear and immediately blood and water came out (John 19:34).

> The presence of any considerable serum and blood clot issuing after a spear wound as described above could only come from the heart or the pericardial sac. Authorities on the subject say that it is extremely rare, well-nigh impossible, for the normal heart muscle to rupture. But the Lord Jesus Christ did suffer as no man before or since has suffered. (Stuart Bergsma)

This real blood and real water that flowed from his side symbolises the effects of Christ's death. It fulfils fills what Zechariah the prophet said, 'they will look on him whom they have pierced' (John 19:37 cf. Zechariah 12:10). Zechariah goes on to say that, 'On that day there shall be a fountain opened for ... sin and uncleanness' (Zechariah 13:1).

This fountain was opened on Calvary. The blood of Jesus Christ is powerful. Perhaps you are reading this book and feel so dirty. Your mind is filthy, the way you speak is unclean and you have done some quite disgusting things. The blood of Jesus Christ can make you clean! (1 John 1:7).

And this blood progressively cleanses you from remaining sin (1 John 1:7 cf. Revelation 1:5b). The water and blood are not stagnant. They flow, so wash daily in this fountain. Your conscience may well accuse you but the blood of Jesus is more powerful than your conscience, so take your conscience to this fountain and wash it (Hebrews 9:14).

One day I will stand before God as my judge. On that awesome day when I stand before him, Jesus Christ will plead for me. He will stand with me and when the devil, the law, my conscience, my past and everyone who knows me will condemn me, he will say as it were: 'look back to before the sun, the moon and all the stars were made, that is when I set my love upon you. Look at those three crosses. On the middle one, I took all your sins upon myself and paid for every one of them! When you confessed your sins to me I was faithful and just and forgave you. When you called upon me I saved you. My blood covers all your iniquities.' Don't look at yourself; trust in the blood that flowed from his wounded side.

Rev. Vernon Higham, pastor of the Heath Evangelical Church in Cardiff, on more than one occasion referred to a lady who attended the Heath Evangelical Church in Cardiff in the 1980s. She had lived a particularly dirty life, but had started attending the Heath Church and realised her sinfulness and trusted the Lord Jesus Christ to save her. She would go back where she was staying with many other women who would taunt her that someone like her should never be going to church and that she could never be forgiven with her past. She felt hopeless and unclean. But she told Mr Higham that one night after a particularly bad evening, it was like the Lord Jesus Christ himself drew near to her and said 'in my sight you are a chaste virgin'.

So do what Elisha Albright Hoffman tells you to in his hymn,

Lay aside the garments that are stained by sin,
And be washed in the blood of the Lamb;
There's a fountain flowing for the soul unclean,
O be washed in the blood of the Lamb!

Surely this is the Son of God?

We have spent the last 7 chapters of this book at Golgotha and watched and listened to all that has gone on as the Lord Jesus Christ hung on that centre cross. Before we leave the scene let me ask you, what do you make of it all? John says that he saw it and that he is telling you the truth about these things that you may believe (John 19:35). So do you?

As we have seen there was a crowd who stood around the cross. Almost all of them there to mock and make fun. But by the end some changed.

One of these was the centurion. He was a perfect witness to all that happened because he would have been there the whole time. Matthew records that after the centurion who was overseeing the crucifixion saw all the things that had happened he said, 'Truly this was the Son of God' (Matthew 27:54). Luke records that he said, 'Certainly this was a righteous Man'. He no doubt said both.

This centurion would do 3 or 4 crucifixions a day. It would just be part of his daily routine. But this one was like no other. It was the only one he had ever left 'glorifying God' (Luke 23:47).

Everything that had happened convinced him that this was the Son of God. He could see from the way Christ conducted himself throughout that he was no criminal and had done nothing wrong. He was a righteous man. The miraculous events that accompanied Christ's death had caused him to fear. When Christ cried out with a loud voice, 'It is finished' and breathed his last, it caused him to sit up and take notice (Mark 15:39).

But it wasn't just the centurion who was affected by what he'd witnessed. Luke says the multitude in general was at least deeply impressed and returned to their homes smiting their breasts (Luke 23:48). They were probably all from Jerusalem and had no interest in Jesus at first but had just come to watch the execution. As we saw in Chapter 8 of this book, at first they were full of contempt and joked and mocked. But as events unfolded, instead of being entertained they were saddened. On the day of Pentecost when the Holy Spirit came in great power (see Chapter 23 of this book). 3000 people believed in Jesus in one day (Acts 2:41). In all likelihood many of those who believed were here at the cross. The crucifixion of Jesus had disturbed them and made them think.

Is that you? You have read about it and considered these things and it has left an impression. You are troubled about your sin and are beginning to see that your only hope is this Saviour. It is beginning to dawn on you that all the pain he went through and the shame he suffered was for you. I urge you, keep thinking, keep looking, keep considering until you say, 'surely this is the Son of God', and trust in his finished work!

15

Dead and buried

Matthew 27:57–61; Mark 15:42–47;
Luke 23:50–56; John 19:38–42

Dead

JESUS WAS DEFINITELY DEAD. IT WAS A LIFELESS CORPSE THAT WAS taken down from the cross between about 5:30 and 6:00 on that Friday afternoon. Mark tells us that Pilate was surprised to hear that Jesus should have already died. And summoning the centurion he asked him whether he was already dead. And when he learned from the centurion that he was dead, he granted the corpse to Joseph (Mark 15:44; John 19:38). Pilate, the centurion, the soldiers (Mark 15:44, 45; John 19:33) and the people we meet in this chapter, all confirm he was dead!

Buried

According to Josephus:

> Under Roman law the bodies of executed criminals were
> normally handed over to their next of kin but not so in the

case of sedition. They were left to the vultures, which was the culmination of indignity and shame. However, the Jews never refused to bury an executed criminal, but they did not allow them to be buried with their relatives. They provided a burial site for criminals just outside the city.

The Jewish authorities just wanted the body down from the cross because a body must not hang on a tree on the Sabbath, especially a special one like this particular one (John 19:31). This had to be done by 6pm as the Jewish Sabbath started from sundown to sundown.

Joseph of Arimathea

But who would do it? Criminals could possibly be buried in unmarked graves, be claimed by their families, or the soldiers would probably just take them down and throw their corpse onto the rubbish dump. But none of Jesus' disciples were there or his family. John had probably gone to bear the news and comfort Mary, the Lord's mother.

Onto the scene steps a man called Joseph of Arimathea. He is mentioned by all four Gospel writers but only in connection with the burial of the Lord Jesus. So who was he and why did he do this?

He was a rich man (Matthew 27:57) from a town called Arimathea which is about 15–20 miles from Jerusalem.

He was a respected member of the Sanhedrin, the Jewish ruling council (Mark 15:43; Luke 23:51) and he used his rank and influence to gain access to Pilate. He was a good and righteous man (Luke 23:50). He had not agreed to the decision or action of the Sanhedrin to put Jesus to death, (Luke) which means he must have stayed away from the Sanhedrin meeting because the vote was unanimous. They 'all' agreed. (Luke 22:70; Mark 14:64).

He was a disciple of Jesus but up until now, secretly, for fear of the Jews (John 19:38). He was frightened that he may be kicked off the council or even out of the Synagogue (John 7:13; 9:22; 20:19).

Like certain others (Luke 2:25; 36–38) he was constantly looking for the kingdom of God (Luke 23:51). He was eagerly waiting for the coming of the long promised Messiah; the one that he read of in the Old Testament and had been promised by God through the prophets. God was at work in Joseph's heart and he was beginning to see that this dead Galilean peasant was this promised Messiah. He saw in some way that when Christ was on earth, the Kingdom of God had come, that the kingdom of God wasn't a geographical kingdom (see chapter 23 of this book) but was spiritual in character; not so much a realm but a rule, set up in the hearts of all those who acknowledge the authority and Lordship of Christ. It would come in its fullness at the end of time when Christ returns to this world and there is a new heaven and a new earth (see chapter 9 of this book). It was all of this, not with real clarity or understanding at this stage, Joseph was constantly looking for.

As these things became more real and precious to Joseph, he took courage and went to Pilate and asked for the body (Mark 15:43). This was brave because he knew the Sanhedrin would find out about it.

I wonder if you are a secret disciple. You are realising more and more that Jesus Christ is God. That he is the only Saviour. You think about your sin and what it deserves. Then you think of what he did on Calvary to forgive you from all those sins and to save you from eternal Hell. You think about his invitation to come to him and find rest, (Matthew 11:28) that he will come to your heart and change you (Ezekiel 36:26). But you are held back by fear. Fear of what others will think. Fear of missing out. Fear of having to deny yourself (Matthew 16:24).

Like Joseph, take courage! Trust him. Do not be afraid (Deuteronomy 31:6; Isaiah 41:10). He will not put you to shame. He says that those who cling on to their lives will lose them, but those who give up their lives will keep them (Luke 17:33). He has come to give life (John 10:10). Life as it should be lived. Real contentment. Real happiness. Real peace. While he doesn't promise that you will not face persecution (2 Timothy 3:12), that you will not have to deny yourself and there will not be a cost (Luke 14:28), he has promised that he will never leave you or forsake you (Deuteronomy 31:6; Joshua 1:5).

Jesus will never put you in a situation that is too much for you to bear (2 Corinthians 12:9). Whatever you have to go through, he will draw near to you.

A Christian man was in the Twin Towers on 9/11 when the terrorist attacks took place. Witnesses who survived say that as people were desperately trying to escape, and panic and fear took hold of everyone, this man, realising that he wasn't going to make it out alive, calmly walked down the stairs and was heard saying to himself, 'Yea though I walk through the valley of the shadow of death, I will fear no evil for thou art with me' (Psalm 23:4 AV). It wasn't the case that this man was naturally braver thank those around him, but his Saviour had drawn near to him and all fear had gone.

People worry that they won't have the courage to face persecution. But trust him that if persecution comes your way he will give you the grace to endure it. You don't need grace for that now because you are not being persecuted. But when it comes he will be with you and give you all the strength you need.

Houghton (1991, p.17, 18) gives examples of Christian martyrs. He tells of Ignatius who was thrown to the wild beasts because of his faith in Jesus. Face to face with death Ignatius of Antioch said, 'I am God's grain, to be ground between the teeth of wild beasts, so that I may become a holy loaf for the Lord'. Soon after the lions were loosed upon him nothing was left but a few gnawed bones. When his friend came to collect his bones for burial they knew that Ignatius 'was with Christ which is far better' (Philippians 1:23).

Another example is Polycarp of Smyrna who refused to say that

Caesar was Lord and was sentenced to death by the Roman consul. He was threatened with wild beasts and with fire but Polycarp remained faithful to the Lord Jesus. He is reported to have said,

> Eighty and six years have I served Christ and he has done me no wrong; how can I blaspheme my king who has saved me? You threaten the fire that burns for an hour and then is quenched; but you know not of the fire of eternal punishment. Bring what you will.

When the torch was applied to the wood, and smoke and flames encircled him, he thanked God for being deemed worthy to receive the crown of martyrdom. It is recorded that the multitude who were watching marvelled at the great difference between Christians and non-Christians.

You must weigh things up. Moses, who was a prince in Egypt, gave it all up. He refused to be called the son of Pharaoh's daughter, choosing rather to be mistreated with the people of God than to enjoy the fleeting pleasures of sin. He considered the reproach of Christ greater wealth than the treasures of Egypt, for he was looking to the reward. By faith he left Egypt not being afraid of the anger of the king for he endured as seeing him who is invisible (Hebrews 11:24–27). The apostle Paul says, 'I count everything as loss because of the surpassing worth of knowing Christ Jesus my Lord. For his sake I have suffered the loss of all things and count them as rubbish in order that I may gain Christ' (Philippians 3:8, 9).

Besides, the Bible says 'do not fear them who can destroy the body but rather fear him who can destroy both your body and soul in hell'. Jesus says of anyone who is ashamed of him now he will be ashamed of them when he comes again (Luke 9:26). Nail your colours to the mast. Stand up and be counted for the Lord Jesus.

A man became a Christian who had previously been 'one of the boys'. He worked in a garage with other typical lads. When he told the boys he worked with that he had become a Christian, they laughed at him and said he would never be able to keep it up and that he would soon be swearing and laughing at dirty jokes and looking at the magazines he used to. One day they grabbed hold of him and pinned him down. Two held his legs and two held his arms while the others got a dirty magazine and put it in front of his eyes. He closed his eyes tight. Afterwards, he was asked what he was thinking of as all of this was going on. He said he was thanking God that he was able to suffer a little for the one who for him had suffered so much.

Daley Thompson was a Gold Medallist in the Los Angeles Olympics in 1984: His event was the Decathlon. As I am sure you know the Decathlon is made up of ten events, track and field. After the first 5 events on day one, things hadn't gone as well as he would have liked. The interviewer asked him what he was going to do on day two to ensure he got the gold medal. Daley Thompson looked down the camera and said 'whatever it takes!'

When fear sets in, or the thought of what other people might say, or being left out, or even persecution, think about these things in the light of eternity and say I'll do, 'whatever it takes'.

And so Joseph took him down from the cross. He pulled the nails out of Jesus' hands and feet and unloosed the ropes. Then he wrapped the sacred body in a clean linen cloth and rapidly carried it to the rock-hewn tomb in the garden close by.

Nicodemus

But Joseph did not act alone. A man called Nicodemus also assisted.

We first meet Nicodemus in John 3: Like Joseph, he had an important position being a ruler of the Jews. He was a member of the Sanhedrin and John would have known Nicodemus and Joseph as prominent Jews.

Nicodemus was a scribe, which is a professional student, teacher and interpreter of the law. In fact he was 'the teacher in Israel'

(John 3:10). He was also a Pharisee. The Pharisees were right on many points of doctrine but they externalised religion. It was all about works; about what a person does to be right with God.

He first came to Jesus by night. This ruler wanted to know in effect how a person could be right with God. Jesus was amazed that 'the teacher' in Israel didn't understand these things. The impression is that Nicodemus knew he was missing something and just hoped Christ could tell him the bits he needed to add. But the Lord Jesus cuts across all his works and religion and tells him that he must be born again (John 3:3). Maybe you are a religious person. You do a lot of good works. You are moral and upright and think these things hold you in good stead before God. But good works and religion, however sincere you are, will not make you right with God. Like Nicodemus, you must be born again.

The famous evangelist, George Whitefield almost always preached on the text, 'You must be born again'. When someone asked him why he always preached on 'you must be born again', he replied, 'because you must be born again'.

Theologians call being born again, regeneration. Regeneration is the work of the Holy Spirit and is essential in a person becoming a Christian. You cannot be a Christian unless the Holy Spirit does a work in your heart. Only the Holy Spirit can produce a spiritual change in a person. The Bible says that we are all 'dead in the trespasses and sins' (Ephesians 2:1). Only the Holy Spirit can give us life. This is called regeneration. According to Packer (1994, p.157) regeneration is 'God renovating the heart, the core of a person's being, by implanting a new principle of desire, purpose and action.' It is a work which only God the Holy Spirit can do. Without his enabling we would have no interest in God and would never put our faith in Jesus Christ or believe the gospel.

The first thing the Holy Spirit does, that we are aware of, is to convict us of our sin and show us our need to be saved. He then points us to Jesus Christ and gives us the faith to believe in him. After we become Christians the Holy Spirit lives within us and makes Jesus Christ more and more real to us and gives us a greater assurance of our faith. He produces within us the fruit of the Spirit which is love, joy, peace, patience, kindness, goodness, faithfulness, gentleness and self-control (Galatians 5:22). As we read our Bible, pray and seek to live lives which please God, this fruit is cultivated and grows (John 15:1–7).

Why do people have no interest in God and find these things irrelevant? Because they haven't been born again. If that is you, pray that the Holy Spirit will give you the faith to believe in the Lord Jesus and the strength to live for him, and that you will have a desire to get to know him and love him more and more.

When Nicodemus first came to Jesus, he came to by night. He didn't want to be seen, plus the night symbolised the darkness Nicodemus was in. But here he has been born again and is stepping out of the darkness into the light. In John 7:50–52 we see Nicodemus tentatively speaking up for the Lord Jesus but here, like Joseph, his faith is out in the open.

Both these men had come to trust the Saviour and wanted to honour the one they had come to love

Nicodemus and Joseph must have worked in collaboration and agreed beforehand what they were going to do. Joseph sought permission from Pilate, took the body down from the cross and provided the tomb and linen cloth. The linen was wound around the body limb by limb as was the custom of the Jews (John 19:40), whereas Nicodemus came bringing a mixture of myrrh and aloes. He brought 100 litres, which is a little less than the 75 pounds specified by the NIV and ESV (John 19:39). The mixtures of myrrh and aloes were laid under and around the body. Inside the tomb the hasty embalmment took place

The tomb

The site of the tomb is probably not the garden tomb where

tourists are directed, even though that is probably what the tomb would have looked like.

The tomb where they laid him was close to Golgotha (John 19:42). It was in a garden (John 19:41) and was new, no one else had ever been laid in it (John 19:41). The tomb was not a natural cave but had been cut out of a rock (Mark). Joseph had prepared this tomb for himself (Matthew 27:60) which fulfils the prophecy of Isaiah that he will be 'with a rich man in his death' (Isaiah 53:9). The entrance to the tomb must have been low because Mary stooped to look in (John 20:11) and Peter stooped when he went in (John 20:5; Luke 24:12).

We know that on the Saturday morning a seal was affixed to the stone at the request of the Sanhedrin (Matthew 27:66); that is a cord with clay or wax on which a seal has been impressed. Importantly, the tomb was safe and secure.

The women

Witnessing everything were the women who had come up with Jesus from Galilee. Matthew says that Mary Magdalene and the other Mary sat opposite the tomb (Matthew 27:61). The other Mary must have been the mother of James and Joses (Mark 15:47). They had followed Joseph, maybe even helped him, and saw exactly where the tomb was, how the body was laid and observed Joseph roll the stone across the entrance of the tomb (Mark 15:46, 47).

They then returned to where they were staying and prepared spices and ointments (Luke 23:56). The intention was that after resting on the Sabbath according to the commandment (Luke 23:56) they would come early on the Sunday morning to anoint the body properly.

16

He's alive!

(Matthew 28:1–15; cf. Mark 16:1–8;
Luke 24:1–12; John 20:1)

1. A hopeless group of sad, pathetic, people

I WONDER HOW YOU ARE FEELING AS YOU START TO READ THIS chapter. What state are you in? Maybe you are sad. Perhaps there are things that are troubling you. There could be something which is frightening you. You may feel abandoned. It could be that you've really messed up and you don't know how you will ever get out of the situation you are in. Or it might well be that you have read this book so far and still don't believe.

Well, this was exactly how the followers of Jesus were feeling early on this first Easter Sunday morning. They were in a terrible condition. They felt sad, troubled, frightened and abandoned. Some had really messed up and all of them were in a state of unbelief. They were a group of sad, pathetic people.

Sad

On Friday evening the group of faithful women who had stood by Jesus' cross, watched Joseph of Arimathea take Jesus down from the cross and then followed Nicodemus and Joseph to the tomb where they laid the Lord Jesus. The women then returned to where they were staying to prepare spices and ointments. They rested on the Sabbath according to the commandment and then planned on returning to the tomb early on the Sunday morning to anoint Jesus' body properly. Nicodemus and Joseph of Arimathea had already bound the body in linen and anointed it with about 75 pounds of myrrh and aloes but it was all done rather hurriedly because they had to get it all finished before the Sabbath. So after the Sabbath had passed, the women wanted to anoint the body properly to show their love for Jesus (Mark 16:1).

Troubled

But not only were they sad, they were also troubled. These women wanted to anoint his body but didn't know how they were going to get to the body because of the big stone that was in the way. The stone was a major problem (Mark 16:3). It would have been like a large silver dollar or two-pound coin and fitted into a groove of the tomb where the body laid. It would have been heavy and very difficult to move.

Frightened

They were also frightened. The disciples were behind locked doors. They were frightened about what the Jewish authorities might do to them (John 20:19). Their leader had gone and they were petrified.

Abandoned

They had been abandoned. Judas who had been one of them for three years had betrayed their Lord and had now killed himself.

Messed up

One of the disciples in particular had really messed up. After making boasts and saying how even if everyone else let Jesus down he wouldn't, Peter denied even knowing him three times. He would have felt a real failure and loser. But none of the disciples had clothed themselves in glory. Nearly all of them had scarpered at the first sign of trouble.

Unbelief

All of them on this Sunday morning were in a state of unbelief. They all thought they had been following a dead Galilean carpenter! The women, despite being loyal and full of love for Jesus, had no understanding nor had come to see the impact, power and full effect of who this Jesus really was.

2. An empty tomb (Matthew 28:6) and a risen Saviour (Matthew 28:9)

But an empty tomb and a risen Saviour was about to change all of that.

Resurrection appearances

We shall see over the next few chapters that Jesus appeared many times after his resurrection to numerous people. On this Easter Sunday morning he appeared at first to Mary Magdalene and later that day he appeared to two disciples on the road from Jerusalem to Emmaus (Luke 24:13–33), then to Peter (Luke 24:34). During the same evening he appeared to ten of the disciples who were gathered in the upper room (Luke 23:36ff; John 2019–23). A week later he appeared to the eleven disciples; this time including Thomas (John 20:24–29). He also appeared to his brother James, 500 people all at once (1 Corinthians 15:6) and then a group of seven disciples when they were out fishing on the Sea of Galilee (John 21). His final appearance was on the Mount of Olives near Jerusalem when he ascended back to Heaven (Luke 24:50–53; Acts 1:1–11).

The women go to the tomb

But in this chapter we will focus on the group of women whom we met in Chapter 11, and look in particular at whether Jesus did actually rise from the dead and all that that means.

He appeared to these women soon after he appeared to Mary Magdalene. Their account is recorded in Matthew 28:1–15, Mark 16:1–8, Luke 24:1–12 and John 20:1. We will put the accounts together to get the fullest picture of what happened.

What they saw

Before the women arrived at the tomb there had been a violent earthquake, for an angel of the Lord came down from heaven, stepped forward, rolled the stone away and was sitting on it. The appearance of the angel was like lightning and his clothes as white as snow. For fear of him the guards trembled and became like dead men (Matthew 28:2–4).

As has already been mentioned, the women, as they walked to the tomb, were wondering how they were going to move the stone but looking up they saw that the stone had been rolled back (Mark 16:3, 4).

They entered the tomb and did not find the body of Jesus. While they were perplexed about this, they saw two men standing by them in dazzling apparel. And they were afraid and bowed their faces to the ground (Luke 24:2–5). Mark says they saw a young man sitting on the right side dressed in a white robe and they were alarmed (Mark 16:5). Mark and Luke are describing angels in human terms. There were at least two angels, probably one by the head and one at the foot of where Jesus would have laid.

One of the angels said to the women 'do not be afraid' (Matthew 28:5). 'Why do you seek the living among the dead?' (Luke 24:5). He is not here he has risen (Matthew 28:6). Remember how he told you in Galilee that he must be delivered into the hands of sinful men and be crucified and on the third day rise (Luke 24:6, 7). Come see the place (Mark 16:5). Matthew records that the angel actually said 'come take a closer look' (Matthew 28:6).

The angels then told them, 'Go quickly tell the disciples (and Peter, Mark 16:7) and look he is going ahead of you into Galilee; there you shall see him (Matthew 28:7) just as he told you' (Mark 16:7).

So the women departed from the tomb with fear and great joy and ran to tell the disciples (Matthew 28:8). By now trembling and astonishment had seized them (Mark 16:8).

And, as they were on their way back, Jesus himself met them and said 'Greetings'. And they came up and took hold of his feet and worshipped him (Matthew 28:9).

Then Jesus said to them, 'Do not be afraid, go and tell my brothers to go to Galilee and there they will see me' (Matthew 28:10). He would appear to them when they were back in the quiet security of familiar Galilee for further conversation and instruction.

3: But is it true?

So that is what the gospel writers say the women saw. The big question is, 'is it true?'

Problems

There are those who say it can't be because there are some apparent discrepancies between the different accounts. These concern in particular the angels, the women and the time of day.

As far as the angels are concerned, in some of the accounts there is one angel and in others there are two. But this shouldn't really concern us. When only one angel is mentioned it is because that angel is the spokesperson and is more prominent than his associate and may be referred to without mention of the others.

Some also point out that Matthew, Mark and Luke record the angels sitting, standing and saying different things. But again this isn't really a problem. It all shows different aspects of the story and record different points of interest.

But not only do the angels cause problems for some people, *the women* do as well. They argue that there are differences in the names of the women who went to tomb early in the morning. Matthew says there were two Marys—Mary Magdalene and the other Mary (Matthew 28:1). Mark says Mary Magdalene and Mary the mother of James, and Salome (Mark 16:1). Luke says that Mary Magdalene and Joanna and Mary the mother of James and the other women went to the tomb (Luke 24:10). John records only

Mary Magdalene but says 'we' which suggests that she was not alone (John 20:1)

The other aspect that causes problems is the *time of day* they arrived at the tomb. Matthew says it took place towards the dawn of the first day of the week (Matthew 28:1). Mark says it was 'very early on the first day of the week when the sun had risen' (Mark 16:2). Luke says it was 'at early dawn' (Luke 24:1) and John says 'it was still dark' (John 20:1)

Solution

So how do we make sense of all this? Are the critics right? Are there inconsistencies which undermine the whole thing? Not at all! As we have already said, that the Bible is without error does not mean it is without difficulties. But it is our responsibility as good students of the Bible to work out these problems.

One possibility is it may have been two parties of women that started out from different places to meet at the tomb. This could account for the slight differences in the details of what they saw and heard at the grave

Even though we cannot be certain, it is plausible that as we put it all together we find that on that first Easter Sunday morning, when it was still dark, at least five women set out for the tomb; Mary Magdalene mentioned by all four Gospels; Mary the mother of James; Salome, Joanna, and other women (which fits in with Luke's reference to other women).

They were going there to anoint Jesus' body. The difficulty they faced was that the tomb had been sealed by a large stone and they had no idea how they could move it.

As they travel it begins to lighten so when they finally draw close to the tomb, probably as they turned the path, they see the stone has been moved. This was something they were not expecting so although it suits their purpose they are nevertheless upset and uncertain what to do.

The open tomb and the fact that the stone had moved distressed Mary and the other ladies. Robbing of graves was common at the time and it would appear they came to the conclusion that these robbers were at it again.

At this point it would seem they sent Mary Magdalene (and possibly some of the other women) back to tell Peter and John about the new development which John himself records, although he doesn't mention the presence of the other women (John 20:2). Possibly, Peter and John each had his own home in Jerusalem (John 19:27; 20:10), perhaps adjoining quarters.

As the women wait for Mary Magdalene to come back the morning grows lighter. Eventually, possibly emboldened by daybreak, the women go forward. Now they see the angels and are sent back by them into the city to tell the other disciples (Matthew 28:5–7; Mark 16:5–7; Luke 24:4–7). They probably returned by a different road to the one Peter and John and Mary Magdalene used on their way to the tomb.

In the meantime, Mary Magdalene found Peter and John who immediately left her behind in their run to the tomb. John arrives at the tomb first (John 20:4) but Peter actually goes in first (John 20:6). As we shall see in the next chapter, John records their view of the grave clothes and points out that it was at this moment that he personally believed (John 20:3–9). Peter and John then left immediately.

Finally, Mary Magdalene arrives back at the tomb again and is the first to see Jesus (John 20:11–18 cf. Mark 16:9).

On the same day, presumably within minutes of his appearance to Mary Magdalene, Jesus appeared to some of the other women as they are returning from the tomb.

There are no inconsistencies, just differences, and this is because the accounts are independent. We should see them as incidents in different newspapers. The main facts are the same but some details different. According to Boice (p.352), 'The accounts evidence a fundamental honesty and accuracy through what we can only call their natural simplicity.'

If the accounts were fictitious these problems would have been eliminated and it would have all been slick and easy. The fact that there are these problems shows the accounts are authentic.

Theories

But as well as people highlighting apparent problems, they also come up with theories about what really happened.

He wasn't really dead
They argue he wasn't really dead when he was taken down from the cross and he simply revived in a cold tomb.

However this really doesn't stand up. Since it was the day of preparation and so that the bodies wouldn't remain on the cross on the Sabbath, the Jews asked Pilate that their legs be broken so that they might be taken away. So the soldiers came and broke the legs of the first criminal and of the other but when they came to Jesus and saw that he was already dead they did not break his legs. But one of the soldiers pierced his side with a spear and at once there came out blood and water (John 19:31–34). As we saw in the previous chapter, Mark tells us, 'Pilate was surprised to hear that Jesus should have already died. And summoning the centurion he asked him whether he was already dead. And when he learned from the centurion that he was dead, he granted the corpse to Joseph' (Mark 15:44). Pilate, the centurion and the soldiers all confirm he was dead!

Wrong tomb
Another theory is that the women went to the wrong tomb. But surely this is clutching at straws as the women saw where Joseph of Arimathea laid him (Luke 23:55). They watched closely as Jesus was laid in the tomb.

Disciples stole his body
A third theory is that the disciples came and stole his body. But

this was impossible as there was no way out. There were soldiers guarding the tomb (Matthew 27:62–66). The Jewish leaders had gone to great lengths to secure this.

Early on the Saturday morning, two groups of the Sanhedrin— the chief priests and the Pharisees gathered before Pilate. The day before, they wouldn't enter Pilate's court because they didn't want to make themselves unclean. They thought he was a Gentile dog but they need him now, so they gather around him and address him as 'Sir'.

The Pharisees believed in the afterlife and knew the resurrection was a possibility. They say to Pilate that they remembered how the deceiver said he would rise from the dead after three days. The problem was they had the chief priests with them who were Sadducees and they didn't, so they had to play the power card. They make the point that if the people think that he has risen from the dead it will be worse than it was before! Unless we stamp this down we'll lose our power. They ask Pilate, therefore, to order the tomb to be secure until the third day in case his disciples go and steal him away and tell the people 'He has risen from the dead'.

And so Pilate orders the guard to make the tomb as secure as they can. To make it secure they sealed it. They took twine or cord, covered it with pitch or clay and attached it to the front of the tomb so they would know in a minute if someone had tampered with it.

Then they took a guard of soldiers to keep permanent surveillance of the scene. This would have been between 12 and 60 soldiers. The soldiers would have thought it was the easiest task they had ever been assigned. Go to a garden and guard a tomb! They would not be expecting anything to happen. Just sit in a quiet garden for a day or two. But it was an impossible task. They might just as well have been told to go outside and stop the sun from rising.

After Jesus rose from the dead some of the guards hurry over to the chief priests to report what had happened (Matthew 28:11, 12). They didn't all go. They had been scattered in all directions and some would have been too scared to face the authorities. The chief priests quickly assemble with the elders and decide what to do next. They bribe the soldiers to spread the rumour that Jesus' disciples had come and stolen the body while they slept, promising that if news of them sleeping while they stole the body reached Pilate, they'd intercede for them (Matthew 28:14).

By the time Matthew wrote his Gospel, this story had been widely spread. Justin Martyr (AD 114–165) in his Dialogue with Trypho writes:

> After you learned that he rose from the dead you have sent chosen and ordained men throughout the whole world and proclaim that a godless and lawless heresy had sprung from one Jesus, a Galilean deceiver … whose disciples stole him by night from the tomb.

But all of this shows the utter foolishness of unbelief. We would rather believe that between 12 and 60 well trained hardy Roman soldiers slept while 11 Galilean fishermen got past them, moved a big stone, unwrapped the body of Jesus, folded up the grave clothes and then walked out of the tomb carrying the body. They must have been the best sleepers ever! And where their story really falls down is if you asked them what happened they'd say that while they were sleeping his disciples came and stole the body, you'd have to say back to them, 'if you were sleeping, how do you know what happened!'

The theory of the disciples coming and stealing the body is impossible.

Compelling evidence

As well as being able to blow apart all the theories and answer all the seeming inconstancies, there is also other compelling evidence to prove it must be true.

Women

If his disciples had made it all up they would never have chosen women to be the first to have seen him. In first century Israel it was impossible for women to give testimony in court because their word couldn't be trusted. If someone was going to make something up the first rule would be, 'Don't use women as witnesses'.

Embellished

Furthermore, if they had made it up surely they would have embellished the story. They would have described the resurrection itself, the descent of the angel, the moving the stone, the appearance of the Lord from within the recess of the tomb. The apocryphal gospels (the gospels according to Hebrews, Peter, Acts of Pilate and others) contain elements of how Jesus appeared to Pilate and confounded him, or how he appeared to Caiaphas and other members of the Jewish Sanhedrin. But these Gospel writers in God's Word don't include any of these 'juicy' bits. Why? Because either they didn't happen or else the writers didn't witness them. The Gospels do not describe the resurrection because no one actually witnessed it, even though it would have made good copy. They just say what they saw.

Disciples

Another compelling argument is the effect it had on the disciples. How did they go from being paralysed with fear behind locked doors, too scared to come out, to boldly preaching on the streets of Jerusalem? The disciples who scarpered at the first sign of trouble would not have died for what they knew was a fabrication.

Plus it wasn't in their minds that he could rise from the dead. Even after the women told the 11 disciples and the rest of the followers of Jesus in the locality, the males still thought the story 'nonsense' (NEB) and they didn't believe them (Luke 24:10, 11). Peter, even when he saw the empty tomb, did not yet believe in the resurrection for he went home 'marveling at what had happened' (Luke 24:12). As the news begun to spread, by and large it was not accepted as true (Mark 16:13; Luke 24:22–25). According to Morris (p.354)

> The apostles were not men poised on the brink of belief and needing only the shadow of an excuse before launching forth into a proclamation of resurrection. They were utterly sceptical. Clearly irrefutable evidence was needed to convince these sceptics.

Body

But the most compelling argument, one that could have put all this to bed in the first century, is the body. If there was a body where was it? The fact is that the body will never be found.

A Hindu and a Christian were travelling together on a boat. As they sailed past a certain place the Hindu turned to the Christian and said, 'Over there is buried the bones of my Saviour'. The Christian replied, 'If you could find the bones of my Saviour, he wouldn't be my Saviour!'

4: So what does all this mean?

Alive

The first thing it means is that Jesus Christ is alive. The angel says to the women, 'Why do you seek the living among the dead?' (Luke 24:5). He is alive! According to DeYoung (2010, p. 91), 'Easter is about a divine Galilean whose heart pumped blood again, whose lungs filled with oxygen again, and whose synapses started firing again.'

The women had gone to a place but they had ended up meeting the person. So many people go to church on Sundays and think they are just going to a place. Others read the Bible and think they are just picking up a book. But in this place and behind this book is a person. Christians are not people who are following someone who lived 2000 years ago. Our Saviour is a living Saviour.

Change

No thinking person really asks is it true anymore. No one buys the theories that he fainted and was resuscitated or the disciples stole him.

Christianity stands up to rigorous investigation. The real reason people don't believe it is because they haven't done the rigorous investigation. But let me press upon you the importance of doing the investigation. Your eternal destiny hangs on it.

But the difficulty in doing the investigation is that within us there are deep layers of prejudice. I don't want it to be true because I will have to change the way I live my life.

People who smoke know it damages their health and can kill them. It is not that they don't believe that, it is just that they enjoy smoking too much. It is not that people don't believe the resurrection happened but they don't want to believe it because of what it means to believe it.

Imagine being a judge and suddenly a case comes before you to do with a company in which you own stock. You can't rule in the case because you cannot be objective. If the case goes against you, you stand to lose a lot of money. It is the same with the resurrection. If the resurrection is true my whole life has to change.

Huxley (1937) said he had motives for not wanting the world to have meaning because it allows the philosopher to do what he wants. It is essentially an instrument of sexual and political liberation—he wants to be able to do his own things.

The Jewish leaders paid the soldiers dearly to spread the word that Jesus' disciples had stolen the body. Anything so that it isn't true! Similarly, people today pay dearly not to have to believe in a resurrected Christ. They have a vested interest for it not to be true. If it is, it changes their whole life. Unbelief is no an intellectual problem, but a moral one.

Fear

But the inescapable fact is that we all must die and stand before Him. We can pretend it isn't going to happen; we can fill our lives with other things so that we don't have to think about it but the reality is that one day I will leave this world and stand before this risen Saviour.

This is a terrifying thought for anyone who doesn't know him as their Saviour. This is seen in the terror which Christ's enemies felt when he rose from the dead. These hardy Roman soldiers shook with fear and became as dead men (Matthew 28:4). When the Angel of the Lord rolled back the stone the guards were so frightened by what they saw, especially by the look and attitude of the heavenly power in the angel, that they were not just merely paralyzed with fear but completely unconscious, totally traumatized by what they had seen.

These men just caught a glimpse of the terror of the Lord. Today we too can get a glimpse of the power and majesty and terror of God. God still speaks through earthquakes and disasters to let people know he is God and to be feared. C.S. Lewis said that suffering was God's megaphone to rouse a sleepy world. Thunderstorms, volcanoes, tsunamis, earthquakes, disasters can cause so much devastation and fear. But imagine what it will be like when the world ends and we have to face God at the judgement.

The judgement of God and Hell awaits everyone who does not trust in the only saviour of mankind, Jesus Christ. In the twenty-first century even as Bible believing Christians we have tried to sanitise Hell and cover it up as some kind of embarrassing family secret, but Hell is as real and terrifying today as it has always been. As you sit reading this book wherever you may be, there are people who once walked this earth and lived and breathed like you, but now find themselves in torment in Hell.

Revelation 6:12–17 symbolically describes the physical catastrophes which will take place at the end of the world when unbelievers face the wrath of God. At this time there will be an earthquake, the sun will become black, the moon become like blood and stars will fall from the sky. It will be terrifying for everyone who is not trusting in Jesus Christ. The kings of the earth, princes, great men, commanders, the rich, the strong, slaves and the free, in fact every kind of person will be so afraid that they will try to hide in caves and want the mountains to fall on them. The question will go out 'who can stand?' (v.17).

Forgiven

The Father and Son are involved in the resurrection. When Christ rose from the dead, it was God's declaration of approval of Christ's work. On the cross Christ cried out, 'It is finished' and the resurrection shows that it is.

The bottom line is, if he is not alive our faith is a waste of time and our sins have not been forgiven. But the resurrection confirms the efficacy of his death. It shows that what he was doing on the cross was successful. The gospel emphasises the cross because there the victory was accomplished. Paul says, 'I decided to know nothing among you except Jesus Christ and him crucified' (1 Corinthians 2:2). He glories in the cross (Galatians 6:14). But the resurrection is the confirmation that the cross was successful. It has brought us an assurance that our sins are forgiven.

The angels say to the women, 'Do not be afraid' (Matthew 28:5). Maybe that is a message for you as you read this book. You are worried that you are too bad to be forgiven. There is that one sin that haunts you. You've got secret sins that keep you awake at night. You know how dirty and guilty you are and can't imagine that you will ever be allowed into Heaven. You feel God stands over you in anger. But if you are trusting in Jesus Christ, his resurrection shows that your sins are forgiven.

Christian you have no need to fear on the last day. Your sins, which are many, have been forgiven (Luke 7:47). If you are trusting Jesus Christ, you are in Christ and so it is as if Christ's death, resurrection and life are your death, resurrection and life. When Jesus perfectly obeyed God for his whole life, God thought of us as having obeyed too. 'By one man's obedience the many will be made righteous' Romans 5:19: He was raised for our justification (Romans 4:25) which means it is 'just as if I'd never sinned'. I am spotless before him, totally clean.

Eternal life

Jesus rising from the dead guarantees eternal life for all who trust in him. He is the first fruits of a new kind of human life (1 Corinthians 15:20, 23). This eternal life will be spent in Paradise for everyone who trusts in Jesus Christ. This Paradise was briefly described in Chapter 10 of this book and in Chapter 19 we will look at what our resurrection bodies will be like.

But Christians do not need to fear death or the judgement. We can say with the apostle Paul,

> We shall not all sleep, but we shall all be changed, in a moment, in the twinkling if an eye, at the last trumpet. For the trumpet will sound and the dead will be raised imperishable and we shall be changed. For this perishable body must put on the imperishable, and this mortal body must put on immortality ... Death is swallowed up in victory. O death where is your sting? O grave where is your victory? (1 Corinthians 15:51–55)

Power

But even on earth we can know and experience the same power in our lives that caused Jesus to rise from the dead (Ephesians 1:19, 20; Philippians 3:10). It is as if the Holy Spirit reproduces Jesus' death and resurrection in our lives when we believe in Christ. The apostle Paul says, 'I can do all things through Christ who strengthens me' (Philippians 4:13). The death, burial and resurrection of Jesus now have real effects in our lives (Colossians 2:12). As Christians we are dead to the demands, attractions, and pressures of our previous sinful way of life so that Paul can say, 'we have died with Christ' (Romans 7:6; Galatians 2:20; 5:24; 6:14; Colossians 2:20). Because the Holy Spirit, the same Spirit that raised Jesus from the dead is at work in our lives, we find ourselves wanting to serve God more. We are dead to sin, alive to Christ (Romans 6:11). Sin no longer has dominion over us (Romans 6:14). We are united to Christ, so because we died and rose with Christ we have power to overcome personal sin more and more (Romans 6:12–14, 19).

This power transformed the disciples. Peter, just over a month after being frightened of saying to a young girl that he knew Jesus, could take to the Jerusalem streets and preach him boldly (Acts 2:22–24). Before the resurrection none of his brothers believed (John 7:5) but they do afterwards (Acts 1:14–1 Corinthians 15:7)

Paul says, it is no longer I who live but Christ lives in me (Galatians 2:20). Christ is in us. It is the real, personal dwelling of Christ in us, not that we merely agree with Christ or that his ideas are in us; he is in us and remains in us through faith (Ephesians 3:17; 2 Corinthians 13:5). The great power that created the world and saved us and raised Jesus from the dead—that same power is now at work in us. We must believe that God is stronger than sexual temptation, sin and addiction. If we believe that God brought a dead man back to life, we should believe that we can change.

So how can I know and experience this power?

We need to set our minds on things above where Christ is (Colossians 3:1–7). We need to think differently. Remember what Christ has done for us, who we now are and all our privileges. We walk in newness of life (Romans 6:4).

To know this power we need to know Christ (Philippians 3:8, 10) and abide in him (1 John 2:28; 3:6, 24). The apostle John says 'whoever abides in me and I in him, he it is that bears much fruit' (John 15:5). We must live our whole life in his presence (2 Corinthians 2:10; 1 Timothy 5:21; 6:13–14; 2 Timothy 4:1). Spend time with God's people. Read the Bible and meditate over it. Listen to his Word being faithfully preached. Pray. Pour out your souls to him and plead for him to draw near to us. Turn away from sin and keep his commandments out of love for him. In these things is where this resurrection power is to be found

Go and tell

These women were told not just to 'come and see' but 'go and tell'. That Jesus Christ died on the cross for our sins and rose again isn't something to be ashamed of or embarrassed about. It is the greatest, most important news in the world. My guess is that many of you reading this book keep quiet about your Saviour and sometimes feel you have to apologise for him. We would rather have a laugh and a joke with people than talk about our Saviour. We don't want to make things awkward and be made fun of or shunned. We don't want to upset people and are worried that in this scientific, technological, cool, trendy age, Jesus of Nazareth just won't cut it. But he is a risen Saviour. He is alive and the whole universe is in his hands. And what is more, he is the only one who can do helpless sinners good.

I taught with a man who I absolutely loved. He was one of the best laughs I have ever met. I remember sitting in the staff room with him and just laughing and laughing and laughing. He retired and within a few months became terminally ill. I never spoke to him about my Saviour. I never told him clearly that Jesus died on the cross and rose again that all my sins could be forgiven. Even when I last saw him just before he died, I didn't urge him to come to this Saviour. I can't be sure where he is spending his eternity but if he has gone to a lost eternity those laughs are not doing him any good now. He would no doubt say to me, 'why didn't you tell me!'

If the resurrection is true, if we believe that Jesus did really die and rose again, then we should be telling others. If there is a Heaven to gain and a Hell to avoid, if unnumbered souls are dying and passing into the night, it should move us to tell as many people as we can.

Recently Muhammad came top of a list of the hundred most

influential people. Darwin was 2nd and the Lord Jesus Christ was 3rd. It was based on the commitment of their followers. As Christians this should shame us and spur us into action. Muhammad or Darwin or anyone else cannot save anyone. There is no other name under heaven given among men by which we must be saved (Acts 4:12). We should therefore say with Paul, 'as much as in me is' (Romans 1:15). 'I'll give it all I've got'.

And when we do go and tell a world that is hurtling to Hell, it is important we tell them clearly and plainly in a language they understand. When Jesus met the women he said, 'good morning'. It was the greeting of the market place or the home. It would have been along the lines of 'Hi'. If ever there was a time for a theological jargon or a religious way of speaking it was when he appeared to people for the first time after he rose from the dead. But he spoke in a plain way. No jargon or frilly language or language from another period of time. When we speak on his behalf we should do the same. We should convey big Biblical and theological truths and never dumb them down. But we have a responsibility to speak about them in the plainest way possible.

But this good news is for everyone. No one is too bad or beyond the pale. Mark records that the angels told the women to go and tell his disciples and Peter (Mark 16:7). Peter is singled out for special mention. Why? Because as we have seen Peter had really messed up. He had really let the Saviour down. Jesus wants him to know that he too can be forgiven. And the same is true for you. Whoever you are. Whatever you have done. If you are reading this book it is because Jesus wants to tell you.

17

Seeing is believing

John 20:1–9; Luke 24:12

The women and the stone

AS WE SAW AND DISCUSSED IN THE PREVIOUS CHAPTER, THE names of the women who went to the tomb of the Lord Jesus vary between the four Gospels.

Matthew says there were two Marys who went to the tomb— Mary Magdalene and the other Mary (Matthew 28:1).

Mark refers to Mary Magdalene and Mary the mother of James and Salome (Mark 16:1).

Luke says it was Mary Magdalene, Joanna, Mary the mother of James and the other women (Luke 24:10).

John only mentions Mary Magdalene (John 20:1) but says 'we', implying there were other women with Mary.

It would seem then, putting it all together, that on that first Easter Sunday morning at least five women set out for the tomb;

Mary Magdalene mentioned by all four Gospels; Mary the mother of James; Salome, Joanna, and other women.

The four gospel writers mention the characters they were most interested in, or the ones that had possibly told them their story. John's focus, as we shall see in Chapter 18 of this book, is on Mary Magdalene.

She, along with the other women, set out while it was still dark to anoint Jesus' body. On their mind was the fact that the tomb had been sealed by a large stone and they had no idea how they could move it. As they travel it begins to lighten, so when they finally draw close to the tomb, probably as they turned the path, they see the stone has been moved.

This was something they were not expecting so although it suits their purpose they are nevertheless upset and uncertain what to do. The open tomb and the fact the stone had moved distressed Mary and the other ladies. Robbing of graves was common at the time and it would seem they came to the conclusion that these robbers were at it again.

At this point Mary Magdalene runs back to tell Peter and John about what had happened.

Peter and John

Once Mary tells them the news, the two disciples quickly get themselves together and head to the tomb. They start walking, then running side by side, then John outruns Peter. John is the younger of the two, so is faster, and arrives at the tomb first but doesn't go in, just stoops to look in; he peeps in. Peter on the other hand, arrives behind John but runs straight in. It is only after Peter had gone in, that John does the same. This little snapshot shows the differences in their personalities. John in his old age recalls it all like it was yesterday!

The tomb and the grave clothes

Joseph and Nicodemus had buried Jesus on the Friday afternoon before the sun went down. They would have removed the body of Jesus from the cross before the beginning of the Jewish Sabbath and then washed it and wrapped it in linen bands. They would have carefully inserted hundreds of pounds of dry spices into the folds of the linen. According to Boice (1986, p.354):

> One of them, aloes, was a powdered wood like fine sawdust with an aromatic fragrance; another, myrrh, was a fragrant gum that would be carefully mixed with the powder. Jesus' body was therefore encased. His head, neck and upper shoulders would have been left bare. A linen cloth would have been wrapped about the upper part of his head like a turban. The body was then placed within the tomb where it lay until sometime on Saturday night or early Sunday morning.

John and Peter stand inside the tomb, which would have been quite a large open space. Jesus' body has gone but it is not the emptiness of the tomb that is making them think. It was the linen cloths; the grave clothes. They are mentioned by John three times almost in the same breath. 'And stooping to look in he saw the linen cloths lying there but he did not go in. Then Simon Peter came, following him, and went into the tomb. He saw the linen cloths lying there and the face cloth that had been on Jesus' head, not lying there with the linen cloths, but folded up in a place by itself (John 20:5–7). Everything was orderly in the tomb.

If he had really died and had just revived, you would expect that he stirred, opened his eyes, sat up and began struggling out of the bandages leaving them torn and unravelled.

If friends had taken the body they would have left the clothes on him not to dishonour him by taking him naked.

If thieves had taken the body they would not have left behind expensive linen and spices.

You can imagine John saying to Peter at this point, 'No one has moved the body or disturbed the grave clothes. They are lying exactly as Nicodemus and Joseph had left them on the eve of the Sabbath. Yet the body is gone. It clearly hasn't been stolen or moved. It must have passed through the clothes leaving them as we see them now. The burial cloth which had been around Christ's head is neatly folded by one who no longer had need of it. Thieves or enemies definitely would not have taken off the clothes and put them there nice and neat. There is only one explanation Peter. Jesus, rose through linen bands, and calmly and majestically put everything in its place and departed from the tomb gloriously alive!'

Seeing and believing

In John 20 the words 'see', 'saw' and 'seen' dominate. In verse 1 Mary Magdalene *'saw'* that the stone had been taken away from the tomb. In verse 5 John peeped into the tomb and *'saw'* the linen cloths lying there. In verse 6 Peter went into the tomb and *'saw'* the linen cloths lying there and the face cloth which had been on Jesus' head, not lying with the linen cloths but folded up in a place by itself. In verse 8 John went into the tomb and *'saw'*. In verse 12 Mary Magdalene *'saw'* two angels in white where the body of Jesus had lain. She turned around in verse 14 and *'saw'* Jesus standing there but at that point thought he was the gardener. In verse 18 she said to the disciples I have *'seen'* the Lord. In verse 20 in the upper room he shows the disciples his hands and his side. Then the disciples were glad they *'saw'* him. A week later in verse 25, they tell Thomas who had not been with them, we have *'seen'* the Lord. To which Thomas replies, unless he *'sees'* in his hands the mark of the nails and places his finger into the mark of the nails and place his hand into his side, he will never believe. In verse 26 Jesus appears to Thomas and says, put your finger here and *'see'* my hands, and place it in my side.

In 1 John 1:1–3 John writing again says, 'that which we have heard, which we have "seen" with our eyes, which we "looked" upon and have touched with our hands … we have "seen" it and testify to it and proclaim to you ... that which we have "seen" and heard we proclaim also to you'.

What's the point? John wrote his Gospel that 'you may believe that Jesus is the Christ, the Son of God, and that by believing you may have life' (John 20:31). And he wants us to know that the things he wants us to believe in, he actually saw.

We say today, 'seeing is believing'. Well these men and women saw and that is why they believed. But today so many people don't want to know what they saw. They are not interested. They dismiss all the witnesses who were there. Can you imagine a judge today saying that in judging the case he is not interested in what the eye witnesses saw? He will come to his own conclusion. But that is exactly what so many, many people do in regard to Jesus Christ and the resurrection today. They say we have no interest in looking at the primary evidence. We will not listen to the eye witness accounts. Instead, we will wait for 2000 years and listen to what the 'experts say'. These theories are way more credible.

Christianity isn't based on theories. Neither is it based on mysticisms or visions or things people just want to believe. It is based on what John and the other eye witnesses actually saw. John wants his readers to believe. Believing is based on evidence and the evidence comes from those who were on the spot.

It is important to note that the stone was not moved from the tomb to let Jesus out but to let the disciples in. They needed to go in and see these graves clothes, to see that he had risen from the dead. Seeing is believing!

And what did they do after they had seen these things? They went home to have a cup of tea! (John 20:10). Seems like such an anti-climax! If they were out to sensationalise it or dramatize it, surely the gospel writers would have ended the story better than that! But that is what they did. It was a lot to take in and they needed to think about it all. It is all very true to human life.

It is at that moment that John sees and believes (John 20:8). He realises Jesus must have risen. In the typical honest fashion of the Gospel writers, John says that at the time he didn't understand the scripture that said Jesus must rise from the dead (John 20:9) but that the resurrection opened a door of understanding. However, by the time he sat down and wrote his Gospel, he understood from scripture that Jesus had to rise from the dead. It all made sense. Jesus had been teaching the disciples for three years but they didn't really understand everything until the Holy Spirit, the Paraclete (helper), came upon them and brought back to their memory all that they had been taught, and gave them understanding (John 14:25, 26; 16:12–15). We will look more closely at the coming of the Holy Spirit in Chapter 23 of this book.

We don't know what went on in Peter's mind at this point. Luke 24:12 says that he 'went away wondering to himself what had happened' (Luke 24:12 NIV). It would seem that Peter didn't fully believe at this time. Again, an example of the straightforward honesty of the Gospel writers and the disciples.

Real life and eternal life

And the reason John wants us to believe is that we might have life. By believing in Jesus Christ we can have eternal life. When we die we go into eternity. For those who don't believe that Jesus Christ is the Son of God and that he died and rose again, they will go into everlasting Hell. They will die eternally without ever actually dying. But for those who do believe these things, when we die we will go to be with God and enjoy eternal life with him in Heaven.

However, life isn't just to be enjoyed after we die. If we believe these things then we can be resurrected with Christ into a new life (Romans 6:3–4). Many people think that when someone becomes a Christian they stop living. But the opposite is true. When we become Christians the life of God is put in our souls. Jesus says that he came that we might have life (John 10:10). New life. The Bible says we go from death to life (John 5:25). Instead of being a slave to sin and my lusts I now live for God. I am now a slave to righteousness (Romans 6:17, 18). I want to do what is right and pleasing to God. I go in a new direction. We have new inclinations. New affections. The old has gone and the new has come. The Holy Spirit gives us a new awareness of sin, a new interest in the Word of God, a new passion for holiness, a new desire for prayer, and a new sense of the majesty of God. Christians are new creations (James 1:18). It is like putting off old clothes and putting on new (Colossians 3:9–10).

I go from darkness to light (Acts 26:18; Colossians 1:13) and instead of being deceived by sin and believing that happiness is found in living for myself and the pleasures if sin, I see things for what they really are. Instead of being left feeling empty and restless; uneasy and guilty I can know contentment, peace and happiness. I know real, deep seated joy not dependent on circumstances. I am at peace with God and therefore at peace with myself. Life!

18

Who are you looking for?

John 20:11–18

Mary Magdalene

As we have seen throughout this book, Jesus' death and resurrection was planned meticulously, every last detail, from before the world was made. Imagine, therefore, being in that council meeting in eternity past, before time began, when God the Father, God the Son and God the Holy Spirit drew up salvation's plan. The question is asked, 'Who shall we choose to be the first person to see the Saviour when he's risen from the dead?' I wonder who you would have chosen. As we saw in chapter 10, in first century Israel it would surely have to be a man. Someone of influence that would give the resurrection credibility and kudos. I don't think for one minute you would have chosen a one-time demon possessed woman!

Her name was Mary Magdalene. As we have seen, she features prominently in all four Gospel accounts of the crucifixion and resurrection. She watched the crucifixion, saw where Jesus' body was laid and set out very early on the Sunday morning to anoint his body.

We first meet her in the Bible in Luke 8:1–3 when the Lord Jesus went on a preaching tour. He was accompanied by his 12 disciples and some women. One of these women was Mary who came from a village called Magdala (meaning the Tower) located on the western shore of the Sea of Galilee and south of Capernaum; about two or three miles north of Tiberius.

We can assume that she was quite a wealthy lady. Mary Magdalene and the other ladies mentioned in Luke 8:2–3 provided for Jesus and his disciples out of their means. In the incident we are looking at in this chapter Mary says to the gardener that if he had carried Jesus away to tell her where he has laid him and she will take him away (John 20:15). The fact she can offer to make the arrangements to fetch the body and give it a proper burial suggests she was a woman of some wealth and standing

Traditionally, some Christians have viewed Mary Magdalene as a beautiful woman who Jesus saved from an immoral life. However, there is nothing in the Gospels to indicate this. We should not confuse Mary with the lady in Luke 7:36–50: If this lady was Mary Magdalene surely Luke would have said so in Luke 8:2: Luke makes no reference to this but says that seven demons had gone out from Mary Magdalene. There is no reason for connecting the demons with immoral conduct: they are more usually associated with mental or physical disorder. In the Bible, demon possession produced effects that were often violent (Mark 9:18) and could cause blindness and dumbness (Matthew 9:32–33; 12:22).

Anyone reading this book who has suffered with any kind of mental illness will have some understanding of what Mary's miserable and troubled existence must have been like. But Jesus had rescued her from this very distressing life.

It is no wonder she loved the Lord Jesus and was so grateful for all that he had done for her. She is an example that those who love Christ most are those who understand how much he has done for them. Furthermore, those who love Christ most diligently and perseveringly are those who receive most privileges from him. That he appeared to Mary Magdalene first shows how much he values love and faithfulness.

J.C. Ryle said, 'Of all the things that will surprise us on the resurrection morning, this, I believe, will surprise us most: that we did not love Christ more'

Why are you weeping?

We saw in the previous chapter, as Mary Magdalene approached the garden early on that Sunday morning that she saw the stone had been rolled away. Alarmed, she ran back to where Peter and John were staying to tell them. The two men immediately go to the tomb. Walking at first, then running, with John out-running Peter. We can assume that Mary went with them but was slower than both of them in arriving at the tomb and by the time she gets there the two disciples have been and gone.

Alone, she stands outside the tomb weeping and stoops down to look inside (v.11). Inside the tomb would have been a stone bench that ran around the wall which may have been a flat ledge under a recessed arch cut out of the inner wall. On this ledge, or bench, the Lord Jesus' body would have been laid.

As Mary peered in she saw two angels in white sitting, one at the head and the other at the feet, where the body of Jesus had been lying (v.12). In the Old Testament, angels regularly, though not frequently, appeared as human visitors. From what Mark says (16:5) this is how these angels appeared. They were dressed in white garments signifying purity, joy, victory; the triumph of life over death, light over darkness and grace over sin. The angels gently reprove Mary by asking, 'why are you weeping?'

She was weeping because not only was she grieving, but now

panic and anxiety had engulfed her. As we saw in chapter 17 of this book, as Joseph of Arimathea and Nicodemus did not have the time to do it properly on the Friday, Mary had come, initially with the other women, to the garden to anoint the body of the Lord Jesus. It was unbearable enough that her master had been killed but now his dead body had gone and she couldn't say goodbye properly (v.13).

It was all becoming too much. From Jesus' betrayal and arrest in Gethsemane, to his trials, to the shameful, barbaric crucifixion and now the disappearance of his body, everything was going wrong. It was a heartbroken Mary who wept alone in the garden that Sunday morning.

I wonder if Mary's condition resonates with you as you read this book.

Perhaps you are a Christian but everything seems to be going wrong. You are finding being a Christian really tough. You try to witness to your family, friends, colleagues, school or university mates, but no one seems interested. Society and our culture appears to be more and more anti God all the time and so out of step with your life and the pressures you face. It seems to have no relevance in regard to your job, family and financial situation.

The church looks to be on the decline and becoming more and more irrelevant. Perhaps the church you go to is small and you have gone through splits and divisions. Reading your Bible is hard and praying even harder. You are worried about the future. Will you increasingly get left out of things on account of being a Christian? Will persecution come your way? Everything seems so difficult.

Perhaps you are not sure if you are a Christian. You're frightened of the judgement to come and of the prospect of going out into eternity. Your past plagues you and you struggle to believe that all your sins are really forgiven. All of this troubles you and even causes you to weep.

Maybe you are not a Christian at all but you feel a bit like Mary.

You're stressed out. At the moment life is tough and everything seems too much. And what is it all for? When you stop and think it all appears meaningless. You are looking for something but haven't found it. Cash, significance, sex—whatever it takes you to get through getting up, getting off, getting up, getting through ... but none of it satisfies. We live in a technological age but you've realised technology won't fix your marriage; technology won't sort out your addiction; technology won't sort out your selfishness. We have never been so entertained but after the music, film, game, play is over, then what? William Shakespeare epitomises this frustration in his play Macbeth when he says, 'life is a poor player that struts and frets his hour upon the stage and then is heard no more. A tale told by an idiot full of sound and fury signifying nothing'. The seeming pointlessness and hopelessness of it all!

Life, whether you are a Christian or not, is causing you right now to weep, or at least feel like weeping.

Who are you looking for?

As you think about Mary on that Sunday morning and you think about how hard life is, you ask, 'so why did the angels gently reprove her? Isn't it perfectly understandable that Mary should be so upset in such circumstances? Haven't you got every right to be feeling the way you do?'

It's the supposed 'gardener's' questions that follow which shed light on why the angels couldn't understand why Mary was weeping.

As soon as Mary answered the angels to say she was upset because they had taken away her Lord and she doesn't know where they have laid him (v.13), she turned around and saw Jesus standing there, although at that point she had no idea it was him (v.14). She probably turned around because she heard someone approaching or maybe the angels pointed at him, bowed down or even suddenly vanished.

As well as asking 'why are you weeping', he goes on to ask, 'who are you looking for?' (20:15). To which Mary, not recognising him or having a clue who he really was, courteously asks him that if he knows where her Lord is, please help (v.15). She then turns back to face the tomb in despair.

By asking Mary, 'who are you looking for?' the supposed 'gardener' is saying in effect, 'what did you expect to find? Who do you think the Jesus you are looking for really is? What kind of Messiah have you been following the last three years? Mary, despite your love and loyalty to Jesus, your view of him is still too small. Haven't you understood anything? If you had a real comprehension of who he is you would not be weeping.'

Mary would have often heard Jesus' prediction of his resurrection but she doesn't say to herself, 'Oh he said he would rise! Could it possibly be?' It doesn't occur to her. Mary needed to understand that Jesus of Nazareth was God! Even after Mary realises that the gardener is the risen Lord Jesus, by the title she uses, 'Rabboni', she still doesn't completely comprehend the full extent of who Jesus is. This title is only given to a few rabbis and often with reference to God, but falls short of full deity.

I imagine as you read this book that is your problem too. You don't fully appreciate who Jesus is. Think about who he is. Really think about it. We say we do, but do we actually believe that the saviour we claim to trust is risen from the dead; that Jesus of Nazareth is the living God? The one who walked by the Sea of Galilee actually built the sky, rolled out the seas and at his command the countries, kingdoms and empires throughout history have risen and fallen. After he stilled a storm by speaking to it, his disciples asked, 'Who then is this, that he commands even winds and water, and they obey him?' (Luke 8:25). He holds the whole world in his hand and here, on this Sunday morning, has even conquered death. Believing this, understanding this, living in the light of this changes everything.

The puritan, John Owen, when asked what he believed was

the church's biggest problem, didn't say how sinful or pathetic or ineffective or rubbish she is. Rather he said it was that she didn't realise her privileges. J.I. Packer in his great book, 'Knowing God', said that the problem with Christians is their inadequate view of God. We are not following a dead Galilean carpenter, not even a wise man, good teacher, someone special. He's God! He holds the whole world in his hand. He controls the future. Abraham Kuyper of Holland (1837–1920) said, 'There is not a square inch in the whole domain of our human existence over which Jesus Christ, who is sovereign over all, does not cry 'mine'.

It is Him we will see first when we close our eyes in death, leave this world and enter eternity. Nothing or no one is outside of his control. You no longer need to be haunted by your sinful past. His resurrection confirmed that his death fully paid the price of the punishment your sin deserved. The blood he shed cleanses your dirtiest sin away. God took out all his anger for sin on His Son so that all those who trust him will never have to face that anger.

There is therefore no need to weep. The most frequent command in the Bible isn't 'Do not murder', or 'Do not steal', or 'Do not commit adultery'. The most frequent command in the Bible is, 'Do not be afraid'. For anyone reading this book whose trust is in Christ, there is absolutely nothing to be afraid of.

This should revolutionise your life, the way you view the world, the Church, everything. As you read your Bible, by mixing it with faith, you believe that what you are reading are words of this great God and living Saviour. You can claim every promise, trust that every command to obey and every sin to avoid is for your good. As you pray, you know that you are not simply getting things off your chest or talking to yourself or the ceiling, but to a living God, and that at his side is the risen Lord Jesus who intercedes on your behalf.

The author Salman Rushdie was invited to meet with Bill Clinton. At the time Mr Clinton was president of the United States of America, the Commander in Chief, the one who had at his disposal the full might of the US military. When he saw Salmon Rushdie he said, 'what can I do for you?' If you are a Christian, the one who is the commander in chief of the whole cosmos says to you, 'what can I do for you?'

The Psalmist says, 'Why are you cast down, O my soul, and why are you in turmoil within me? Hope in God' (Psalm 42:5).

The same but not the same

As we have seen, Mary turns around from peering into the tomb, looks at Jesus, supposes him to be the gardener, answers his question and then turns back to face the tomb in despair (John 20:15). The question has to be asked, why didn't Mary recognise the Lord Jesus when she turned around and saw him? Why did she suppose him to be the gardener?

One possibility is that her eyes were so full of tears she couldn't see properly.

Another is that she clearly did not expect to see Jesus alive. This is important because it is another pointer that shows the resurrection must be true. It was the last thing any of those early disciples expected; it wasn't something they dreamt up. It hadn't crossed their minds. Even after Mary had seen Jesus and gone to tell the disciples he was alive, they still didn't believe it (Mark 16:9–11).

While both these reasons could be factors why Mary didn't recognise Him, the main reason is that Jesus did not look exactly the same.

On the one hand there is a considerable degree of continuity between the physical appearance of Jesus before his death and after his resurrection (Luke 24:15–18, 28, 29; Matthew 28:9; John 20:20). Jesus' body could be touched and handled (Luke 24:39) and bore the wound marks, (John 20:20, 25, 27) could cook and eat fish (John 21:9; Luke 24:41–43, Acts 10:41).

On other hand, he was different. After his resurrection he rose through the grave clothes, and appeared and disappeared (Luke 24:31, 36). He came through locked rooms (John 20:19, 26). He was able to appear, vanish and move unseen from one location to another. His body had been made perfect, no longer subject to ageing or death but able to live eternally. A man who had lived a life of suffering and grief and hardship, now has a body that has been restored to its full youthful appearance (1 Corinthians 15:42–44). Jesus looked different (Mark 16:12; cf.9:3); yet still human. His body now has no scars from his beatings and death, only the nail prints and side wound to act as an eternal reminder of his sufferings and death for us. His body is glorified and deathless (Philippians 3:21; Hebrews 7:16, 24)

The exciting prospect for those who are 'in Christ', that is, have placed their faith in him, is that he is the first fruits of a new kind of human life (1 Corinthians 15:20, 23). What is true of him will be true of all those who have put their faith in him. Our bodies grow old and tired. We have aches and pains. Hair falls out in places we don't want it to and starts growing in places we really don't want it to! Some of you reading this book have serious health issues and disabilities. At the moment our bodies hinder us; we lust, are self-centred and easily distracted. But one day we will be raised in power, full of energy, healthy, no more tiredness. We'll have bodies dominated by the Holy Spirit. We will be like the Lord Jesus Christ, sinless and perfect. Bodies capable of running and riding, catching and kicking, diving and jumping, throwing and hitting. We will receive perfect resurrection bodies (1 Corinthians 6:14; 1 Corinthians 15:12–58; 2 Corinthians 4:14). According to Macleod, (Macleod, 2002 p.331) 'The scenario is a thrilling one: brilliant minds in powerful bodies in a transformed universe. With energy, dexterity and athleticism here undreamed of, we shall explore horizons beyond our wildest imaginations'.

Miriam

However, even though Mary didn't recognise Jesus because he

didn't look the same, it is also true that Jesus' disciples didn't recognise Him until he revealed himself to them (Luke 24:31).

It was only when the Lord Jesus called Mary by her name that she knew it was him. It was spoken in the way Jesus had always uttered it, in those well remembered accents. With infinite tenderness and warmth, in a tone that resembled former days. He says, 'Miriam'. Her name in her native tongue. Can you imagine the feeling this heart-broken lady had when she heard his voice? In one word, everything had gone from being all wrong to being wonderful.

There is nothing nicer than hearing the voice of the person you love the most calling your name in their affectionate way. I have a son called Jack but I very rarely call him Jack. I call him 'amigo'. It's my affectionate name for him. If he hears 'amigo' in the way I say it, he knows it is me and I am specifically calling him.

When Jesus called 'Miriam' she recognised his voice. It was unmistakably his. If you are a Christian reading this book, do you remember when Jesus first called you? Maybe you were listening to a man preach from the Bible and through that preaching, the preacher's voice faded and you heard the voice of Jesus calling you. Maybe a friend was explaining the Bible to you or you were reading the Bible yourself and you heard his voice calling you. You knew that what was being said or read was for you, and as it called out to you, you responded by calling out to the Lord Jesus in prayer.

You may, however, be reading this book, have sat through sermons, read the Bible, discussed these things with your Christian friends, family members or colleagues and never heard his voice. You have heard about Jesus' death on the cross and his love for underserving sinners. You have heard about Heaven and Hell and the fact that everyone of us will stand before the judgement seat of God and it has no effect. Nothing. Why? Two people can be sat right next to each other. The one hears the voice of Jesus, the other doesn't. Why?

Theologians distinguish between the general call and the effectual call. The call to repent and believe on the Lord Jesus Christ goes out indiscriminately (the general call). But because of sin all human beings are naturally dead to God (Ephesians 2:1). They can't hear his voice or see anything in Jesus Christ or the Bible. They are dead to it. However loud you shout, you cannot get a dead person to hear. The preacher calls out but he is calling out to spiritually dead people, so it is ineffectual.

But in effectual calling God quickens, rouses, wakes the dead. As the general call is communicated through the reading, explaining and preaching of the Bible, the Holy Spirit makes the call effectual by enlightening and renewing the heart of sinners chosen by God (Romans 1:6; 8:28, 30; 9:24; 1 Corinthians 1:24, 26; 7:18, 21; Galatians 1:15; Ephesians 4:1, 4; 2 Thessalonians 2:14). In other words, as the preacher preaches, or the Bible is read, God himself calls some people by name and those people call back to him in prayer.

If you are a Christian, it is not primarily because you called out to God to save you, it is first of all because God called out to you by name.

If you are reading this book and do not believe what you read; you do not take it to heart; you are not thrilled by it or understand the eternal significance of the message. (1 Corinthians 2:14), pray that, like Mary, he will call you by your name and would give you the faith to believe. Jesus, by his Spirit, could be stood right next to you and you can't see him. So say with Frances Jane Van Alstyne (Christian Hymns, 2005, No. 561).

Pass me not O gentle Saviour
Hear my humble cry
While on others thou art calling
Do not pass me by

Things are different now

John 20:17 is one of the most difficult verses in the New Testament. As soon as Mary realises that it is Jesus, she grabs hold of him. She had probably fallen to her face and grasped him by the feet (cf. Matthew 28:9). Jesus tells her to stop holding on to him. Conversely, however, he actually tells Thomas to handle and touch him and doesn't rebuke the other women who took hold of his feet and worshipped him (Matthew 28:9). So why does Jesus say to Mary, 'Do not cling to me for I have not ascended to my Father' (John 20:17).

Thomas was told to touch because he had not yet believed Jesus was risen from the dead. Jesus invites Thomas to touch him so he can see it really is him. It would seem Mary grabbed hold of Jesus because she thought that by grabbing him she could keep him always. She'd lost him once and wasn't about to lose him again. In her enthusiastic and relieved grasping of Jesus she does not really comprehend what is transpiring.

Jesus wanted her to know that he is not about to disappear any second, but equally he is not going to be around forever in the same way he was before. By saying to her, 'I am ascending to my father and to your father' he was saying to Mary that while his final, dramatic, decisive ascension from this world was still to take place (see Chapter 23), this process of ascending had begun. He was spelling out to Mary that earth was no longer his abode. It was going to be different now. He will appear to his disciples many times during the 40 days between his resurrection and ascension but he will not be with them continually as the days before his crucifixion. He will no longer be constrained and restricted like he was in the days of his flesh (Hebrews 5:7).

Mary didn't want to lose him again; she wanted things to be like they were before and carry on like it forever. However, even though he won't be with them physically as before, in an even better way than before, he won't be leaving them at all. He will send his Spirit and they (and us) can enjoy his presence morning, noon and night!

He is going to be as close to her now as ever before, but through his Spirit. It is going to be better, because whereas before the Lord Jesus could only be in one place at a time, now he can be with his people everywhere, all the time. But this uninterrupted fellowship for which she yearns must wait a little while until he has ascended to be forever with his father. This happened ten days after he ascended to Heaven by the sending of the Holy Spirit (see chapter 23). The disciples then, and Christians ever since to a greater or lesser degree, have enjoyed Christ's presence.

But as you read this book, you may be thinking that you have never really felt the presence of the Lord Jesus. You wonder what it would feel like and how you can know his presence. You may know of some people who claim to have had lots of experiences of feeling Christ's presence, whilst you know of others who are suspicious of any 'experiences'.

The Bible teaches plainly that every Christian has the Holy Spirit within them. You cannot be a Christian unless the Holy Spirit is at work in your heart. He is convicting you of sin, giving you faith to believe, strength to overcome temptation, longings to be holy, a deepening love for God and producing the fruit of the Spirit in your life—love, joy, peace, patience, kindness, goodness, faithfulness, gentleness and self-control.

The Lord Jesus said, 'where two or three are gathered in my name, there am I among them' (Matthew 18:20). Every time Christians meet together, even just two, he is there with them as much as they are there with each other.

When he gave his disciples the great commission (see chapter 23), to go into all the world and make disciples of all nations, he went on to promise them, 'And behold, I am with you always, to the end of the age'. (Matthew 28:20). As Christians do door to door, stand up for him in work, witness for him in school or university, the Lord Jesus is with them.

When a person is dying, the Lord Jesus promises to draw very near to them. Psalm 23:4 says, 'Yea though I walk through the valley of the shadow of death I will fear no evil for You are with me.'

But not only is the presence of Christ a doctrine to be believed, it is also an experience to enjoy. Christianity affects the emotions. It is something that must be known and felt. In 2 Timothy 4:17, standing in the dock, the apostle Paul says he felt the presence of Christ as he defended himself against the Emperor Nero.

But how can we feel his presence? As a rule, the Lord Jesus will make his presence felt through the Bible. He will bring it alive and make it real as we read it or hear it preached and expounded. At times he will even cause our hearts to burn (Luke 24:32). The Lord Jesus Christ will come to us, not physically but by his Spirit. It follows, therefore, that the more robust and theological our thinking is the more likely we are to experience the felt presence of the Saviour we love. What goes on in our thought should be of supreme importance. He will bring back to our memories things we have read and heard.

It is also true that we will not feel his presence if we live in a way that grieves him. By fleeing from sin, Jesus will draw near.

Therefore, any experience we claim to have that does not spring from God's Word must always be suspect, and any inward emotion that is not matched with outward obedience is not an emotion on which our Lord smiles.

My brothers

Mary is also told to stop clinging onto Jesus because it was a time for joy and sharing the good news, not for clutching him. He wants her to go and tell his disciples that he has risen from the dead and is alive.

A few days earlier they had all abandoned him in his hour of deepest need—despite them having been full of bravado, especially Peter (Matthew 26:33; John 13:37). They had slept when they should have been praying and on the look-out (Mark 14:37–42). At the first sign of trouble in the Garden of Gethsemane they all bolted as fast as they could. As he stood trial before the Jews and then Pontius Pilate they were nowhere to be seen. Peter is remembered in history as the one who denied knowing him but at least he followed Jesus, with John, to the High Priest's palace. The others went AWOL. As he hung on the cross suffering a shameful, excruciating death, they all, apart from John, had abandoned him.

But Jesus doesn't ditch these fellows. He doesn't say to Mary, 'Go and tell those good for nothings, those quarrellers, those quitters those losers, those cowardly deserters'. Neither does he say 'go and tell my disciples' or even 'go and tell my friends'. He says 'go and tell my brothers'. Brothers! He calls this gutless band of no hopers, his 'brothers'. Jesus calls them by a new name, even more intimate than friends. They are part of the same family. He wants them to know that his father is their father, and his God is their God (John 20:17).

I imagine as you are reading this book, like me, you feel a real failure as a Christian. You keep committing the same sins time and time again. You let the Lord Jesus Christ down so often. You know you don't love him anywhere near enough as you should. As you try to pray you really feel you can't because you are so aware of how unworthy you feel, and think that he must be sick of you. Like these disciples you have had so many privileges but still keep falling into those sins of lust, self-indulgence, gossip, anger and so on. But this same kind Saviour says to you 'brother' or 'sister'.

This is wonderfully illustrated in the opening verses of 1 Corinthians. In the ancient world, to be a Corinthian was to be immoral. The people of Corinth were known for having filthy minds, ideals and ideas. Like us, the Corinthians lived in a sex crazed society. John MacArthur says 'Corinth was such an immoral city that its name became a byword for sexual vice; the verb to "Corinthianize" meant to commit sexual immorality'. They were rotten to the core. Many in the Corinthian church to which Paul wrote had come from this kind of lifestyle and hadn't quite shaken it off. The church in Corinth was in a right mess. Some of the members were immoral, and others were divided and confused. Snobbery existed and there was no regard for authority. I wonder how would you start a letter to a church like this? Paul begins his letter by telling the Corinthians, 'I thank God for you' (1 Corinthians 1:4)! The Lord Jesus Christ calls people like this, 'brothers' and says his God is their God and his father their father.

Just pause and think about that for a moment. By trusting the Lord Jesus Christ, God is your father. Mary is told to tell his disciples 'I am ascending to my father and to your father'. For all who trust him he says not to think first of all that God is your creator or your judge but your Father. The Lord Jesus Christ didn't say, 'when you pray say 'Our creator who art in Heaven' or 'Our judge who art in Heaven' but 'Our Father' (Matthew 6:9). God says 'think of me as your father' and the Lord Jesus Christ says 'think of me as your brother'.

Some of you reading this book might have bad experiences of your father. But God is the perfect Father; what a father should be like. In the play, 'An Inspector Calls', the son falls into all sorts of trouble. The dad at the end asks him why he didn't tell him or come to him for help. The son says 'because you're not the sort of father I can turn to when I am in trouble'. Can I tell you on the authority of God's Word that your Heavenly Father is. When you've messed up, failed again, feel dirty and rubbish, you can turn to him again and again and again.

Remember how the Lord Jesus presents God in the parable of the Prodigal Son (Luke 15:11–32). The son had moved far away from home, as far away from his father as possible but not before getting his share of the inheritance. He spends all the money on partying, prostitutes and generally living riotously, and then a famine came. No money, no friends, just a pigsty and the left-over food from the pigs. He is in want and decides to go back to his Father, say how sorry he is and see if his father will take him on as one of his workers, living in the village near-by but just coming onto his father's estate to do some menial work. But the story says that while he was still a long way off, a dot in the distance, the Father spots him (no doubt he'd been looking out for him every day he was away) and runs to meet him. In that culture distinguished Middle Eastern patriarchs just did not run. Children did, women were known to, young men might, but not dignified pillars of the community. But in this parable, God is pictured picking up his robe, bearing his legs like some young boy and sprinting. He then pounces on his son in love not only before he has a chance to sort out all the mess he's caused and proved he's changed, but even before he can get out his 'sorry' speech. And the same God right now in Heaven will tuck up his robe and run to all his children who call out to him, however much of a mess they are in. He will also come to anyone who calls out to him for the first time.

Furthermore, we often say to ourselves that God is our Father. But the other way around is true too: Our Father is God! Think of that. Your Father is God! Children often brag about their fathers. They say, 'my dad can throw a football about a mile!' or one will say 'my dad makes a million trillion pounds a year' to which another responds 'that's nothing mine makes a million trillion pounds a day!' Imagine a dad who could throw all the miles a football could travel and owned all the money in every bank in the world! Jesus says, 'My father is greater than all' (John 10:29). And through faith in him, his Father is also your Father.

19

Hearts on fire

Luke 24:13–35; Mark 16:12–13

On the road to Emmaus

Up to this point in his Gospel, Luke has not reported any appearance of the risen Christ. He has reported the empty tomb (Luke 24:2, 3), the message of the angels that 'he is risen' (Luke 24:4–6) and Peter's visit to the tomb (Luke 24:12). But he hasn't recorded any sightings of the risen Saviour. However, in Luke 24:13–35 he gives a vivid account of Jesus appearing to two disciples as they walked from Jerusalem to Emmaus on the day of the resurrection. According to Morris (2008, p.355):

> This charming story is one of the best loved of all the resurrection narratives. There is something very moving in one of the Lord's few appearances given to these humble, quite unknown disciples.

We cannot be certain where Emmaus was but know it was 7 miles from Jerusalem (Luke 24:13). Neither is it stated why these disciples were going to Emmaus, but it can be reasonably inferred from Luke 24:28, 29 that they lived there. Probably the two had been in Jerusalem for the Passover and were now, early that spring afternoon, on their way home.

The two disciples

We don't really know who the two disciples were. They may have been from the wider circle of disciples (Luke 10:1–12).

We know the name of one of them was Cleopas but don't know much else about him. According to Morris (2008, p.356) Cleopas 'is not known to us apart from this story'. While others (Hendriksen 1978, p. 1061) feel there is no good reason to identify him with the Clopas of John 19:25:

However, others (Boice 1986, p.357) think that the Cleopas of Luke and the Clopas of John are one and the same with slightly different spellings of their names. This would make the Cleopas on the Road to Emmaus the husband of the Mary who stood by the cross (John 19:25). This seems unlikely as surely they would have left Jerusalem together and Luke would surely have named them both.

The one who is not named could very well have been Luke. The vividness of the account could be down to the fact that it was Luke's personal recollection. All four Gospel writers leave their signature in their accounts. Matthew is the publican in Matthew 5: Mark is probably the young 'streaker' in Mark 14:51, 52: John is the 'disciple who Jesus loved' (John 13:23). Could this unnamed disciple here be Luke? Possibly. Although in his preface to his Gospel, Luke distinguishes himself from those who were eye witnesses 'from the first' (Luke 1:2). However, I don't think this necessarily means that Luke had no direct encounter with the Lord Jesus.

Whoever they were, the two disciples give us a picture of the state of those early disciples. Sad (Luke 24:17), hopeless and confused.

Jesus draws near

As the two men travelled from Jerusalem to Emmaus they talked together of all the things that had happened (Luke 24:14). 'All these things' must refer to the events of the last three days, (Luke 24:18) Gethsemane, the trials, the crucifixion. The two men had also been in communication with Peter and John who had gone to the tomb and found it empty. It would seem they had heard about the testimony in bits and pieces of the women who had been to the tomb had seen angels and who had said he was alive. They clearly hadn't got the full picture and found it all hard to believe and put together (Luke 24:22–24). These two men were deep in conversation about all of these things as they walked together on that spring afternoon.

As they talked and reasoned, Jesus himself drew near but they did not recognise him. Acting as a stranger, Jesus asked the two men what these things are they are talking about. This caused them to literally 'stand still' (Luke 24:17). This 'stranger' must be the only person in Jerusalem not to know about the things that had happened there in the last few days (Luke 24:18). They were the topic of conversation in the capital city at the time.

But Jesus is a wise counsellor (Isaiah 9:6). He wants to give Cleopas the opportunity to unburden himself (Luke 24:18). Jesus listens before he speaks. He wants this man who is so sad (Luke 24:17) to tell him all about it. Before Christ speaks to these men to help them he wants them to speak to him to find out what help they need.

This is a great example for us to follow. Too many of us in trying to help others rush in with our advice without really listening to what is on the person's mind and heart. We try to solve the problem without understanding what the problem is, or try to make the situation better without grasping what the situation really is.

We should let them talk and talk. Tell their story one, two, three times without interrupting unless to clarify certain points. And as they talk, pray that God would guide our thoughts and give us wisdom in what to say.

Kept from recognising him

As we have seen, the two men didn't recognise Jesus at first. The implication is that the disciples were prevented from recognising him. Jesus was walking right next to them but they didn't know it. In the same way we cannot see the risen Christ, even though he is not far from anyone of us (Acts 17:27), unless he discloses himself to us.

We need faith to see him. So today, if these things mean nothing to you, if you don't see that you are a sinner; if the judgement to come doesn't trouble you; if you cannot see that Jesus Christ is the Son of God, that you need to be saved and he is the only one who can save you, then ask him to give you the faith to believe.

Concerning Jesus of Nazareth

And so the two men proceed to tell this 'stranger' all 'the things' they were talking about. 'The things' were concerning Jesus of Nazareth (Luke 24:19).

They saw Jesus as a prophet mighty in word and deed (Luke 7:16; John 4:19, 44; 9:17; Acts 3:22; 7:37). They knew he was special. They had no doubt seen some of his miracles, listened to his parables and heard him speak with such power and authority (John 7:46). They had observed the way he had lived, how kind and righteous he was and that he had grown in favour with all men (Luke 2:52).

They had even hoped that he was the long-awaited and prophesied one who had come to redeem them (Luke 24:21). But how could this be when their own rulers and chief priests had delivered him up to death and crucified him? (Luke 24:20). He had been dead three days.

To add to the confusion, these men, who were probably in the outer circle of disciples, had heard the report that some women had been to the tomb and found it empty, as had Peter and John, but as far as these men knew, no one had actually seen Jesus (Luke 24:23, 24). The women had even seen angels but because they hadn't seen Jesus, it threw doubt on what they said. These men just don't know what to make of it all.

I wonder if that is how you feel as you consider all these things. You just can't seem to piece it all together.

You think there is something in Christianity. You have met Christians and can see that they have got something you haven't. However, you haven't yet seen that Jesus Christ is God. You are not yet fully trusting that Jesus Christ is the only Saviour. You see Jesus on a par with, or just slightly higher than other religions and great men, and are yet to be fully convinced that no other religion or person, or trying your best, can get you to God. Furthermore, you read the Bible and as you read it you can see that it is a book like no other, but are still reluctant to accept completely that it is the inerrant Word of God, especially when it says things that go against the thinking of the day and cut across things you want to do. You are also confused about the trouble and suffering that is in the world and can't reconcile how an all-powerful, loving God could allow these things to be. And then you look at the church and think it is ineffective and weak. You might know Churches that have split and Christians who have abandoned the faith, and it all seems so confusing.

You also struggle to realise that he is able and willing to save you. You feel you need to make yourself better, add some of your own good works, do something towards your own salvation. You are yet to see there is nothing you can add or contribute towards your salvation. Jesus Christ is able to save you completely. You are struggling to see that his death and resurrection means that all your sins can be forgiven and you can be right with God, and that all you need to do is trust him.

You need, as these men do, to study the Bible and ask Jesus, by his Spirit to give you the understanding and the faith to see these things clearly. This is exactly what happened next on the road to Emmaus!

Necessary

After listening to them, Jesus says to them 'O foolish ones, and slow of heart to believe all that the prophets have spoken. Was it not necessary that Christ should suffer these things and enter glory?' (Luke 24:25, 26).

He as good as says to them, 'How dull are you? Don't you realise this is exactly how it is all meant to be? Everything has happened exactly to plan.'

And to show them he gives them a systematic Bible study. Beginning with Moses and all the Prophets, he interpreted to them in all the scriptures the things concerning himself (Luke 24:27). He shows them that the prophecies regarding the Messiah are not just about his glory but also about his suffering. We don't know what parts of the scripture he opened up to them, but we can guess.

Maybe he started with Genesis 3:15 to show that as soon as man fell into sin, a Saviour was promised. He would crush Satan's head, but in doing so Satan would bruise his heel. The Saviour would conquer sin and death and hell but it would not be without pain.

He could then very well have taken them to Genesis 12:3 and reminded them of the promise to Abraham that one of his descendants would be the Messiah (cf. Matthew 1).

From Genesis he might have gone to Exodus 12:3 and explained that the blood of the lamb that saved the Hebrews from slavery in Egypt, was a picture of how this promised saviour would save mankind from the slavery of sin. God's plan to save mankind would be accomplished through the sacrifice of a Lamb. The problem of sin and all the results of the fall would be dealt with by a Lamb. In the Old Testament lambs were sacrificed to take away the sins of the people. These all were types and shadows of the Lamb of God who would one day come to take away the sin of the world (John 1:29; Isaiah 53:7, 8).

He then no doubt reminded them that the Messiah would become a man and be born of a virgin (Isaiah 7:14) in a place called Bethlehem (Micah 5:2). He would grow up in a place held in contempt (Isaiah 9). A messenger would come preparing the way for him (Malachi 3:1). The Messiah would open the eyes of the blind, the ears of the deaf and make the lame to leap, (Isaiah 35:5, 6) and that is precisely what Jesus of Nazareth did.

He probably said to them to think about it. The Messiah would come riding on a donkey and bringing salvation (Zechariah 9:9). He would be betrayed for 30 pieces of silver (Zechariah 11:12). The prophets said that he would be struck and at that point all his disciples would desert him (Zechariah 13:7).

Why were they surprised that the rulers and kings of the earth took counsel together and set themselves against him? That is precisely what the Psalmist said would happen (Psalm 2:2).

The prophets said that the Messiah would be numbered with the transgressors, and, true to this prophecy, he was crucified between two thieves (Luke 23:33). He would be with a rich man in his death and he was buried in a rich man's grave (John 19:38–41). He would be pierced (Zechariah 12:10). The Psalmist said that he would be forsaken by God (22:1) and that they would divide his garments among them and cast lots for his clothes (22:18).

There is little doubt he took them to Isaiah to show that all that happened on the cross was part of God's great plan. The Saviour's appearance would be so marred it would be beyond human recognition (Isaiah 52:14). He would be despised and rejected; people would weigh him up and conclude that he is worthless (53:3;

Psalm 118:22). He had to be wounded for our transgressions and crushed for our iniquities (53:5). The Lord would lay on him the iniquity of us all. On that cross he was bearing the sins of many (Isaiah 53:6).

But despite the suffering and shame, this Messiah's kingdom will last forever (2 Samuel 7:12, 13). It won't be like an earthly kingdom that lasts for a period of time but will be an eternal one. Kingdoms will rise and fall but the kingdom he will establish will last forever (Daniel 2:44).

And when he referred to himself as the Son of Man it was the one spoken of by Daniel (7:13, 14).

All of this shows three things:

1. Salvation has been meticulously planned from start to finish

2. All the Bible is about Christ. Christ is the key to understanding the whole Bible. In the Old Testament he is expected. In the Gospels he is revealed. In Acts he is preached. In the New Testament letters he is explained and in the last book, Revelation, he is expected. Or another way to look at it is to see that in the Old Testament Jesus is seen prophetically, in the Gospels biographically, in Acts historically, in the letters theologically and in Revelation apocalyptically.

3. If we want to help people, open up the scriptures to them. Let our advice come from God's Word. To help these two, Christ explained the scripture, which should be our pattern. So we need to know and understand the scriptures and when we speak to people, pray that parts of Scripture come to mind, parts that we have not read recently and have largely forgotten. We should try to explain Scripture's teaching and apply it to their situation. Maybe a doctrine has to be taught, a duty to underline, a fear quelled or an encouragement given. But none of this will be possible unless we know it and understand it ourselves.

Stay with us

We can only begin to imagine what a great Bible study it was, and how the two men must have hung on his every word. At the beginning of the afternoon they no doubt had dragged their feet as they left Jerusalem for Emmaus. But it felt like no time and they were back in Emmaus.

Jesus makes out that he is going further (Luke 24:28), but being in his company was so wonderful that they ask him to stay. They strongly urge him to lodge with them. They would have tried to convince him by saying that it was getting late and travelling at night was dangerous for a whole variety of reasons—robbers, the rough path, wild animals, but the real reason is that they just want to be in his company. The last thing they wanted at first was to be in the company of this stranger, but now they don't want to let him go.

This gives a glimpse of how much Christ loves to be entreated by his people. The Bible says that the ones who find him are those who diligently seek him (Hebrews 11:6), who seek him with all of their hearts (Jeremiah 29:13). He wants to know that you are serious about him.

So he went into stay with them. And when he was at the table with them, he took the bread provided for supper and blessed it and broke it and gave it to them. And at that moment their eyes were opened and they recognised him (Luke 24:30, 31). How exactly we don't know. Was it the way he broke the bread or was it the nail prints in his hands? Whatever it was, they suddenly, all at once, realised it was him!

And then he vanished from their sight (Luke 24:31)!

Hearts on fire

They say to each other, 'Did not our hearts burn within us while he talked to us on the road, while he opened to us the scriptures?' (Luke 24:32).

When was the last time your heart was on fire as you read the Bible or heard it preached?

Why do we read the Bible and listen to preaching? Isn't it so that the same Jesus will draw near to us? It isn't just that you may learn things and put things into practice, even though that is part of it. If that is the only way you view the Bible, it is just a book, and an old one at that. The real purpose for reading the Bible is that you may find Christ and then get to know him better and better and better.

As you read the Bible you need to mix it with faith that what you are reading is the words of the living God to you. The promises are for you. His death is for you. The power that raised him from the dead can be in you. All he accomplished—sins forgiven, peace with God, a home in Heaven—is for you.

If you are a Christian, he has promised to be with you always but you don't always feel his presence. But the reason for that may be that you are too taken up with this world—job, family, friends, house, pleasures. If you draw near to him, he will draw near to you (James 4:8). Pray that he would show himself to you and that as you 'turn your eyes upon Jesus and look full in his wonderful face that the things of earth would grow strangely dim in the light of his glory and grace'. The more time you spend with him and listen to him in his Word and attend the preaching of it, the more your heart will burn within you. Pray that you will really know and feel his presence. Pray to him in the words of the hymn writer, 'for closer communion I pine' and as you read his Word say 'beyond the sacred page I seek thee Lord'.

The God of the Bible doesn't need to be some far off remote being. He can be your friend. Abraham was known as 'the friend of God' (James 2:23), Moses talked to God like a friend talks to a friend (Exodus 33:11). You too can know this God. According to Tozer (1993):

> a loving personality dominates the Bible ... men can

know God with at least the same degree of immediacy as they know any other person or thing that comes within the field of their experience.

Ran back

The same hour they returned to Jerusalem. They ran seven miles because they had an urgent, exciting message to tell. It was probably about 9 o clock by the time they got back to the disciples and those who were with them gathered.

For these men, Jesus' death and resurrection had changed their lives. Their hearts burned within them. They were excited and couldn't wait to tell others. The question is, does the message excite you? Are you desperate to tell others? Is your heart on fire?

20

My Lord and my God!

Mark 16:14; Luke 24:36–43; John 20:19–25
and Thomas (John 20:26–29).

When

WE ENDED THE LAST CHAPTER WITH THE TWO DISCIPLES WHO
had been on the road to Emmaus, running back to Jerusalem to tell
the disciples and those who gathered with them (Luke 24:33) that
Jesus was alive and had appeared to them. But before the two men
could get their words out, the others said that Peter had just seen
him. You can feel the excitement and sense the drama!

The events of this chapter follow hard after this. In fact 'as they
were talking about these things, Jesus himself stood among them'
(Luke 24:36). It was Easter Sunday and by now it was probably
late evening (Luke 24:29, 33, 36). John refers to it as the 'first day
of the week' (John 20:19) reinforcing the fact that after Christ's
resurrection Sunday is the most important day of the week, and
by the time he wrote his Gospel this was the day of the week
Christians met together.

Who

Gathered together were the eleven, those who associated with them and now the two who had been with Jesus on the road to Emmaus. The eleven is a term used to describe Jesus' disciples. We know that one of them, Thomas, was not there. Those who associated with them would include the women and the likes Nicodemus and Joseph of Arimathea, Lazarus, Mary and Martha etc. (Luke 10:38–42; John 11). We can totally understand why they had met together. Given everything that had happened there was so much to talk about.

Where

In a locked room in Jerusalem. The disciples and those with them were scared of the Jewish leaders and what they might do to any followers of Jesus, so they had locked the outside and inside doors of the place where they were (John 20:19). They were having food (Mark 16:14) and discussing the various appearances of Christ. They now thought for sure that he had risen from the dead based on what Mary Magdalene and Peter had said, but still did not really understand the resurrection. As they were talking about these things, Jesus came and stood in the midst of them.

Two different versions of the same event

Luke (Luke 24:36–43) records what happened as does John (John 20:19ff). They are talking about the same appearance. Mark also briefly refers to this appearance by saying that he appeared to the disciples as they sat at the table, and that he rebuked their unbelief and hardness of heart because they did not believe those who had seen him after he had risen (16:14).

Even though Luke and John are describing the same account there are differences, but these differences simply show how both accounts are independent. In both accounts Jesus shows the disciples the mark of his wounds. Both accounts say that Jesus greets the disciples by saying, 'Peace'. However, Luke records nothing about Jesus breathing on the disciples and makes no reference to the Holy Spirit. John mentions the locked doors whereas Luke says that Jesus suddenly appeared. But nothing in the accounts are contradictory, they just bring out different aspects.

If we put the two accounts together it would seem that Jesus came through the locked doors and appeared suddenly to them (John 20:19; Luke 24:36, 37). They are scared and think he is a ghost (Luke 24:37). He says to them 'Peace to you' (Luke 24:36; John 20:19) and asks them why they are troubled and have so many doubts (Luke 24:38). He invites them to see his hands and feet so they can see it is really him (Luke 24:39; John 20:20) and then asks if there any food there for him (Luke 24:41). They give him fish which he took and ate. He tells them that as the Father has sent him so he is sending them (John 20:21). Then he breathed on them and said 'receive the Holy Spirit'. He gave them authority such that whoever they forgive is forgiven and whoever they don't forgive isn't (John 20:22, 23). Let's consider some of these things in more detail.

Suddenly appeared through locked doors

As they are gathered together talking about all that had happened, Jesus suddenly appeared in the midst of them. He had come through locked doors. They were startled and frightened and thought he was a ghost.

Some may ask why were they so frightened to see him when Peter had just seen him, and the Emmaus two were in the middle of telling their story; surely it would not have been that much of a shock? But it goes to show that they still didn't really understand what was going on. Plus it would be a shock to anyone to see someone suddenly appear when you hadn't seen them enter the room and the doors were all locked!

Peace

To these frightened, on edge disciples, he says 'Peace be with you'.

They were living in fear of the Jews and confused about everything that was happening. They were embarrassed about the way they'd let the Saviour down, but Jesus says to them, 'peace be with you'. The gracious words with which the Lord Jesus introduced himself to his disciples after his resurrection were not 'let's sort a few things out' but 'peace be with you'.

Peace is the one thing we all want. To have peace of mind. To sleep well at night. Not to be on edge, churned up inside and full of cares. The late Freddie Mercury, lead singer of the pop group Queen, said in one of his last songs, 'I don't want you to see me cry, I long for peace before I die.'

I wonder as you read this book if you long for peace. There is so much in life to be troubled about. A past that haunts you. Secrets you live in fear of being discovered. The uncertainty of the future. Failings that plague you. Times you can't forget when you really let the Saviour down. You worry about persecution and the cost involved in being a Christian. You worry about whether you can live the life and keep it up.

Most importantly, the Bible says that one day the Lord Jesus will suddenly appear again (Matthew 24:44) and this really worries you. What if he came today? What if he called you to eternity today? How could you possibly stand before him given the life you've lived? But if you are trusting him, Jesus says to you, 'Stop worrying. There is nothing more to fear. Everything has been taken care of'.

The 'peace be with you' on this Easter Sunday evening complements the 'It is finished' (John 19:20) of Good Friday. All your sins were laid on him (Isaiah 53:6). His blood can cleanse the foulest of them (1 John 1:7). He conquered death and Hell and will present you faultless when you stand before God (Jude 24). The God who holds everything and everyone in his hand is for you. And if he is for you, who can be against you (Romans 8:31). So trust your life into his hands and be at peace.

Nothing can separate you from the love of God. Not tribulation, or distress, or persecution, or famine, or nakedness or sword. In all things we are more than conquerors through him who loved us. Paul says, 'I am sure that neither death nor life, nor angels nor rulers, nor things present nor things to come, nor powers, nor height nor depth' (and just in case someone says, 'but what about this?') 'nor anything else in all creation, will be able to separate us from the love of God in Christ Jesus our Lord' (Romans 8:38, 39). In other words, Paul is saying, 'Whatever you are worrying about, stop. Nothing, absolutely nothing, can separate you from the love of God if you are trusting Jesus Christ as your Saviour. The one who died on the cross and rose again is for you and says "Peace be unto you"'.

And the peace he gives isn't dependent on circumstances. In the National Eisteddfod in Wales, the Art competition one year was to draw a scene that depicted peace. The runners up drew pictures of summer evenings and still lakes with boats gently bobbing on them and such like things. But the winner drew a picture of a raging storm. Black clouds, strong winds, loud thunder, waves crashing against the rocks and boats being thrown around the sea. But in the cleft of one of the rocks was a little chick safely snuggled under her mother's wing. The chick was warm and safe. At peace! That is the peace that you can have by trusting in Jesus Christ. No matter what is going on in the world or what your circumstances are, you can know a peace which passes understanding which guards your heart and your mind. You can rest in Jesus Christ. Even at the final judgement when the waves and winds and storm of God's wrath will blow and crash, you can be totally safe and know peace.

Maybe you find that hard to get your head around. When you think about yourself and what you are like and the mess you feel your life is, it is impossible to grasp that Jesus Christ would say 'peace' to you. You can't understand how someone who knows everything about you would be willing and able to be at peace with you. But if you are a Christian, God looks at you and deals with you, even in the state you are in, as if you have lived the life Jesus

Christ lived. He loves you and thinks your life is as beautiful as the Lord Jesus Christ's. A great exchange has taken place. On the cross he took your sin and guilt and shame and gave you his perfect, spotless life.

Christ looks at his Church and the first thing he says is 'Peace be unto you'. The church is made up of failed, broken, messed up people, but it was for this church he gave his life and to this church he says, 'peace'.

A couple had been married for many years and the wife was taken ill with cancer. In the latter stages of the illness, the cancer had ravaged her body. As she was approaching death the husband took the minister to see her in hospital. By this time she looked dreadful and was completely disfigured. As they stood by her hospital bed, the husband turned to the minister and said, 'Isn't she beautiful'.

Even today, in the state we're in, God looks at the church and says, 'Isn't she beautiful'. In the same way, the disciples who Jesus appeared to on that Sunday evening would have felt anything but beautiful. They were in a bad way. But to Christ they were beautiful and precious. And what is even better is that one day we will be made beautiful and precious. The Church will no longer split and have divisions; no longer will the people of God gossip and hurt one another; no longer will we fall into sin and be plagued by it. We will be beautiful. He died and rose again to make us beautiful and so that we can enjoy perfect peace.

So rest in Jesus Christ. Trust yourself completely into his care and nothing that happens to you will be anything other than for your good (Romans 8:28), in this life and the next. Be at peace. When worries come and fears take hold of you, remind yourself that God is your Father and the Lord Jesus Christ is your Saviour. What is there to fear? J.C. Ryle said that faith rests best on the pillow of God's omnipotence (all-powerfulness). As the hymn writer said, 'be still my soul: the Lord is on your side'. Or even better, the Psalmist says, 'In God I have put my trust: I will not be afraid. What can man do to me? (Psalm 56:11).

It's really me

The disciples were still troubled and full of doubts so he asks them, 'Why?' (Luke 24:38). Jesus brings these disciples' doubts out into the open and deals with them. Most Christians have doubts. And the best thing to do with these doubts is to bring them out into the open.

To still these doubts and fears, Jesus tells them to look at him, touch him, handle him (Luke 24:39). He shows them his hands and his feet. He wants them to know he is a real man, that he is flesh and bones. He even asks for food and sits down and eats some fish with them.

When we are full of doubts and fears this is exactly what we should do. Take them to the Lord Jesus. Tell him all about it. Lay them all out before him. Then look to him, knowing that he is a man and remembers what it is like to be us. He knows our frame and remembers that we are dust (Psalm 113:14).

The doubts you have can be taken to the Saviour who is alive and invites you to cast all your care upon him because he cares for you (1 Peter 5:7). He graciously says to us, 'Come now let us reason together ...' (Isaiah 1:18). Let's talk everything through. Let's sort all of this out. But the answer is found in Jesus Christ. So think about him, consider him, meditate upon him, call out to him in prayer.

No wonder the disciples 'disbelieved for joy'. It is almost too good to be true. Jesus Christ provided remarkable evidence of his own resurrection and that he is still the 'man Christ Jesus' (1 Timothy 2:5). The man who walked beside the Sea of Galilee is still the same man who is in Heaven and ever lives and pleads before God on my behalf. He is still a real man. 'A spirit doesn't have flesh and bones' (Luke 24:39). He is the one who one day

I will see and be like (1 John 3:2). The hymn writer, Joseph Hart (1712–1768) put it wonderfully.

> A Man there is, a real Man
> who once on Calvary died.
> His blood for guilty sinners ran
> From hands, and feet, and side.
>
> 'Tis no wild fancy of our brains
> No metaphor we speak
> The same dear Man in heaven now reigns,
> That suffered for our sake.
>
> This wondrous Man of whom we tell
> Is true Almighty God
> He bought our souls from death and hell
> The price, His own heart's blood.
>
> That human heart He still retains
> Though throned in highest bliss
> And feels each tempted member's pains
> For our affliction's His
>
> Come, then, repenting sinner, come
> Approach with humble faith
> Owe what thou wilt, the total sum
> Is cancelled by His death!
>
> His blood can cleanse the sin stained soul
> And wash our guilt away
> He will present us sound and whole
> In that tremendous day.

Authority

The disciples were the twelve men Jesus had called to be his apostles (Luke 6:13), now eleven after the betrayal by Judas. An Apostle is one who has been sent or commissioned, and after his death and resurrection these men would have the responsibility of spreading the good news of Jesus Christ (the Gospel) across the whole world, starting in Jerusalem. As apostles they would carry out this task with not only the authority of Heaven behind them, but, as we shall see later in this chapter and in chapter 23 of this book, the help of the Holy Spirit.

He says to them 'as the Father has sent me even so I am sending you' (John 20:21). These men receive the same commissioning authority as the Lord Jesus. The authority he spoke with, they will speak with. The message these men will proclaim is the same message Christ preached. The difference is that Jesus through his death and resurrection makes it possible; the apostles simply proclaim it.

Jesus came into the world to heal the sick, help the needy and preach repentance and the forgiveness of sins. These men were given the authority to do the same. The miracles they performed (Acts 5:12) were to prove they had this God given authority (cf. Matthew 9:1–8).

For us today that reinforces the importance of the Bible. Even though the New Testament was written down by these apostles, it is the Word of God; these men were writing under divine inspiration. You cannot say (as some do) 'I like the words of Jesus in the gospels but don't pay as much attention to the letters as they were just the opinions of his disciples and the early church'. The words found in the Bible, written and preached by these men, are the very oracles of God. They carry infinitely more weight than what people say and think today. The Word of God is more important than the traditions of the church, our own human reason and any feelings or leadings we may have. What we do in churches, the view of the church on issues such as laws that are passed, and our view of God has to be based and built on what the prophets in the Old Testament and the Apostles in the New Testament wrote down. This is how we are to judge whether or not a church is really a church. Is the Bible their sole authority for belief and practice? If what they do and say is based on tradition or human reason or experiences, then, for all their good intentions, they are not the true church of Jesus Christ.

The apostles were given authority to expel people from the church who were not behaving like Christians and showing no repentance, and of restoring sinners to fellowship.

It is this apostolic authority that church discipline is built upon today. How do we know if someone is a Christian or not? How do we know if someone is forgiven or not? On what basis should someone be admitted to church membership? What is the basis for church discipline? The answer to these questions is found in the apostles teaching and on the authority of what they wrote down in the Bible. It is not what society thinks and feels but on what the Word of God says that has come to us through these apostles.

There are no apostles now as one of the qualifications to be an apostle was to have seen the risen Saviour (Acts 1:21, 22). But today the church is governed by elders, an office appointed by the apostles (Acts 14:23; Titus 1:5). Churches, therefore, should be under the authority of elders. These men lead the church and church members submit to their authority of the elders as long as they are doing and teaching what the Bible says.

These elders are to look after the people as shepherds look after the sheep (Acts 20:28–31; 1 Peter 5:1–4), leading them by example (1 Peter 5:3) away from all that is harmful into all that is good. In virtue of their role, elders are also called shepherds or pastors (Ephesians 4:11) and overseers (Acts 20:28) and are spoken of as leaders (Romans 12:8; 1Thessalonians 5:12; Hebrews 13:7, 17, 24).

The congregation, for its part, is to acknowledge the God-given authority of its leaders and follow the lead they give (Hebrews 13:17).

Elders must have mature and stable Christian character, and a well-ordered personal life (1 Timothy 3:1–7; Titus 1:5–9). Some elders are also called to preach and teach as their full-time calling in life (1 Timothy 5:17; Titus 1:9; Hebrews 13:7).

The other office recognised by the church of the New Testament is that of Deacon (Philippians 1:1; 1 Timothy 3:8–13). But the function of deacons is more practical; administrative and financial mainly.

Breath of God

The Lord Jesus blew on them, which symbolised that he would give them the Holy Spirit. It was a visible sign of the pledge that after he had ascended to Heaven the Holy Spirit would come and be with them. He 'breathed' or 'exhaled' and said, 'receive the Holy Spirit' (John 20:22).

And boy, did these men need the breath of God! They were going into a hostile world to tell them that they were sinners and needed to be saved from the judgement to come. How were they going to convince people to stop living for themselves, repent of their sins and trust in the Lord Jesus Christ? How was this pathetic group of cowards, locked up in a room for fear of the Jewish leaders, going to take to the streets and stand before thousands and preach to them? How were they going to ensure that the words they used would never grow stale? Only by relying totally on the Holy Spirit. And through the Holy Spirit, these men 'turned the world upside down' (Acts 17:6).

As we think about our society, family members, work mates, friends, the task seems impossible. How can the gospel penetrate into their lives? How can we convince them that they are sinners in the hands of an angry God? How can we get them to see that the things of eternity are more important than the things of time? That the hereafter is more real than the here and now? How can we compete against pubs and clubs and hundreds of television channels, game consoles, the internet? How can get people to give up their sin; to turn away from drunkenness, sexual promiscuity; to stop children being cheeky and disrespectful; to stop violence and prevent marriages splitting up? How can we change people's thinking from being seduced by the culture of the age, to believe the Bible? How can we stand as a Christians in this environment with so much to attract and distract us?

We can never do it in our own strength! We need the Holy Spirit to really come upon us. We need to pray as the hymn writer put it, 'Breathe on me breath of God, fill me with life anew'. And when he does, hundreds will be saved. Salvation with man is impossible. But with God, all things are possible (Matthew 19:26). 'And I can do all things through Christ who strengthens me' (Philippians 4:13).

In the West, we live in days where God and the Lord Jesus Christ and the church seem irrelevant. Christians are seen as a small, out of fashion, pitiable group. But there have been times in the past just as bad, if not worse. According to Dallimore (2001) life in England between 1730 and 1740 was foul with moral corruption and crippled by spiritual decay, very similar to the condition of the West in our day and age. People thought then that the church had had its day: sin was too rampant. But during this dark time, 'England was startled by the sound of a voice' (Dallimore, 2001, p.31). It was the voice of the preacher George Whitefield. God came down upon Whitefield and used him and others, including John and Charles Wesley, to make his church rise again. Wouldn't it be amazing if in these days we were startled again by the sound of a voice!

Such times are known as revival. Duncan Campbell (Edwards, 2004 p.26) described a revival as a 'community saturated with God'. Surely we should be pleading with God for times like this!

Up and down my homeland of Wales there are churches which are derelict, or are now used for other things—carpet warehouses, mosques and night clubs. Imagine a day when we can go back to the people who now own these buildings and say 'we need our churches back'. We'll even pay over the odds but we desperately need the buildings back for God's people to meet in.

My Lord and my God!

If imposters or deceivers had compiled the Bible they would not have recorded how Thomas, one of the first founders, behaved (John 20:24–29). He was not there when Jesus appeared to the other disciples, and when the disciples told Thomas that they had seen the risen Jesus, Thomas said that 'unless I see in his hands the mark of the nails, and place my hand into his side, I will never believe' (John 20:24, 25). Thomas doesn't believe a word of it!

But after a quiet week had passed, when the disciples were gathered again Jesus came and appeared this time to Thomas as well. It was a Sunday and the '8 days later' referred to by John (John 20:26), counted the two Sundays.

Thomas probably did do as Jesus commanded and actually put his finger in the holes where those nails had been, and put his hand into the side where that spear had been thrust. And at that point, Thomas says 'My Lord and my God!' (John 20:28).

This was the fullest expression that Jesus of Nazareth was God. For a Jew this was a remarkable confession. This first century Jew called Thomas, steeped in the Old Testament monotheistic scriptures, stood face to face with another first century Jewish peasant, a Galilean carpenter, and says, 'You are actually, really God! You are the same one who created the cosmos, who is the God of our fathers, Abraham, Isaac and Jacob (Exodus 3:6; Acts 3:13). You are the one who Isaiah had to hide his face from in the Temple because of your holiness (Isaiah 6:1–7), you are the one who when Moses saw your glory, just the back of you, his face shone (Exodus 33:18 cf. 34:29). Jesus of Nazareth, you are the Lord God of Heaven and earth, the only true and living God'.

The purpose of John all along in his Gospel is to show that Jesus is the Son of God (John 20:30) and here this man who had said that unless he gets cast iron evidence will not believe, believes. If Thomas believed it, it must be true!

Put yourself in the way of good things

It is also an encouragement to meet with God's people and put ourselves under the preaching of the Word of God and prayer. Thomas probably wasn't there the first time with the other ten because he had not been that interested in meeting. Maybe he had better things to do. Perhaps he was disillusioned with it all and thought, 'what's the point?' I wonder if that is how you feel about the church prayer meeting, or going twice on a Sunday or attending a Bible study. You're busy, got other things to do, don't want to really mix with Christians right now. But you never know when Jesus will really draw near. Imagine God really came down in a Church meeting and you missed it because you were watching Coronation Street or on the golf course!

Blessed

Jesus is patient and kind to Thomas. But he does ask 'have you believed because you have seen me?' (John 20:29) and he went on to say how blessed were those who believed without seeing the resurrected Lord.

I imagine that you would love to have seen him and put your hands in his nail prints and in his side but Jesus says that when we believe without seeing, we are blessed. The same Saviour that Thomas saw is the one you are trusting in if you are a Christian, or you are invited to trust in if you are not. He is real and close to each one of us (Acts 17:27) and has promised to richly bless all who come to him. He will never leave you or forsake you in this life, has washed away all your sin, will give you peace and has prepared an eternal home for you in Heaven for all eternity.

21

Breakfast on the beach

John 21:1–24

And there's more!

JOHN CHAPTER 20 FEELS LIKE THE END OF THE BOOK BUT THERE is a Chapter 21. This has led some to claim that Chapter 21 wasn't really part of the original book. However, John has said in Chapter 20 verse 30 that Jesus did 'many other signs in the presence of the disciples which are not written in this book'. So you feel that in order to prove that there is so much to know that isn't contained in the Gospel, John gives another story. John 21 begins, 'After this …' As if to say, there's more, so much more, so let me give you one more. He then finishes Chapter 21 by saying, 'Now there are also many other things that Jesus did. Were every one of them to be written, I suppose that the world itself could not contain the books that would be written' (John 21:25)

Who, where and when

It is extremely difficult to place all the resurrection appearances reported in the New Testament in chronological order. John says this was the third time Jesus was revealed to the disciples in this gospel (John 21:14). The appearance to Mary Magdalene isn't counted. Therefore, the three appearances John is referring to are: the first time he appeared to the disciples in the locked room, then the time he appeared eight days later to the disciples and Thomas, and now this time.

On this occasion, Jesus appears to seven of the disciples—Peter, Thomas, Nathanael, James, John and two unnamed disciples (John 21:2).

By now the disciples had left Jerusalem and are back in Galilee; back home in familiar green Galilee by that old familiar blue lake! They probably left Jerusalem after the Passover in dribs and drabs, not in a big caravan of pilgrims. John says that Jesus appeared to them by the Sea of Tiberius (John 21:1) which is an alternative name for the Lake of Galilee.

Gone fishing

So, back in Galilee, Peter said to the others, 'I'm going fishing' and they all go with him (John 21:3). Some have concluded this shows that Peter had turned his back on being a disciple of the Lord Jesus and returned to his old way of life. He had abandoned the faith. But this seems a little harsh. These men had to eat and support themselves. Besides Jesus had told them to go back to Galilee and wait for him (Matthew 28:9, 10).

However, it is hard to imagine Peter going fishing after Pentecost (see chapter 23 of this book). The truth is probably somewhere in between. Peter hadn't completely turned his back on being a disciple, but neither was it as important in his life as it might have been. This episode doesn't read like the lives of men on a Spirit-empowered mission to turn the world upside down (Acts

17:6). Furthermore, Jesus had said to these men to leave their nets and follow him.

And as it turned out, it was quite an unproductive fishing trip as they didn't catch anything (John 21:5). Maybe this was God showing them that this was no longer what they should be doing. He would make them fishers of men not fishers of fish. They were now to go out and instead of bringing in fish, bring in men to the kingdom of God (Matthew 4:19). Their job was to cast the gospel net throughout the whole world and catch men and women, boys and girls for the Lord Jesus Christ.

What is refreshing to see, is that these early disciples who would turn the world upside down were working class fishermen. The church isn't meant to be full of middle class professionals, kitted out in Abercrombie and Fitch and Jack Wills! It is for sinners from all backgrounds and walks of life; all rubbing shoulders with each other and loving one another with no cliques or divisions or classes. Jesus could have chosen anyone to be his disciples, from any socio-economic background, and he chose working class fishermen from Galilee!

Jesus appears

As was the case back in Luke 5, the men had been fishing all night and caught nothing (Luke 5:1–10). Jesus stood on the shore but the disciples did not recognise him, probably because the dawn was only just breaking or maybe, as with some of the previous appearances, they were kept from recognising him. Jesus said to them, 'You haven't caught anything have you?' The way he asks them shows he still loved these men so much. When he asks them if they have any fish, he refers to them as 'lads' or 'boys'. It is affectionate and warm.

And when they told him they hadn't, he told them to cast the net on the right side of the boat and they would find some. Even though they didn't recognise him, they still did it. Perhaps they thought he was someone who had come to see what they'd caught so he could buy some fish off them or even just a well-meaning 'expert' offering some much needed advice; what did they have to lose? And immediately they were unable to haul it in because of the large number of fish. In fact there were 153 fish! Peter pulled the net ashore and the disciples counted them. You can imagine them saying to each other, 'Can you believe it, I wonder how many there are? Let's count them up. Wow, there are 153!' Again this specific detail is the touch of an eye witness.

Although there were so many the net was not torn (John 21:11). This little detail is not there for the sake of it. It is to show that when these men go out and fish for men and women, boys and girls, the gospel net will never break. Peter in Acts 2 is going to take to the streets of Jerusalem and thousands are going to be saved but the net won't break. It can still catch more. Throughout the centuries millions have been saved. Lambert (2006) talks about China's Christian millions. In Operation World (Mandryk, 2010) documents how this gospel net has been cast in almost every land and people group and it still hasn't broken. Until the one who commissioned these disciples to go and catch men returns, the net will always be able to take more.

Different

John is the first to realise who it is who stands at the shore. He says to Peter, 'It is the Lord!' (John 21:7). At which point Peter jumps in. He would have been wearing nothing but an outer garment loosely draped around him, so before jumping in he would have wrapped it around him and tucked it up.

John is the first to discern. Peter is the first to act. As in John 20, John gives us a glimpse of the different characters of the disciples.

All of the disciples were different. But Jesus carefully picked each one of them. He stayed up all night before choosing them. Some are famous, some we know very little about. Some were pessimistic some were over confident. They came from different backgrounds. Simon the Zealot was a nationalist, and Matthew the tax collector would have been viewed as a traitor to his country. Some point others to the Lord and then get overshadowed by them. If you had seen them walking down the street in first century Israel and someone had pointed them out as the men Jesus had chosen to be his apostles, you would have thought, 'really? This lot?'

It is the same in the church today. We have all been given different characters and temperaments and gifts. Some can discern things and see the issues straight away. Others act and get things done. We must never wish we were like somebody else or be jealous. God has made us exactly how he wanted us to be. We are fearfully and wonderfully made (Psalm 139:14) and God has given us specific gifts for the role he wants us to carry out.

Later on in this account, Jesus and Peter walk along the beach. Jesus is telling Peter what is ahead of him. Peter turns around and sees John following. He is concerned for his junior and asks Jesus 'what about him?' (John 21:21). Jesus tells him it is none of his business. There is work to be done, souls to be reached, a task to be accomplished. Just focus on this. Jesus has a plan for each one of us; we just need to follow him.

Cooked breakfast on the beach

In John 21:12 we have one of the most wonderful scenes in the Bible. A cooked breakfast around a charcoal fire at daybreak on the Sea of Galilee, cooked by the Son of God (John 21:9). He already had bread and fish prepared and said to them, 'Come and have breakfast'. These men had caught nothing by themselves to eat for breakfast, but Jesus had got it all ready for them.

It is like a little picture of Heaven. Beautiful setting. Great food (Revelation 19:6–9). With friends in the company of the Son of God.

Do you love me?

Painful
On the night Jesus was betrayed, Peter had stood around a charcoal fire in the High Priest's courtyard and denied Jesus three times. And now here, again with a charcoal fire, Jesus is going to ask Peter three times if he loves him; really loves him. He had denied him three times and now he wants Peter to tell him three times that he loves him. The three times would also remind Peter of how he had denied him following big boasts and claims (Matthew 26:33). It was painful and it grieved Peter, but he had to look deep and think hard.

So when they had finished breakfast, Jesus walked away as though to vanish from the group. Peter, maybe taking literally the words, 'follow me' walks after Jesus down the beach with John following behind in ear shot (John 21:20). Peter and John were intimate friends and always together.

Examine yourself
As they walked Jesus asked Peter, 'Do you love me more than these?' (John 21:15). What were the 'these'? Was he looking at all the fish and the fishing gear? Or is he asking Peter do you love me more than the other disciples love me?

Peter responded with a word but not total commitment. Jesus wants Peter to be sure that he loves him. He doesn't just want Peter to love him, he wants him to love Jesus more than anyone or anything else. And he doesn't want Peter just to say it in his impulsive way. He asks him three times so he could be really sure and really had to think about it.

How do you know if you are not loving Christ as you ought? It is such an important question and one that requires self-examination because we can so easily drift. The signs to look for are that prayer ceases to be a vital part of your life. The quest for biblical truth ceases and you do not apply what the Bible says to your life. Thoughts are predominately earthly and not heavenward. Going to church and being with God's people loses its delight. Spiritual discussions are a source of embarrassment or are uncomfortable. Sins can be committed with little or no violation of the conscience. Aspirations for Christlike holiness cease to dominate your life and thinking. Your mind is focused on the acquisition of money and goods. Enjoyment of pleasure and leisure is what your life is mainly all about. Personal sins are excused by a belief that the Lord understands. Nothing is done to relieve the misery and suffering which exists around you; there is no concern for the lost or sharing the gospel. These are all signs that you do not love Christ 'more than these' (John 21:15).

Thomas Guthrie said,

> If you find yourself loving any pleasure better than your prayers, any book better than your Bible, any house better than the house of God, any table better than the Lord's table, any person better than Christ and any indulgence better than the hope of Heaven, take alarm'.

He knows

Peter had been humbled and felt that he could never be as close to Jesus again. Peter says to him, humbly, 'You know all things'. Despite my bitter failings, I love you and you know that I love you.

Maybe you feel that you can't be too committed because of your failings. You have badly let the Saviour down. But you still love him, but can't believe that he still loves you. Or if he does, you can never be close to him.

But he so wants you to be reconciled to him. However, you must tell him everything, look into your heart, leave no place out of bounds to him. It will be painful but it is the only way to be fully restored and have intimate communion with the Saviour. Examine your heart (Lamentations 3:40). Confess and repent of any known sin (1 John 1:8–9).

He wants to draw near to you. He doesn't want anything

between you. He wants you to serve him fully. He says to you 'Return to Me, and I will return to you,' (Malachi. 3:7).

Care for them

Christ told Peter that if he loved him he should feed his sheep' (John 21:17). Because of your experiences and your sincere sorrow, consider the members of my church to be your lambs and feed them. I want you to love them Peter and I want you to shepherd them. I want you to pastor them Peter. Take care of them Peter.

Peter was never the same again. He never forgot how he had let the Saviour down. But he was better for it. Peter's denial was overshadowed by his fruitful ministry and martyrdom. What better person to shepherd God's people than someone who had failed like Peter! Because of how badly he had messed up, there was no one better to shepherd and care for people who will fail and falter.

Cost

In AD 30 when Christ spoke these words to Peter, he was middle aged. Jesus says to him when you were younger you did whatever you wanted. But when you are older you will have to raise your arms so that rope can be tied around you to crucify you (cf. John 21:18, 19). By the time John wrote his Gospel Peter had already passed from the scene of history.

According to Eusebius (2011):

> But Peter seems to have preached in Pontus and Galatia and Bithynia and Cappadocia and Asia, to Jews of the Dispersion, and at last, having come to Rome, he was crucified head downward for so he himself asked to suffer.

In the Antidote for the Scorpion's Sting (XV) Tertullian says, 'At Rome Nero was first who stained with blood this rising faith. Then is Peter girt by another when he made fast to the cross'

The middle aged man who was frightened to say he even knew Jesus, in his old age, full of the Spirit of God, now wants to die an even more painful death than the Saviour he had denied. He says in effect, if my Saviour died upright, crucify me upside down.

And throughout the centuries, as we saw in Chapter 15 of this book, Christians have been given the same courage to die for their Saviour.

Now

The Lord Jesus takes Peter right back to when he first called him in Luke 5 and says 'Follow me' (John 21:19). He is showing Peter that whatever has happened is behind him, the future will be exciting and the end hard, but don't worry about anyone else or anything else, just follow me.

And that is a message for all of us. We spend so much time worrying about others, are crippled by our past, living in fear of the future, but Christ says to us to just focus on today and 'follow me' (John 21:22).

22

The Great Commission

Matthew 28:16–20

Forty days of teaching

So far we have considered several of Jesus' post resurrection appearances: Mary Magdalene, the other women, the two on the road to Emmaus, the disciples, then a week later the disciples and Thomas, and his appearance to seven of the disciples on the beach in Galilee.

But he made other appearances as well. He appeared to Peter on the same afternoon he appeared to the two on the road to Emmaus (1 Corinthians 15:5). He appeared to five hundred all at one time (1 Corinthians 15:6) and to James his brother (1 Corinthians 15:7).

In fact, he appeared to his disciples regularly during the forty days after his resurrection, teaching them the scriptures (Luke 24:36ff).

Some think that the teaching in Luke 24:44–49 was all given to the disciples on Easter Sunday evening. Lenski (1961, p.1203) for example thinks that the events of Luke 24:36–49 took place on

Easter Sunday evening, and that John 20:21–23 corresponds with Luke 24:44–49.

However, it is more likely a summary of all the things Jesus taught his disciples over the whole of the 40 days from his resurrection to his ascension. In Acts 1:3, Luke (who wrote Acts as well as his gospel) says that 'Jesus presented himself alive to [the disciples] after his suffering by many proofs, appearing to them during forty days and speaking about the kingdom of God'. But, at the end of his gospel there is no mention of Jesus appearing to his disciples during 40 days, which have led some to think that Luke is contradicting himself. However, at the end of his gospel, Luke is giving a condensed account of many of the resurrection appearances.

The important teaching that Jesus gives his disciples is that all the Law (the first five books of the Old Testament), the Prophets and Psalms are about him. As we saw in Chapter 19, he showed them that he is the key for understanding the whole Bible. He explained to them that he had to suffer and to rise from the dead on the third day. He would send the Holy Spirit to help them in the work he was commissioning them to do and they were to wait in Jerusalem for him to come (Luke 24:44–49).

The work that he commissioned them to do is what we will look at in this chapter. It is known as the great commission.

Luke says that starting in Jerusalem and working out into the whole world, the disciples were to preach repentance and forgiveness of sins in his name (Luke 24:47). But as we have established, Luke was summarising all that Jesus taught his disciples in the 40 days after his resurrection. The particular occasion when this commission was given is found in Matthew 28:16–20: Luke 24:47 probably occurred when Jesus was talking to the disciples in Galilee (cf. Matthew 28:19).

The setting

The eleven disciples went to Galilee to a mountain which Jesus had directed them to (Matthew 28:16). Jesus had sent the women who he had appeared to on that first Easter Sunday morning, to tell his brothers to go to Galilee and there they will see him (Matthew 28:10). And so the eleven disciples met Jesus on a mountainside in Galilee. It was only fitting that the great commission should take place in Galilee on a mountain. The mountain would have been quiet, picturesque and reminiscent of earlier days. Jesus had prayed all night on a mountain before he chose the twelve (Luke 6:12–15).

Maybe this occasion coincides with 1 Corinthians 15:6 when Jesus appeared to 500 people at one time. In the true, warts and all fashion of the New Testament, Matthew says, 'And when they saw him they worshipped him, but some doubted' (Matthew 28:17). At first, as Jesus started to walk towards them, some found it hard to believe it was actually him until he came close to them.

Make disciples

Jesus gathers the apostles on the mountain in Galilee. He is about to commission them to go into the world and make disciples. Even though the implication is that people will need to be converted, that is changed into Christians, the apostles are to go into the world and make disciples.

The emphasis is definitely on making disciples. Men and women, boys and girls who will follow the Lord Jesus Christ. They will listen to his Word and keep his commandments (John 14:15), be witnesses for him in the world (Matthew 5:13–16), love God with all their hearts and their neighbour as themselves in the recognition that everyone is their neighbour (Luke 10:27). Jesus Christ wants the apostles to go into the world and tell people that they must deny themselves, take up their cross and follow him (Matthew 16:24) and no longer live for themselves but for him. They need to repent of their sins and put their trust completely in him. Jesus is commanding his apostles to go into the world and tell people to turn their whole lives around. That is what being a disciple of Jesus Christ is all about.

It is not just about getting people to make a decision to follow Christ, or even to simply believe the gospel. Disciples are those who live it out. There are too many 'unconverted believers' today. They believe it but it has no impact on their lives.

The command Christ gave to, 'Go therefore and make disciples of all nations, baptising them in the name of the Father and of the Son and of the Holy Spirit, teaching them to observe all that I have commanded you' (Matthew 28:19, 20) has one imperative verb, and three supporting participles. The main verb is not 'to go'; the main verb is the command to 'make disciples'. The three participles explain how the command is to be fulfilled: they are to make disciples by going, teaching and baptising.

But before we look at how they are to fulfil the command, let's look at why we should obey the command.

Because

To 'make disciples' has been the mandate for the church ever since the great commission and will be right up until the end. But it is a huge ask. And the question is, 'Why should the world listen to the message of these apostles that has been handed down throughout Church history? Why is Christianity right and everything else wrong? Who are Christians to say what they believe is right? Why should you believe the Bible? Why can't people do what they want and please themselves? If people want to believe Islam or Hinduism or humanism or nothing at all, why does it matter?'

It matters because the one who commissioned these apostles is the Son of God. His resurrection, which we saw in previous chapters really happened, is proof that what he did on the cross was accepted by God and therefore he is able to say, 'All authority in heaven and on earth has been given to me' (Matthew 28:18). It is the only thing that God accepts and recognises. Trusting in his

Son's death and resurrection is the only hope of having my sins forgiven and getting into Heaven. Other religions who promise their adherents acceptance with God have not got the authority to do so. All authority has been given to the one who rose from the dead. Furthermore, would you really trust your eternal soul to what you or others think or feel? What is your or their authority?

Besides, because he is the all-knowing and all powerful and all loving God, he knows, can do, and wants, what is best for us. So what he commands is for our good which should encourage us to trust him.

Go

Christ tells them to make disciples, they had to 'Go' (Matthew 28:19). He didn't say wait here and I will send people to you who you can preach to. He said 'go'.

Maybe today the reason so many of our churches are empty is because we are waiting there patiently for people to turn up and listen to us preach. The message we give is 'you come and get it' but that is not the way. We need to 'go and give it'.

We do that in our work place, inviting people to church, witnessing by the way we live and what we say; going to where people are and preaching to them, in the open air, knocking on doors, joining clubs and societies, getting to know and love people, going to wherever people are and talking to them about our Saviour. Winsomely, urgently and clearly.

We cannot sit in our churches and bemoan the state of the nation, complain about young people today, how bad our politicians are and so on. We need to go out and declare to them that there is a God, a judgement, a Heaven and a Hell. We need to tell them that they are sinners but Jesus Christ died to be their Saviour. We need to urge them, implore them, plead with them to repent of their sin and trust him.

We must love people. If we haven't got a burden for the lost, then we need to ask God to give us one. Evangelism pulsates through God and our pulse rate needs to be the same. When Christ saw the multitude he had compassion on them (Matthew 9:36), and we need to have the same love for people.

Importantly, we need to get the gospel into all nations (Matthew 28:19). 'God so loved the world' (John 3:16). At times we can be guilty in the West of thinking that Christianity is for white middle class Westerners. But we forget that it actually started in a Middle Eastern country and moved out and out and out. So we need to keep moving it out!

A missionary spoke at the Heath Evangelical Church in Cardiff a few years ago. He told us about his parents who were among the first missionaries to go to Indonesia. As these Indonesians were told about the cross and resurrection hundreds and hundreds of them were saved. One of the chiefs of the tribes asked the missionaries how long ago did Jesus die? Last week, last month last year? When the missionaries said he died 2000 years ago, the people couldn't believe it and asked them why it had taken them so long to go and tell them!

And the encouraging thing for the apostles was that in this hostile world they were about to go into, were people that God had chosen and set apart to be his disciples. They would find people, many, many people, who would become disciples! And that should be our encouragement to 'go' today.

As the apostles spread this message, such people would hear it and repent of their sins and trust the Saviour. The apostles would go into the world and preach indiscriminately to everyone, but the ones God had chosen, his elect, would come to him.

The biblical doctrine of election is that before creation God chose for salvation a great number of our fallen human race and sent Christ into the world to save them (John 6:37–40; 10:27–29; 11:51, 52; Romans 8:28–39; Ephesians.1:3–14; 1 Peter 1:20). The elect are the Father's gift to the Son (John 6:39; 10:29; 17:2, 24). Jesus testifies that he came into the world specifically to save them (John 6:37–40; 10:14–16, 26–29; 15:16; 17:6–26; Ephesians 5:25–27) and now he was specifically sending his apostles out into the world to bring them in.

This doctrine has caused some controversy throughout church history, but it is unnecessary. God does not punish anyone unjustly. We are all sinners by nature and deserve God's wrath. But God in his mercy saves some and in his justice condemns others. The one who is condemned must acknowledge that he is receiving only what his sin deserves. It is important to remember that no one is sent to Hell because they were not elect. People are in Hell because they would not come to Jesus Christ. No sinner has ever come to Jesus Christ and been turned away. No one will be able to say on judgement day to Jesus Christ, 'I called to you but you would not listen'. Even though election is on every page of the Bible, it is equally true that 'everyone who calls upon the name of the Lord shall be saved' (Acts 2:21) and that God takes 'no pleasure in the death of the wicked', but that the wicked turn from his way and live' (Ezekiel 33:11). Whoever wants to can come to Jesus Christ!

The elect have done nothing to merit or earn God's favour. It is all of grace (Ephesians 2:8). It is the reason why Christians are so full of praise. Why should he choose to save any of us? Christians are no better in and of themselves than the ones who face the terrible judgement of God. The only difference is that God has set his love upon this multitude. He has graciously saved them. They have done nothing to contribute towards their salvation. They were dead in trespasses and sin and could do nothing to save themselves. They would never have chosen God.

But it is important to acknowledge that election and predestination are things that are really beyond our ultimate comprehension. The same Saviour who came to save the elect is also the same one who, when he looked out at Jerusalem said, 'Oh Jerusalem, Jerusalem, the city that kills the prophets and stones those who are sent to it! How often would I have gathered your children together as a hen gathers her brood under her wings and you would not! (Matthew 23:37). This wasn't a cold, calculating Saviour who thought, 'Well these are not the elect and so these not coming to me is simply part of the eternal redemptive plan'. He was heartbroken and says he would have loved to have gathered them, but they would not. How do we reconcile election with a God who is heartbroken with the unrepentant? I don't know. My mind is tiny and God is infinite, but all I know is that if I am a Christian, it is because God chose me and if I am not a Christian then if I come to him he will never turn me away.

The late Rev. Derek Swann said that there was a time when he fought against God's sovereignty and predestination but then he began to live off it! When someone asked Spurgeon how he reconciled God's sovereignty and man's responsibility he said that he never reconciles friends.

Instead of arguing with it and protesting against it, just come! Come now. Come as you are, your tale of sin confessing. Your past will be forgiven and forgotten; you'll have a guide, a friend and protector through life, and a glorious hope for the future! All who come will find mercy (John 6:35, 47–51; 54–57; Romans 1:16; 10:8–13).

But the question someone may have is, 'how do I know I am one of the elect?'The Bible says plainly that election is known by its fruit (1 Thessalonians 1:3–6; 2 Peter 1:5–7).

And among the elect are some seemingly unreachable people. We may look at some people and conclude that they are un-saveable. But it is not down to us to save them. Of course they are too much for us. But if God has set his love on them they will be irresistibly drawn to him. In 1960 the Humanist society in Cambridge was at its apex. The Christian Union (CU) prayed for the most unlikely people to be saved. The president of the Humanist society came to the CU mission to cause trouble and was saved! The humanists called an extraordinary meeting and appointed his successor and then his successor was saved!

But for all of that to happen we have to 'go' and tell them.

Teach

To make disciples the apostles had to 'go' but when they do 'go' what were they going to do to make disciples? Jesus told them by 'teaching them to observe all that I have commanded you'. (Matthew 28:20). To make disciples, the apostles would preach the gospel.

Preaching is the only means ordained by God. He says that it is through the preaching of the word that people will be saved (1 Corinthians 1:21; Romans 10:14). The mistake we make in the twenty first century is we adopt other methods in our attempt to reach people, but we need to rely on the means appointed by the commissioner.

We just have to preach him. The danger we have is that in this sophisticated and trendy age we try to make our message more impressive. We try to make out that Christianity is cool so that people will think Christianity can cut it in today's world. Whatever the world does we have to try and copy. Whatever methods they use, we try to use. But we can never compete with them on their terms. They will always do things bigger and better. We need to trust in the tools that have been given to us—prayer and preaching. These are the only two means that God has promised to bless.

We must avoid thinking that the message we have is not credible or impressive enough and then try to make to more impressive. The King of Glory was born in a stable not in a palace; not royalty but a working class family; reared in a country village, in the back of beyond a place that was a byword for all that was contemptible and unworthy. It was said, 'can anything good come out of Nazareth?'

The temptation has always been to try to market the 'product' better. But that is not the way. Even the miracles were primarily there really to prove that Jesus and the apostles had the authority to say and do the things they did (Mark 2:10, 11). But now we have the Bible as our authority. And the way to make disciples is taking this book and teaching it and then relying on the Holy Spirit to do the work that only he can do.

It is also important that in our preaching we preach the whole counsel of God (Acts 20:27), that is the whole Bible. We cannot just talk about the bits we like. To appeal to people we take out the hard, unpalatable bits. Don't talk too much about sin, never mention Hell. Some churches take out the supernatural. Anything that might be looked down on or sneered at by the intellectuals, they take out. They try to explain away the miracles and don't hold to the biblical ground over creation. But the Bible is a supernatural book about a supernatural God. We mustn't apologise or be embarrassed about it. We mustn't have an inferiority complex in the face of science and modern thinking. The Bible stands up to intense scrutiny and we must remember that even the brightest, cleverest mind is still a finite human being who knows so very little. Science a hundred years ago is laughed at today. We are discovering new things all the time. Whereas God is infinite and eternal. If I don't understand Mathematical equations, the problem isn't with the mathematical equation. It is with my understanding of it. The same is so much truer as I try to understand the mind of God.

Preaching is to be built on the scriptures. It is to bring people to salvation, teach them sound doctrine, correct us from going wrong in what we think and in how we behave and train us in right behaviour (2 Timothy 3:16).

In making disciples there are different emphases in using the Bible. The evangelist preaches with the aim of bringing those who are not saved to a saving faith. The Bible teacher's aim is to teach people the scripture and doctrine. The Bible study leader is to apply these truths to people's real lives and situations. But really, the work of the preacher is to embrace all of these concerns.

It is also important in preaching and making disciples, to preach to people where they are at, not where they ought to be. We need to preach to people in the state they are in, in a language they understand, according to the knowledge they have and the time they find themselves in.

Above all we are to preach the majesty of a holy God and the glory of the Lord Jesus Christ.

Baptize

Why?

Jesus commands his apostles to make disciples and to do that they needed to 'go', 'teach' and 'baptise' them. This shows that baptism is important. According to Masters (1998, p.11):

> [Jesus] does not merely suggest we should be baptised. Neither does he advise or recommend it. The Lord who bled for us looks upon us with that kindness and love which is beyond describing—and commands it.

Disciples are to be baptised in the name of the Father, Son and Holy Spirit. Baptism confers acceptance by and commitment to all three persons of the Godhead. Baptism into the name of the triune God signifies control and direction by God himself. So important.

What?

But the outward sign of baptism does not automatically or magically convey the inward blessing that it signifies, and the professions of faith of those who are baptised are not always genuine (cf. Acts 8:13–24).

Baptism pictures or symbolises:

- Obedience. It is following in Jesus' footsteps (Matthew 3:13–15).

- Forgiveness and inward cleansing from sin. Immersion in water illustrates the washing away of the whole body of sin (Acts 22:16; 1 Corinthians 6:11; Ephesians 5:25–27).

- New life (in which the imagery of burial and rising again

illustrates the radical change of having died to the old life, to receive a new, converted life (Titus 3:5).

- Identification, union with Christ in his death, burial and resurrection (in which we tread in the steps of our Saviour and forerunner to show that we are now more closely identified with Him than with anyone or anything on earth (Titus 3:5).

- The abiding presence of the Holy Spirit as God's seal testifying and guaranteeing that one will be kept safe in Christ forever (1 Corinthians 12:13; Ephesians 1:13–14).

Which?

All Christians accept that baptism is important but the church has been divided throughout the centuries between infant baptism and believers' baptism. There have been very good men who have believed in believers' baptism and others in infant baptism and both have based their convictions on the scriptures. Therefore, one cannot be too dogmatic on the subject. It is also important to stress that this is a secondary issue, and what someone believes about this does not determine their eternal destiny. As we have seen, the dying thief didn't have opportunity to be baptised!

In saying all of that, it would seem that the baptism Jesus commands here and which is spoken of in the New Testament is believers' baptism. There appears to be no evidence on the pages of the New Testament to support infant baptism and no examples of infants baptised in the Bible. All the people named in the New Testament in connection with baptism were believers.

Those who hold to the conviction of infant baptism assume that when the Philippian jailer was baptised in Acts 16:33, his infant children were baptised with him, but there is no evidence they were infants. His household may well have consisted of older children and servants. In fact Roman jailers were often older ex-servicemen so it is almost certain his children would be grown up. Acts 16:34

implies that these children were old enough to understand the message that Paul and Silas preached to them.

Another text used by infant baptists is Acts 2:38 where Peter calls people to repent and be baptised, promising the gift of the Holy Spirit to all who do so. He goes on to say that the promise 'is for you and for your children and for all who are far off, everyone whom the Lord our God calls to himself' (Acts 2:39). However, it would seem that this doesn't refer to the fact that babies should be baptised, but refers to subsequent generations, the ones 'the Lord our God calls to himself'. People who hear the call of God must repent in order to receive the Holy Spirit. Infants can neither hear the call or repent. Plus, Acts 2:41 says they that gladly received his word were baptised. This assumes they were not infants.

Two other texts are given by those who advocate infant baptism—Acts 10:48 and Acts 16:5. But in Acts 10:48 the people gathered with Cornelius were his kinsmen and near friends who heard the word (Acts 10:24, 44), not his infants. In Acts 16:15, Lydia does not even appear to be married so her household consisted probably of adult servants, capable of believing.

It seems that baptism follows repentance (Acts 2:38) and is exclusively a sign of faith and conversion.

In saying all of that, God loves to save families, but it appears more appropriate that Christian families should dedicate their children to God, commit them to him, promise to bring them up in the way of good things, and pray that what they have been taught and modelled will become real to them, so they will show that publicly one day by repenting and being baptised.

How?

As for how people are to be baptised, there seems to be no prescription of a particular mode of baptism found in the New Testament. The command to baptise may be fulfilled by immersion, dipping or sprinkling; all three modes satisfy the meaning of the

Greek verb *baptizo* and the symbolic requirements of passing under, and emerging from, cleansing water.

However, it would appear that total immersion was the mode used in the New Testament. John 3:23 says that John the Baptist was baptising in Aenon near to Salim because there was much water there (John 3:23). According to Calvin,

> From these words it may be inferred that baptism was administered by John and Christ by plunging the whole body under water … here we perceive how baptism was administered … for they immersed the whole body in water.

With you, always

The disciples were going into a hostile world. They would be rejected, mocked and nearly all of them would be martyred. But wherever they went and whoever they stood before, Jesus was with them. He says, 'And behold I am with you always, to the end of the age' (Matthew 28:20). Remember, he says, I am with you day in day out until the close of the age.

And he is with us too. As you sit in the 6th form common room, he is with you. On the factory floor, in the staff room, the board room, the university lecture hall, the classroom, he is there with you. He said 'He will not leave you or forsake you' (Deuteronomy 31:6). As you try to speak up for him, tell a friend or colleague or family member about him, mustering up all the courage you can, he is with you; right next to you.

Dr Martyn Lloyd-Jones, was one of the most famous Welsh preachers ever, and the minister of Westminster Chapel, London in the last century. Indeed he is known throughout the world and his books have helped millions. So someone once said, 'wouldn't it be great to do door-to-door if Dr Martyn Lloyd-Jones was with you?' No doubt it would, but a far greater than Lloyd-Jones has promised to come with you every time you speak up for Jesus Christ. He himself is with you and he holds the one who you are witnessing to in his hand!

23

Where is Jesus now —the Ascension

Mark 16:19, 20; Luke 24:50–53; Acts 1:9–12

Introduction

OVER THE LAST 22 CHAPTERS WE HAVE LOOKED AT WHY JESUS came to earth; his agony and arrest in Gethsemane; his trials before the religious leaders and Roman authorities; his crucifixion and resurrection. But the question remains, if Jesus is alive, where is he now? And what is he doing?

In Luke 24:50–53 and Acts 1:9–12 says that Jesus ascended to Heaven. We will look at this by asking and answering 9 questions.

1. When and where did it happen?

The ascension took place after Jesus had commissioned his apostles. Jesus had given the disciples the Great Commission on a mountain in Galilee. Sometime after that they had left Galilee and gone back to Jerusalem. Maybe just before he ascended he reminded them once again of the Great Commission he had given them in Galilee (Luke 24:47, 48).

In his Gospel, Luke says that Jesus led them out as far as Bethany, and lifting up his hands he blessed them and while he blessed them he parted from them and was carried up into heaven (Luke 24:50, 51). In Acts 1:12 Luke says that Jesus ascended up into heaven from the mount called Olivet which was near Jerusalem, a Sabbath day's journey. Again there is no contradiction here. Jesus didn't take them to Bethany but out towards Bethany. The Mount of Olives would have been in that direction, about 1 kilometre walk which was permitted on the Sabbath and would have taken them about 15 minutes.

2. Who saw it?

When the Lord Jesus ascended it was in front of the apostles (Acts 1:6–8). It was just the apostles who witnessed the ascension.

But later that day they were joined by others (Acts 1:13–16). They no doubt gathered in the upper room where they had eaten the Last Supper (Luke 22:12), which was possibly the upstairs room in the house of Mary, John Mark's mother. It was in that same house that later many of the Jerusalem church gathered to pray (Acts 12:12).

We know that soon after the ascension, 120 believers gathered together (Acts 1:15). Among these were no doubt Mary Magdalene, Joanna (whose husband managed Herod's household) and Susanna—the three ladies mentioned by Luke (8:2–3). The others who went to the tomb were also there as were his brothers (Acts 1:14) and his mother.

It was during these days that they replaced Judas (Acts 1:15–26). They needed to do this to fulfil the scriptures (Acts 1:15–17, 20). To be an apostle you had to be an eyewitness of all that Jesus had done, from his baptism right through to his ascension (Acts 1:22). Two men were put forward and after praying over it and asking God to guide them, Matthias was chosen. We know that Jesus appeared to 500 at one time, probably in Galilee, and no doubt Matthias was one of those.

After praying they cast lots. This way of discovering God's will doesn't seem to have been used after the Holy Spirit had come. Today Christians are guided through prayer and reading the Word of God, along with sanctified common sense that we exercise in the light of the Word of God and the situation we are facing. It is clear the apostles did this in making decisions (Acts 1:21–26).

3: How did it happen?

Jesus led the eleven (Acts 1:13) out towards Bethany on the eastern slope of the Mount of Olives. Previously he had been arrested in a garden, tied up and held in custody by the religious leaders and Roman governors; he had been mocked and beaten by soldiers, nailed to a cross of shame. His lifeless corpse had been taken down and put in a cave. But now he is leading his disciples out to a mountain so they can watch him ascend to his Father. He is the conqueror.

Having arrived there he busily engaged in conversation with them. He corrects one of their errors about when he is coming back (see below) and he repeats the promise that they will receive the Holy Spirit who will qualify them for the task they have been commissioned to do (Acts 1:6–8).

In full view of the disciples he was lifted up into the sky. They saw him ascend until a cloud hid him from their sight (Acts 1:9). The account of the ascension is very matter of fact. It isn't embellished or dramatized. Luke just states the facts. Stott (1991, p.48) says 'It reads like history, and as if Luke intended us to accept it as history'. Haenchen (cited in Stott (1991) p.48) says, 'the story is unsentimental, almost uncannily austere'.

Before he left them he lifted up his hands and blessed them (Luke 24:50). This is significant. It was the archetypal pose of the High Priest in the Old Testament. When he had offered a sacrifice for sin, he would come out of the holy of Holies and raise his hands and bless the people to signify that the sacrifice had been accepted by God. By lifting his hands, Jesus is saying that everything that needed to be done to secure their eternal salvation from sin, guilt, death and hell has been accepted by God; once and forever. It is done. The ascension, and how he ascended, shows mission accomplished! Sinners can be friends with God; better still, they are children of God (John 1:12; 1 John 3:1).

It was actually while he was blessing them that he left them. How you leave is important. He left them with blessing ringing in their ears and hearts.

4: Why did it happen?

As we have seen, for forty days since his resurrection, Jesus had been teaching his disciples. He had appeared, disappeared and reappeared many times during that period, giving them important instructions on the task they were about to carry out.

He told them to wait in Jerusalem until the Holy Spirit came and clothed them with power (Luke 24:49). Before ending his personal ministry on earth, Jesus deliberately made provision for its continuation on earth (through the apostles), and from heaven (through the Holy Spirit).

However, when he led them out to the Mount of Olives he wanted them to know that this time his departure was final, and he wanted everyone to see it and know that. He wasn't coming back to earth until the Second Coming (Matthew 24:30, 31).

His ascension into heaven also marked the sending of the Holy Spirit. Even though the disciples couldn't see Jesus anymore, they would have his Spirit. This would be even better. The man Christ Jesus was localised. He was confined to a particular area at a particular time. He must have gone to bed at night and thought of all the people he didn't reach but now, by his Spirit, he can be everywhere at once.

5: Where did he go to?

He returned to Heaven. He went to a real place. And excitingly, Jesus' ascension foreshadows our ascension to Heaven. It is a promise of our future heavenly home.

One day we will disappear from view. We will leave this world behind. But we will live on, we will go to a place, a real place, a much better place. Right now, as we go about our business on planet earth, there are people in Heaven. It is the place Jesus went to when he disappeared out of the disciples' sight. Though we can't see him, he is alive and real in a place that is alive and real!

Even now we are sat with Christ in the heavenly places (Ephesians 2:6). When Christ ascended to heaven all the glory he received and everything he accomplished is already ours. All that is Christ's is mine. They are stored in Heaven for us (1 Peter 1:3–5; Colossians 3:3–4; Ephesians 1:3). God thinks of those blessings as rightfully ours, just as if we had earned them ourselves. This is called union with Christ. (Romans 6:3–10; Colossians 2:12, 20; 3:1). If we are trusting Jesus Christ we are united to him which also brings us into union with the Father and Holy Spirit.

Through Christ, we have been adopted into God's family (Galatians 3:26; 4:4–7). The apostle Paul says in Galatians 3:26, 'for in Christ Jesus you are all sons of God through faith' and again in Galatians 4:7, 'so you are no longer a slave, but a son, and if a son then an heir through God'. Packer describes our status as sons of God in his brilliant book, Knowing God (1993). He says:

> In Paul's world, adoption was ordinarily of young adult males of good character to become heirs and maintain the family name of the childless rich. Paul, however, proclaims God's gracious adoption of persons of bad character to become 'heirs of God and fellow heirs with Christ'

(Romans 8:17). The adopted status of believers means that in and through Christ, God loves them as he loves his only begotten Son, and will share with them all the glory that is Christ's now (Romans 8:17, 38–39).

Christ has ascended to the highest heaven and one day we will be with him. Therefore we may pray to God as father (Matthew 6:5–13) and trust him as such (Matthew 6:25–34).

All this is terrific, but how do we know that we are united to Christ? How can we know that all these blessings are ours?

The evidence is in our sanctification, which is the way I am being changed day by day and year by year to be more like Jesus Christ and more fitted for Heaven. Heaven is in us before we are in Heaven. It is a lifelong process where Christians become increasingly Christlike.

That is not to say that Christians are perfect. They find a tension in their lives and find within them contrary urgings (Romans 7:14–25). 'The Spirit sustains their regenerate desires and purposes; their fallen, Adamic instincts (the flesh) which though dethroned are not yet destroyed, constantly distract them from doing God's will and allure them along paths that lead to death' (Galatians 5:16–17; James 1:14–15). But Christians are, according to the Westminster Shorter Catechism (Q.35), 'enabled more and more to die unto sin and live unto righteousness'. The moral profile of Jesus is progressively formed in them (2 Corinthians 3:18; Galatians 4:19; 5:22–25). So, 'whoever says he abides in him ought to walk in the same way in which he walked' (1 John 2:6). Keeping his commandments is an indication that we are united to Christ.

Someone who is a real Christian and is united to the ascended Christ, dies to self (Mark 8:34). They have a deep dependence on Christ. Their confidence is not in themselves but in Christ (Galatians 2:20; Romans 15:18; Philippians 4:13). They abide in him (1 John 2:28; 3:6, 24), that is they spend time praying, reading, meditating on his Word and doing the things that please him.

John's Gospel says, 'Whoever abides in me and I in him, he it is that bears much fruit' (John 15:5).

The Holy Spirit also bears witness to us that Christ is in us (1 John 3:24). He is the great source of spiritual strength that is within us (1 John 4:4).

Furthermore, those united to the ascended Christ are prepared and ready to suffer with him (1 Peter 2:21).

These are all characteristics that a person displays who is united to the ascended Christ and one day will ascend to be with him.

6: What happened when he got there?

It is hard to imagine the glorious scene that greeted the Lord Jesus Christ when he returned to his Father and re-entered heaven. He had enjoyed heaven as the Son of God but he was now returning as the Son of Man. His divine nature was now permanently joined by a human nature.

The picture the Bible gives is of the hosts of heaven looking out from the towers of the heavenly Jerusalem to see the Lord Jesus as he ascends through the clouds, accompanied by an entourage of angels chanting, 'Open the city gates and let the king of glory in'. And from the city towers came the response, 'But who is the king of glory that we should fling open the gates of the heavenly Jerusalem for him?' To which the answer would come: 'The Lord, strong and mighty in battle. He is the king of glory. Open the doors that the king of glory may come in' (Psalm 24:7–10).

And so the Son of Man comes to the Ancient of Days. He comes from the bloody scenes of Calvary and the victory of his resurrection to receive the kingdom and the power and the glory.

Jesus refers to himself fifty or so times as the Son of Man. One latent meaning of Son of Man is 'here is a true man'. 'Son of' is a Hebrew way of saying 'possessing the properties of', 'being characterised by, exhibiting the marks of'. Adam was the first son of man and failed, but now *The Son of Man* has beaten the devil and all the powers of darkness.

This is a precursor to when Christ returns to earth again. On that occasion he will come to judge the world. Those who have rejected him will be consigned to Hell forever. But those who are trusting him will be taken with him into glory. This is known as glorification.

Glorification is something which all the people of God will enter together at the exact same point in time.

When a believer dies they enter Paradise (1 Thessalonians 4:16, 17; 1 Corinthians 15:51, 52). But at the moment they are spirits; the 'spirits of the righteous made perfect' (Hebrews 12:23). According to the Shorter Catechism,

> The souls of believers are at their death made perfect in holiness and do immediately pass into glory: and their bodies, being still united to Christ, do rest in their graves until the resurrection.

But our glorification will happen when Christ comes again. It refers to the immediate change that will take place for all Christians at the Second Coming. Christ will descend from Heaven with a shout of triumph and all his people, from the four corners of the earth and from throughout history, will have new bodies and enter the new heaven and new earth together. The whole of creation will be renewed (Romans 8:21). Satan and all his angels will be cast into Hell forever, never to trouble the people of God again. No chance of sin re-entering. Glory!

Christ ascension to Heaven gives a glimpse of what it will be like.

7: When is he coming back?

As Jesus led them out to the Mount of Olives, they ask him, 'Lord, will you at this time restore the kingdom to Israel?' (Acts 1:6).

They are saying in effect 'when are you coming back to set up the kingdom of heaven?'

They were still mistaken about the nature of the kingdom of heaven. They didn't want Christ to go and wanted him to stay and set up the kingdom of heaven on earth. They failed to understand the true nature of the kingdom of God.

It is a kingdom that really has three dimensions.

Firstly, when Christ was on earth, he told people that the kingdom of heaven was among them (Luke 17:21). That is, wherever he was, the kingdom of God was.

Secondly, the kingdom of God is also spiritual. It will never figure on any map. It is not a realm but a rule; a rule in people's lives. It has no borders but is international. The apostles were being sent out into the whole world to make disciples of all nations. The kingdom will include people from every tribe and people and language and nation (Revelation 7:9).

The kingdom of God is wherever the rule of God is set up in people's hearts and lives. Disciples' lives will be changed by kingdom values. However, even though it isn't geographical or in that sense tangible, it will, or should have radical political and social implications. If Christians live out and hold to kingdom values they will collide with secular values. Moreover, Christians should seek to make a positive impact on the world around them (Matthew 5:13–16).

Thirdly, there is also a future dimension to the kingdom of God which will be established at the end when the Saviour returns. It will be heaven. When that is though, only God knows and it is none of our business (Acts 1:7). The disciples wanted it to happen there and then. They say 'at this time' (Acts 1:6). It was a mixture of curiosity and impatience. 'When?!' 'Can it happen today?!'

But Jesus tells them that all they need to do is get on with the task of making disciples of all nations. All they need to know is that Jesus Christ is coming back one day. Until he does he will send his Holy Spirit to be with them as they go, teach and baptise. They are to build the kingdom that will expand gradually until eventually all the elect are gathered in and then he will return. Their only business is to go on a world-wide mission and be his witnesses, and the task is urgent. There is no time to sit about wondering when he might come back.

Acts 1:10, 11 says, 'And while they were gazing into heaven behold two men stood by them in white robes and said, "men of Galilee why do you stand looking into heaven? This Jesus who was taken up from you in heaven will come in the same way as you saw him go into heaven"'

The message is that Jesus is coming back. And he is not coming back on his own. It will be nothing like his first coming. He will not return alone but with millions of holy ones with him—both human and angelic (Matthew 25:31; 1 Thessalonians 3:13).

So stop heaven gazing and look out on a world in compassion that needs the Saviour. Get on with it!

8. What is he doing until he comes back?

Jesus ascended to Heaven. One day he is coming back to this earth. Until he comes again he has commanded first his apostles, then Christians throughout the ages to make disciples of all nations. He has sent his Holy Spirit to help with this huge task. But the question remains, what is Jesus doing now?

1. Presiding over the universe

He is presiding over the whole universe (Hebrews 1:3). He ascended far above; above all the kings, presidents, the royal family, thinkers, scientists, philosophers and the good and the great of this world; they are all below him. One day every knee will bow and every tongue will confess that Jesus Christ is Lord (Philippians 2:10). He was taken up and a cloud took him out of their sight (Acts 1:9).

He is higher up than them all and has authority over the universe (Ephesians 1:20, 21; 1 Peter 3:22). He is actually in Heaven. The president of the USA lives in the White House, decisions are made in the Oval office; he has at his disposal the whole might of the US military. He's the commander in chief and knows the nuclear codes. Impressive and powerful. But Jesus is in Heaven. He has at his disposal the whole might of Heaven and holds in his hand the whole world.

It was said of Bill Clinton, former president of the United States, that he had such a huge presence and was such a charismatic figure that when he walked into a room he owned it. Well Jesus Christ is far above Bill Clinton and every other president and king and he really does own every room—the staff room, university lecture hall, common room, office, factory floor, board room. He presides over all things.

2. Ruling his Church

Not only is he presiding over the universe but he is also ruling his church. It is not the pope, or any bishop or cardinal or council that should decide the doctrine or ethics of the church. It is the Lord Jesus Christ, and he has clearly set out how things should be done in his Word. The church shouldn't take her lead from the society of its day, human reason or traditions or feelings, but from the commands of her ascended Lord and Saviour who rules from on high.

That Christ is ruling his Church is so comforting and reassuring for Christians because even though he presides over the universe, he governs it all in the interest of his church. The church isn't some side show; it is the very centre of history. Everything that takes place in history is all for the good of the church (Romans 8:28).

I have been to see my son in numerous school plays. There have been hundreds of other children on the stage at the same time as him, but my eyes for the whole time are on him. There are 7 billion people on planet earth. Great nations. Powerful leaders. But the

Lord Jesus Christ has ascended to the highest heaven and is ruling his church. His eye is on her the whole time.

3: Being our Great High Priest

Jesus is in Heaven pleading our cause and interceding on our behalf before God. He is in Heaven at God's right hand mediating between us and God (1 Timothy 2:5). He is my Great High Priest.

The idea of Jesus as our Great High Priest would have been familiar to Jews who had become Christians. They would have known all about priests and sacrifices and the tabernacle and the temple. But to any of us Gentiles (non-Jews), living in the twentieth century, these things may be alien concepts. So for us to appreciate that the ascended Jesus is in Heaven now as our Great High Priest, we need to have some understanding of the Tabernacle/Temple and the Old Testament priesthood.

High Priests

The Old Testament priesthood showed how awesome a thing it is to approach God. It was serious and if one approached him in the wrong way it resulted in death. In Exodus and Leviticus it specifically states how people can approach God. It was only through the High Priest and the sacrifices they made on behalf of the people. Exodus 28, 29 and the book of Leviticus describe the dress, consecration and duties of the priests. Everything had to be done meticulously.

People couldn't just approach God any old how. God is holy and we are sinners. He can't even look at sin so if we came before him on our own, we would be destroyed. Therefore, God appointed priests in the Old Testament to represent people before him. They offered sacrifices for sins on behalf of the people (Leviticus 1–7). The priesthood gave 'types', or pictures of spiritual realities and had no permanent value. The priesthood and sacrifices themselves did not atone for the people but showed three things: forgiveness is costly, punishment for sin is death and without shedding of blood there is no forgiveness for sin.

Tabernacle/Temple

In the same way that the High Priest and the sacrifices he made could not actually take away sin but were just types and pictures of what the Messiah would do when he came, the Temple, and before it the Tabernacle, were visual aids of God's presence. They were pictures.

In the Old Testament, God instructed Moses to make a sanctuary that was an earthly copy and shadow of what was in Heaven. God did this to convey to our poor minds some idea of invisible and spiritual realities.

It was called the Tabernacle. Exodus 25–27 and 35–40 describe the fabric, furniture and construction of it.

It was a tent pitched in a large courtyard. It had two rooms which were separated by a veil. The one was the Holy place. Only the priest could enter here; the people had to remain in the courtyard outside.

But the other room in the tent was the Holy of Holies. Inside the holy of Holies was kept a box, the Ark of the Covenant. Inside the Ark of the Covenant were the two tablets of stone on which the Ten Commandments were written and above it were sculptures—the two cherubim of glory overshadowing the mercy seat. The priest never went into Holy of Holies. Only the High Priest went in, and only once a year. The veil symbolised God's inaccessibility to the sinner and could only be penetrated on this one day, the Day of Atonement and by no other person than the High Priest, and by no other condition than the shedding and sprinkling of blood.

The temple was built along the same lines as the Tabernacle. It consisted of a Holy Place and a Most Holy Place, though the latter no longer contained the Ark of the Covenant. The two areas were divided by a great curtain or veil. A huge altar of burnt sacrifice stood in the front of the temple. The temple was surrounded by a number of courts, each more exclusive than the last. Gentiles were only admitted into the outer courtyard. There was also a Court of the Women.

There was so much imagery and symbolism, but the overwhelming message in the Old Testament period, before the Saviour came, was that people couldn't approach God on their own. They couldn't just enter his presence. Sinners were not allowed to approach him directly, because God is holy. The High Priest needed to represent their case before him, sacrifices needed to be made and the message, loud and clear, was so far, but no farther!

A Great High Priest that has passed through the heavens

But as a result of Jesus' finished work on Calvary (John 19:30), and his ascension to the right hand of God, it has all changed. There is no longer need of a tabernacle or a temple or a High Priest. We can come directly to God and enter his presence because Jesus is there. We no longer have need of a High Priest in a temple in Jerusalem because we have a great High Priest who has ascended to heaven and is in the presence of God all the time. When Christ cried out on the cross, the veil in the Temple was ripped from top to bottom. God ripped it. The message loud and clear is that sinners, through Jesus Christ, have direct access. We are all a kingdom of priests (1 Peter 2:5).

It is so much better in so many ways. This is emphasised in the title given to the Lord Jesus Christ. In the Old Testament era one priest was differentiated from the others by being called great or high. But Jesus Christ is called a great High Priest (Hebrews 4:14). So much greater and higher than all others!

The Old Testament priests were sinners and had to offer sacrifices for their own sins as well as for the sins of the people, but Jesus Christ was and is the sinless Son of God (Hebrews 7:26, 27). And whereas the High Priest offered animal sacrifices on behalf of the people, Jesus Christ offered himself as a sacrifice to God (Hebrews 9:11–14). He was the final sacrifice. The one all the millions and millions of other sacrifices had pointed to. There is no longer any need for sacrifices because he was the Lamb of God who took away the sin of the world (John 1:29). God's wrath has been turned away and justice has been satisfied. Christ has finished his work.

In the Old Testament the priests in the temple never sat down because their work was never finished. The sacrifices they made were only types and pictures of what Christ did on Calvary and so the work that needed to be done was never completed. But when Christ cried out, 'It is finished' everything that you and I need to be right with God is finished, and so he is sat down (Hebrews 1:3; 10:11, 12). Everything is done!

But the Jews who had become Christians through the apostles' preaching found all this difficult to come to terms with and coupled with the persecution they were suffering as Christians, some were in danger of going back to Judaism. They had loved their temple and the fact that they could go to the priest. It was visible, tangible and grand. Christianity seemed plain compared to Judaism and all its trappings. They would be taunted by their old Jewish friends that this 'new' religion had no High Priest to intercede for its misguided adherents. A.W. Pink in his commentary on Hebrews (2003 edition) says that nothing had a stronger hold on the imagination and affection of the Jews than 'the gorgeous apparel, solemn investiture, mysterious sacredness of the High Priest, the grandeur of the Temple in which he ministered and the imposing splendour of the religious rites which he performed'. All these operated like a charm in enticing them away from the simple, spiritual, unostentatious system by which it was superseded.

This is why the book of Hebrews in the New Testament was written. It was a letter to Jewish Christians and the author is at pains to say to these Jews, 'don't go back because, despite its simplicity, Christianity is so much better. The priesthood and temple and sacrifices were only pictures of something far, far greater.'

The Christians' High Priest is invisible because he has 'passed through the heavens' (Hebrews 4:14). Jesus of Nazareth who was born in Bethlehem, raised in Nazareth and died on Calvary is no longer visible because he has ascended to Heaven and is appearing in the presence of God on our behalf (Hebrews 9:24). Our hope of entering Heaven is founded on the fact that our High Priest has already entered it. We need him to be there. The temple was just a picture, a visual aid for Heaven and the presence of God. Far better to have a High Priest you cannot see if he is actually in Heaven, in God's presence, at his right hand (Luke 22:69) interceding on our behalf continually. The High Priest was allowed into the Holy of Holies once a year. Jesus Christ is in God's presence continually which means I can approach God 24/7!

By shedding his blood he made peace for us (Ephesians 2:16; Colossians 1:20). We can now come before God boldly and intimately because Jesus is there making it possible. All hostilities between us and God are over. We no longer need to fear in his presence (John 12:32; Romans 15:18; 2Corinthians 5:18–21; Ephesians 2:17). We come into God's presence without fear. Moreover, we are encouraged and welcome to come to him! (Hebrews 4:14–16).

A Sympathetic High Priest
But even though Jesus is great and in Heaven, he is not beyond my reach. He is also a sympathetic High Priest (Hebrews 4:15). He is able to enter into our struggles and sympathises with our weaknesses. As we saw in Chapter 1 of this book, he still remembers what it is like to be me and you. He still remembers Gethsemane! In fact the Bible says that the Lord Jesus learned obedience (Hebrews 5:8). Jesus never did anything wrong. He was perfect so this cannot mean he learned how to be good. It really means he learned what it was like to be human. He learned what it was like to be me and you.

There is nothing that you go through that he cannot sympathise with you about. He bore all your sins on the cross. He suffered the guilt and shame and torment that your life and sins deserve. Even though he never sinned he felt the consequences of those sins. In fact he experienced far worse than us. Because he never gave in to temptation, he knows the power of temptation far stronger than we do. He also knows total abandonment by God. When he was suffering the eternal torment of guilt and sin God turned his back on him.

Maybe you are a Christian and you are going through a really hard time. Perhaps it has been going on a while and you feel no one understands. It seems unbearable. Heaven is silent and you feel forgotten by God. Jesus Christ says to you, 'I know, I've been there'. The one we come before remembers his own time of need on earth, strengthened by his father and ministering angels (Mark 1:13; Luke 22:43). Jesus became flesh—real, weak but without sin. He stepped into our shoes. When I pray, I need him, want him, must have him as close as possible to God but at the same time, I need him to remember what it was like to be me. His time on earth, especially in Gethsemane and on the cross, means he does.

So come boldly

The fact that the Lord Jesus has ascended to Heaven and is right now interceding for us as our Great High Priest should really encourage us to come to him.

Perhaps you are finding it really hard being a Christian at the moment. The attraction of the world, being left out and not being part of the crowd are all a bit much right now. Perhaps there are particular temptations you face, or sins you really struggle with or a particular person is giving you a hard time because you are a Christian. The state of the Church gets you down and leaves you feeling discouraged.

You could even be at the point of giving up. You look at the world and think how impressive it is; its universities, pop concerts, state buildings, sports stadiums, board rooms, theatres. Everything is so visible, tangible, real and impressive. Then you come to the church, and it is all a bit invisible and hard and unimpressive. You feel that you, other Christians and the Church seem so rubbish in comparison with the world and all that it has to offer.

But think. The one those eleven disciples saw ascend up through the clouds has gone to Heaven to be at God's right hand to intercede for us as our Great High Priest. We can come with boldness and confidence and find grace to help in our time of need. We have direct access to the throne room of God. Far better than the White House or Downing Street or Buckingham Palace or anywhere else! My voice isn't just getting heard in congress, or parliament or in the oval office or around the cabinet table; Jesus Christ is praying for me in Heaven. We have the ear of God!

When I have been too busy to pray; when I am so troubled and overwhelmed that I cannot put my prayers into words; when I am afar off, he is praying for me and that should really encourage me. Robert Murray McCheyne once said: 'If I could hear Christ praying for me in the next room, I would not fear a million enemies.' But far greater than him praying in the next room is that he is praying in the presence of God for you.

So when we pray we know that he is interceding on our behalf. That should motivate us to come to him. Come broken. Come empty. Come confused. Don't come pretending you are something you are not. Don't think he won't listen to you because of all the sins in your past. Ask him where the car keys are. Ask him to save your children. Ask him for health. Ask him for holiness. Ask him for everything!

The writer to the Hebrews repeatedly uses the verb 'to have' (6:19; 8:1; 10:19–22, 34; 13:10, 14). These people had forgotten their privileges. That is good for us to be reminded of today. We haven't got to grit our teeth and get on with it until we get to Heaven. Every day I have access to God; the maker and sustainer of the universe, my loving Father whose presence I can enjoy and be at home in because of Jesus Christ.

I can come to him for help and strength. He is interceding for me that my daily sins may be pardoned, that I may be kept from the accusations and temptations of Satan and that I may be progressively sanctified.

The ascension means that Jesus is accessible to all who come to him (Hebrews 4:14) and he is powerful to help them, anywhere in the world (Hebrews 4:16; 7:25; 13:6–8).

9: What happens on Earth in the meantime?

The Holy Spirit is with us

After Jesus ascended to Heaven there were ten days before he sent the Holy Spirit to earth. The disciples were told to wait in the city until they had been clothed with power from on high that would enable them to carry out the great task they had been commissioned to do (Luke 24:44–49). Until they receive this great gift they must remain quietly in Jerusalem (Acts 1:4).

So after the Lord Jesus ascended, they then returned to Jerusalem to wait, with great joy. You may have thought that having seen Jesus leave them they would be sad but they had come to realise that they had lost nothing and gained more. They had Jesus for a while but now by his Spirit they have him forever until he returns in glory (Acts 1:11). The Jesus of history began his ministry on earth, but the Christ of glory has been active through his Spirit ever since. He has kept his promise to be with his people always, to the very end of the age.

The coming of the Holy Spirit came at Pentecost which was a Jewish Festival. According to the Jewish historian Josephus (Maier 1988) the normal population of Jerusalem was 150,000 people but it often swelled to more than a million during Pentecost. The suburbs were also crammed with people as were the hills surrounding Jerusalem, on which people were camped. Far more people were in the city at this time than ever heard the Lord Jesus speak. It is no accident that the Godhead chose this time to send the Spirit.

The coming of the Holy Spirit concerned especially the 11 (soon again to be the 12, Acts 1:26). Pentecost is unrepeatable. It is the same as the birth of Christ, his death, resurrection and ascension. They can never be repeated. Pentecost brought the apostles the equipment they needed for their special role of making disciples of all nations (Matthew 28:18–20). It was the inauguration of the new era.

Peter's preaching in Acts 2:14–36 illustrates the power of the Holy Spirit and how he enabled them to be true and effective witnesses. As Peter preached on the streets of Jerusalem, in one day 3,000 were converted. No doubt many of those who were converted were present at Calvary (Luke 23:48).

However, even though the coming of the Holy Spirit was a unique and unrepeatable event, it has significance for every believer. All the people of God can now, always and everywhere, benefit from his ministry. The promise of the Holy Spirit is for every Christian (John 14:16, 17, 26; Acts 1:8).

The same Holy Spirit that came upon the disciples at Pentecost is the same Holy Spirit that is in every Christian. In fact we are totally dependent on the Holy Spirit.

The work of the Holy Spirit is essential in a person becoming a Christian. You cannot be a Christian unless the Holy Spirit does a work in your heart. Only the Holy Spirit can produce a spiritual change in a person. The Bible says that we are all 'dead in trespasses and sins' (Ephesians 2:1). Only the Holy Spirit can give us life. This is called regeneration and according to Packer (1994, p.157) regeneration is 'God renovating the heart, the core of a person's being, by implanting a new principle of desire, purpose and action.' It is a work which only God the Holy Spirit can do. Without the Holy Spirit we would have no interest in God. We would never put our faith in Jesus Christ or believe the gospel unless the Holy Spirit enabled us.

The first thing the Holy Spirit does that we are aware of is to convict us of our sin and show us our need to be saved. He then points us to Jesus Christ and gives us the faith to believe in him.

After we become Christians the Holy Spirit lives within us and makes Jesus Christ more and more real to us, and will give us a greater assurance of our faith. He produces within us the fruit of the Spirit which is love, joy, peace, patience, kindness, goodness, faithfulness, gentleness and self-control (Galatians 5:22). As we read our Bibles, pray and seek to live lives which please God, this fruit will grow (John 15:1–7).

It is important for us to remember that even though the Holy Spirit does not have a body he is a real person. He teaches (John 14:26); he testifies (John 15:26); convicts (John 16:8); guides (John 16:13); can be grieved (Ephesians 4:30); lied to (Acts 5:3). These are the actions of a real person not a mere power or influence.

While the Holy Spirit is in every believer, there are also times when the power of the Holy Spirit is more felt than other times. These are known as times of revival (see Chapter 20); times when the Holy Spirit comes down in real power and Christians are convicted of their sin and have a greater reality of God, sinners are saved in numbers and society in general is affected for the good.

Didn't just sit back

Even though the Lord Jesus had promised to send the Holy Spirit, the apostles didn't just sit back and wait. They prayed. Throughout the ten days they were united and persevered in prayer. They prayed constantly, were busy in prayer. Christ promised the Spirit, but that motivated them to pray. They didn't not pray because they thought it would happen anyway.

The way the apostles and early Christians conducted themselves as they waited for the Holy Spirit to come and after he came, is an example for us to follow.

As they chose a new apostle they prayed to Jesus. They said, 'You, Lord, who know the hearts of all' (Acts 1:24—literally, 'heart knower'). They knew that even though he was out of the world he was still accessible. And as their prayers were built on the scriptures (Acts 1:15ff) so should ours be.

We should pray. We should claim God's promises and pray

them back to him. His promises should stimulate our prayer. How they prayed should also determine the way we pray.

Furthermore, as well as praying, they met together as believers (Acts), helped and cared for each other (Acts 2:44, 45), worshipped God (Luke 24:52, 53) and preached Christ (Acts). So should we.

The events over these hours, days and weeks in the Spring of AD 30 are the most significant in history, in the life of the Lord Jesus Christ, in your life and in the life of all those around you. Make sure you have come to trust in what Christ accomplished during this time. Hold onto the fact that right now he has ascended to Heaven to the presence of God for you. He is coming back but until he does he has sent his Spirit. Pray to feel the presence and power of his Spirit more and more and preach this great message to all!

Until he comes!

References

Books

Barth, K. (1956–57) *Church Dogmatics* ed. G.W. Bromiley and T.F. Torrance, tr. G.W. Bromiley. T. & T. Clark

Blanchard, J. (2012) *Major Points from the Minor Prophets.* Evangelical Press. Darlington

Boice, J.M. (1986) *Foundations of the Christian Faith.* IVP Academic.

Bruce, F.F. (1984) *The Epistles to Colossians, Philemon and Ephesians.* Eerdmans

Brunner, E. (1934) *The Mediator: A Study of the Central Doctrine of the Christian Faith.* The United Society for Christian Literature

Bunyan, J. (1997) *Pilgrims Progress.* Banner of Truth Trust. Edinburgh.

Calvin, J. (2014). *Institutes of the Christian Religion.* Banner of Truth

Carson, D.A. (ed) (1999) *From Sabbath to Lord's Day.* Wipf and Stock. Eugene Oregon.

Christofides, A. (2002) *The Life Sentence.* Paternoster. Carlisle

Dallimore, A. *George Whitefield: The life and times of the great evangelist of the 18th century revival,* volume 1. Banner of Truth.

Edinburgh.

Dawkins, R. (2007) *The God Delusion*. London. Black Swan

DeYoung, K. (2010) *The Good News We Almost Forgot*. Moody Publishers. Chicago

Edersheim, A. (2004) *The Life and Times of Jesus the Messiah*. Hendrickson

Edwards, B.H. (2004) *Revival: a people saturated with God*. Evangelical Press. Darlington.

Eusebius, P. (2011) *Ecclesiastical History*.

Grubb, N. (1934) *C.T. Studd Cricketer and Pioneer*. The Religious Tract Society. London

Grudem, W. (2007) *Systematic Theology*. Inter Varsity Press. Nottingham, England

Hendriksen, W. (1971) *The Bible on the Life Hereafter*. Baker.

Hendriksen, W. (1978) *New Testament Commentary Luke*. Banner of Truth. Edinburgh

Houghton, S.M. (1991) *Sketches from Church History*. Banner of Truth. Edinburgh

Huxley, A. (1937) *Ends and Means*. Chatto & Windus

James, L. (1998) *The Rise and Fall of the British Empire*. Abacus. London

Lambert, T. (2006) *China's Christian Millions*. OMF. Sevenoaks

Leahy, F.S. (1999) *Great Conversions*. Ambassador. Belfast.

Lenski, R.C.H. (1961) *St Luke's Gospel*. Augsburg Publishing House. USA

Lewis, C.S. (1952) *Mere Christianity*. HarperCollins. London

Lewis, C.S. (1950) *The Lion the Witch and the Wardrobe*. Geoffrey

Bles

Lewis, C.S. (1992) *The Screwtape Letters*. HarperCollins. London

Lloyd-Jones, D.M. (2002) *The Church and the Last Things*. Hodder & Stoughton. London

Maier, P.L. (1988) *Josephus: The Essential Writings*. Kregel Publications. Grand Rapids

Mandryk, J. (2010) *Operation World*. Biblica. Colorado Springs, USA

Macleod, D. (2002) *A Faith to Live by*. Mentor. Great Britain

Masters, P. (1998) *Baptism: The Picture and its Purpose*. Sword and Trowel. London

Morris, L. (2008) Tyndale New Testament Commentaries *Luke*. IVP

Olyott, S. (2014) *Something Must be Known and Felt*. Bryntirion Press.

Packer, J.I. (1993) *Concise Theology*. IVP. Leicester, England

Packer, J.I. (1993) *Knowing God*. Hodder & Stoughton. Kent, Great Britain

Pink, A.W. (2003) *An Exposition of Hebrews*. Baker. Grand Rapids. USA

Ramachandra, V. (1996) *Gods That Fail*, Downers Grove, Ill: InterVarsity,

Reymond, R. (1998) *A New Systematic Theology of the Christian Faith*. Thomas Nelson

Sanders, O. (1971) *The Incomparable Christ*. Moody Press. Chicago

Stott, J.R.W. (1991) *The Cross of Christ*. Inter-Varsity Press. Leicester, England

Tozer, A.W. (1993). *The Pursuit of God*

Webster, D. (1957) *In Debt to Christ.* Highway Press

Wroe, A. (2001) *Pontius Pilate.* Modern Library

Articles

Levy. P., (2015) *Dangerous Calling—A Review.* Reformation 21. Available at http://www.reformation21.org/featured/dangerous-calling-confronting-the.php. (Accessed on 15th July 2015)

Newspapers and Magazines

The Times (18th October 2010)

The Week (11th December 2010)

Websites

Bible History Online. Available at http://www.Bible-history.com/empires/pilate.html. (Accessed on 14 July 2015)